A History of Ireland in
100 Episodes

A History of Ireland in
100 Episodes

ANCIENT, MEDIEVAL AND MODERN IRELAND

JONATHAN BARDON,
COMPLETED BY FERGAL TOBIN

Gill Books

Gill Books
Hume Avenue
Park West
Dublin 12
www.gillbooks.ie

Gill Books is an imprint of M.H. Gill and Co.

978 07171 90003

Designed by Graham Thew
Print origination by Liz White
Edited by Conor Kostick
Copy edited by Esther Ní Dhonnacha
Proofread by Simon Coury
Printed and bound by Hussar Books, Poland
This book is typeset in Masqualero and Freight Display.

The paper used in this book comes from the wood pulp of sustainably managed forests.

A CIP catalogue record for this book is available from the British Library.

5 4 3 2

For permission to reproduce artwork, the author and publisher gratefully acknowledge
the following:
© Alamy Stock Photo: 11, 14, 16, 22, 34, 38, 40, 45, 52, 62–63, 95, 97, 116, 118–119, 126–127,
135, 138, 139, 143, 153, 156, 161, 169, 172–173, 175, 178, 180, 193, 205, 209, 218, 222, 231, 234,
239, 246–247, 250, 253, 257, 266, 270–271, 276, 281, 283, 287, 290, 301, 304–305, 309, 313,
316, 323, 335, 344, 347; © Andrii Yankovskyi: 191; © Getty Images: 49, 58–59, 66, 83, 90–
91, 101, 108–109, 111, 123, 130, 148, 150, 199, 200, 207, 215, 260, 262, 274, 326–327, 329, 333,
340–341; © Granger/Shutterstock: 241; © iStock/Getty Premium: 6–7, 21, 26–27, 31, 54,
69, 76, 79, 87, 105, 164, 185; © Morphart Creation/Shutterstock: 1, 189, 225; © National
Library of Ireland: 72, 292, 296; © RTÉ Archives: 319; © Sergey Kohl/Shutterstock: 228.

Contents

Introduction viii

Preface ix

Episode 1   The Irish landscape: the last Ice Age and after 1

Episode 2   Pioneers of the Stone Age: from hunter-gatherers to the first farmers 4

Episode 3   Megalithic monuments and the beginning of metalworking 9

Episode 4   The coming of the Celts 12

Episode 5   Preparing for the Otherworld in pre-Christian Ireland 15

Episode 6   Patrick the Briton 19

Episode 7   The early Irish Church 22

Episode 8   Kings, nobles, 'men of art' and commoners 25

Episode 9   'Not the work of men but of angels' 29

Episode 10   Colmcille, Aidan, Columbanus, wandering Irish and marauding Vikings 33

Episode 11   'There came great sea-belched shoals of foreigners': Ireland and the Vikings 36

Episode 12   Brian Boru and the Battle of Clontarf 39

Episode 13   'At the creek of Baginbun, Ireland was lost and won' 43

Episode 14   The first time an English monarch sets foot in Ireland 47

Episode 15   Creating the Lordship of Ireland 50

Episode 16   John, Lord of Ireland: 'dreading the fury of the king' 53

Episode 17   The feudal transformation of Ireland 56

Episode 18   When Edward Bruce 'caused the whole of Ireland to tremble' 60

Episode 19   Pandemic: The Black Death 64

Episode 20   King Art, King Richard and the Pale 68

Episode 21   The rebellion of Silken Thomas 72

Episode 22   Turbulence under the Tudors 75

Episode 23   Shane the Proud 78

Episode 24   'Warring against a she-tyrant': holy war in Ulster and Munster 82

Episode 25   The wreck of the Armada 86

Episode 26   'The wild Irish are barbarous and most filthy in their diet' 89

Episode 27   'A fit house for an outlaw, a meet bed for a rebel, and an apt cloak for a thief' 93

Episode 28   Granuaile: the Pirate Queen of Connacht 96

Episode 29 The Nine Years' War begins 100

Episode 30 'We spare none of what quality or sex soever' 103

Episode 31 The Battle of Christmas Eve 106

Episode 32 The Treaty of Mellifont 111

Episode 33 Borderers: 'A fractious and naughty people' 114

Episode 34 The Flight of the Earls 118

Episode 35 A bizarre beginning: planting Down and Antrim 122

Episode 36 The Plantation of Ulster 125

Episode 37 'Great things move slowly' 130

Episode 38 London companies and 'the scum of both nations' 134

Episode 39 From smouldering resentment to a failed plot 137

Episode 40 The *Eagle Wing* and the Black Oath 139

Episode 41 The 1641 Massacres 142

Episode 42 A world turned upside down 147

Episode 43 The curse of Cromwell 149

Episode 44 'To Hell or Connacht' 152

Episode 45 Cromwell and the Scots in Ulster 155

Episode 46 Three kings and thirteen apprentice boys 159

Episode 47 'No surrender!' 163

Episode 48 Enniskillen and the Boyne 167

Episode 49 Galloping Hogan, Sarsfield and the walls of Limerick 170

Episode 50 Athlone, Aughrim, Limerick and a treaty 174

Episode 51 'Seven ill years' 178

Episode 52 The Penal Laws 180

Episode 53 Scots 'are coming over here daily' 184

Episode 54 'Jet-black prelatic calumny' 187

Episode 55 'Like a contagious distemper' 190

Episode 56 Bliadhain an Áir: 'Year of the Slaughter' 193

Episode 57 Flaxseed and prosperity 197

Episode 58 The second city of the Empire 200

Episode 59 'The Irish gentry are an expensive people' 203

Episode 60 'In America they may get good land' 206

Episode 61 Volunteers, Grattan and the madness of King George 209

Episode 62 The United Irishmen 213

Episode 63 General Lake and the Orange Order 216

Episode 64 Rebellion: Wexford and Antrim, 1798 220

Episode 65 The Act of Union 224

Episode 66 Daniel O'Connell and the road to Emancipation 227

Episode 67 Mass movement politics and Catholic Emancipation 230

EPISODE 68   The Tithe War 234

EPISODE 69   Repeal of the Union 237

EPISODE 70   On the eve of the Great Famine 240

EPISODE 71   'The food of the whole nation has perished' 244

EPISODE 72   Black '47 249

EPISODE 73   Fenians and disestablishment 253

EPISODE 74   The Industrial Revolution in east Ulster 256

EPISODE 75   The Ulster apogee 259

EPISODE 76   The Land Question 262

EPISODE 77   Charles Stewart Parnell 265

EPISODE 78   The birth of Ulster unionism 268

EPISODE 79   Parnell ascendant 272

EPISODE 80   Committee Room 15 275

EPISODE 81   After Parnell 279

EPISODE 82   Rural revolution 282

EPISODE 83   New beginnings: 1905 285

EPISODE 84   Home rule again 288

EPISODE 85   Lockout and citizen armies 291

EPISODE 86   The Great War 295

EPISODE 87   The Easter Rising: an Ireland transformed 299

EPISODE 88   The new Sinn Féin and the conscription crisis 303

EPISODE 89   War of Independence and treaty 308

EPISODE 90   The partition of Ireland 312

EPISODE 91   Green against green 315

EPISODE 92   The Irish Free State 318

EPISODE 93   Fianna Fáil in power 321

EPISODE 94   Emergency and Blitz 324

EPISODE 95   Clann na Poblachta and post-war Ireland 328

EPISODE 96   The 1950s and the change of generations 331

EPISODE 97   All change, all change 334

EPISODE 98   Troubles 338

EPISODE 99   The tide turns, slowly 342

EPISODE 100   The Republic to the millennium 345

Epilogue 348

Acknowledgements 360

Publisher's note 361

Selected bibliography 362

Index 365

Introduction

JONATHAN BARDON DIED IN 2020, having completed 60 per cent of this book. It is based on his masterly *A History of Ireland in 250 Episodes*, with a brief to reduce its content accordingly. In my publishing days, I had commissioned and published 250, so I was both surprised and flattered to be invited in retirement to complete Jonathan's work. The latter part of the book you now hold in your hand is the result.

I remain very conscious that this is first and foremost Jonathan's book, not mine. Accordingly, I have tried as far as possible to maintain his temperate tone without, I hope, totally suppressing my own voice, more given when left to itself to the vociferous and the opinionated than his. It is for the reader to judge the degree to which I have succeeded in that endeavour. I have retained, as far as possible, the exemplary quotations – emblematic of his method – from 250, substituting my own only when more appropriate and urgent ones, as it seemed to me, came to hand.

I was proud to know Jonathan and to publish him. He was a gifted scholar who wrote with wonderful clarity. He had the gift, given to very few, to make complex historical issues comprehensible to the general reader without dumbing down or condescension, the gift of the eloquent précis. His schema in this book required him to reduce the content of 250 – already as tight as a drum – by 40 per cent. I have retained what I hope is the essence of his structure, method and diction. I have no desire to be a post-mortem ghostwriter, but not to do this to some degree might have resulted in a pantomime horse of a book with distinct fore and hinder parts. I have had, as one might say in context, a desire for unity.

Fergal Tobin
Dublin 2022

Preface

THIS BOOK IS LARGELY based on scripts written for a BBC Radio Ulster series entitled *A Short History of Ireland*. The aim of each broadcast – eventually 300 of them, each one lasting five minutes – was to tell a story from Irish history which was sufficiently self-contained for those listeners who had not heard the previous broadcast. In the same way, the reader should be able to open this book at random to enjoy a fully understandable snippet of Irish history. In turn, the hundred episodes selected here and revised, read in sequence, provide a narrative history of Ireland.

Trawling through the archives is a core activity for the professional historian. Historians must also consult and build on the scholarly work of their predecessors and contemporaries. In a book of this scope, spanning all of the time that humans have been in Ireland, the author is especially reliant on the published findings of specialists. It has been a real privilege to be reminded of the vigorous good health of historical research in Ireland.

Material useful to the historian can be found beyond libraries and record offices. Here are some examples.

'I got the essay done!' And a good essay it was too. A police officer in the Royal Ulster Constabulary, he explained with a broad smile that he had written it in the back of a Land Rover before going in, truncheon in hand, to deal with rioters in north Belfast. It was April 1969 and I was teaching adult students about the First World War in the Jaffe Centre, a former Jewish primary school on Belfast's Cliftonville Road – a building subsequently reduced to ashes during convulsions accompanying the Drumcree crisis in July 1996. At the end of the class another student, Kathleen Page, came up to me with a single sheet of paper: this was a letter written by Herbert Beattie in July 1916 which vividly described the first days of the battle of the Somme. No doubt the seventeen-year-old's idiosyncratic spelling enabled the letter to escape his officer's censoring pencil.

I spent much of my spare time in my teens in the 1950s at the end of the West Pier in Dún Laoghaire. Here I fished with former employees of the gasworks, who had been presented with orange-painted bicycles on retirement. In the winter dark, while rats formed a great semicircle round us (waiting for us to throw them an undersized whiting or two), one man gave me a vivid account of the great Dublin Lockout of 1913 and how members of the Dublin Metropolitan Police batoned people all round him when listening to Jim Larkin in O'Connell Street.

Shortly after being asked to write articles for a Sunday newspaper to commemorate the fiftieth anniversary of the Battle of the Somme in 1966, I was rushed to hospital to have my appendix removed. After the operation, I found six veterans of the battle in my ward, and one of them had also fought in the Boer War. Naturally, I recorded as many of their memories as I could. One of them recalled little: he was a Catholic who had enlisted in what had been a temperance battalion of the Ulster Volunteer Force, and he drank the tots of rum his comrades refused before going over the top. The former water keeper of the Argideen river in west Cork, Johnny Murphy, recounted in detail for me how in his youth a neighbouring family had resisted eviction by boiling up a cauldron of porridge and hurling spoonfuls of it at the bailiffs.

Every home, I used to say to students, has material of historical interest within it. Included in my own are photographs taken by my maternal grandfather, Donald Whiteside, of Edward VII's visit to Dublin in 1907, with the GPO in O'Connell Street draped in Union flags; a photograph I took at the request of a farmer in Co. Wicklow at the age of twelve, showing a steam threshing machine in action; a copy of the *Baghdad Times* from 1922 which contained a detailed account of the bombardment of the Four Courts written by an eyewitness, my father, then aged sixteen; and a fragile typescript entitled 'An Irishman in Iraq: Ten Years in Mesopotamia', written on the banks of the River Tigris by my paternal grandfather, Captain James Bardon – no doubt little remains today of the many bridges he built there in the 1920s. Memories and memorabilia do much to enliven the past and – if treated with suitable caution – add to our understanding of it.

The Irish landscape: the last Ice Age and after

. . .

Mountain hare (*Lepus timidus*) or blue hare or tundra hare or variable hare or white hare or Alpine hare or Irish hare. Trousset encyclopedia (1886–91)

IT IS AN ARRESTING thought that human beings had been living in Australia for at least 40,000 years before the very first people came to live in Ireland. Indeed, Ireland became inhabited very late in all the time that *Homo sapiens* has roamed the earth. The explanation for this is the last Ice Age.

Today Ireland is a detached fragment of the Eurasian landmass, from which it is separated by shallow seas. It was not always so. Around two million years ago severe cold conditions set in over north-western Europe. Then the ice relented to give way over the last 750,000 years to alternating cycles of warmth and cold. The Munsterian Ice Age, lasting between 300,000 and 130,000 years ago, covered the entire country with two great elongated domes of ice, in places a mile thick. So much water was still locked up in ice sheets in the Northern Hemisphere that the sea level remained low – low enough to keep both Britain and Ireland not only connected to each other but also to the European mainland.

A thousand-year 'cold snap', as scientists refer to the last manifestation of the Ice Ages, seems to have come to a rather sudden end around twelve thousand years ago. The ice sheets began to dissolve about 15,000 BC, and 3,000 years later they had all but disappeared. They left behind a landscape which had been smoothed and scoured by flowing ice. Retreating glaciers carved out U-shaped valleys and steep-sided corries. Soil and rock had been shifted enormous distances and dumped as rubble in huge mounds of boulder clay, known as drumlins, which number in their tens of thousands, particularly around Clew Bay and stretching across southern Ulster from Strangford Lough to Donegal Bay. Meltwater flowing under the ice left behind sinuous ridges of gravel, known as eskers; often several miles long and up to twenty metres in height, these provided invaluable routeways later on across the boggy midlands.

As temperatures and the oceans rose, Ireland became an island for the first time. This was long before the English Channel was formed to sever Britain from the rest of the continent. The thousand-year cold snap had all but killed off grasses, sorrels, dwarf willows and other pioneering plant species. Around 8000 BC the process of colonisation had to begin again. From now on plants and animals had to find their way across the sea westwards to Ireland. As the permafrost melted the tundra, grasslands attracted willow, juniper, birch and hazel, and the larger trees soon followed.

While the Irish Sea widened it was now a race against time for plants and animals to reach the island. Oak, wych-elm, holly, yew, ash, hawthorn, blackthorn and alder succeeded in establishing themselves, but other trees such as beech and sycamore remained on the British shore until brought over by human beings in the Middle Ages. By the beginning of the twenty-first century archaeologists had reached a startling conclusion: only fourteen land mammals can be considered native to Ireland. A few had been able to survive the thousand-year cold snap. They included: the hare, stoat and wood mouse which subsequently evolved into distinct Irish species; otters able to swim across; and brown bears, wild cats, lynx and wolves, later driven to extinction by human hunters.

In Britain, Stone Age hunters had a wide choice of game, such as wild cattle, red and roe deer, wild boar, badgers and beavers. The first arrivals in Ireland discovered that these creatures, up to then forming the main part of their diet, were simply not there. Even the range of freshwater fish was limited to a handful of migratory species such as eels, shad, lampreys, salmon and sea trout, with landlocked trout, char and pollan transformed into freshwater fish as the ice retreated. Certainly, shellfish were gathered from the shore, and hazelnuts, raspberries, blackberries, crab-apples, water-lily seeds, fungi, edible bracken, goosegrass and vetch could be harvested in season from the woods. But human pioneers in Ireland found the fare on offer was disappointingly limited. For example, it would have required 250 eels to provide the same number of calories as a single wild boar.

'Bring Your Own' is the arresting title given by the archaeologist J.P. Mallory to his explanation that, almost from the outset, the first hunter-gatherers to settle in Ireland felt they had no choice but to transport animals from Britain to bring comfort and variety to their lives. By far the most important were wild boar – even if half their young were killed and eaten, enough remained to breed and multiply. Foxes, red squirrels and pine martens were probably brought over for their fur. Badgers came too (in the eighteenth century the Irish gentry relished 'badger flambé'), while 'native' red deer do not seem to have been carried over by boat (probably as fawns in wicker baskets) until the beginning of the Bronze Age. Perch, pike and other freshwater coarse fish had to await later introduction by monks.

Pioneers of the Stone Age: from hunter-gatherers to the first farmers

. . .

JUST SOUTH OF COLERAINE, a great ridge of basalt lies in the path of the Bann, and after a serene passage from Lough Beg, the river is funnelled between bluffs to cascade in rapids and through weirs and sluices into a long estuary leading north west to the Atlantic. Here in 1973, where waters draining off nearly half the surface of Ulster meet the tide, archaeologists began to unearth evidence of the very first human presence in Ireland.

In 1973, Peter Woodman and his archaeological team began what seemed a routine investigation at Mount Sandel near Coleraine only to discover – after carbon dating of charred hazelnut shells – that human beings had dwelt here between 7000 and 6500 BC. The generally accepted date of the arrival of people in Ireland had been put back by more than a thousand years. The slope of post-holes showed that large saplings had been driven into the ground and bent over to form domed roofs covered with bark or hide to create four huts in an artificially enlarged hollow. Around six metres wide, each hut gave shelter to perhaps a dozen people gathered around a bowl-shaped hearth in the centre.

Since the sea level was around five metres lower than it is today, the falls by Mount Sandel must then have made a majestic sight; below them, in early summer salmon waited in thousands for a flood to take them upstream to spawn, and sea bass foraged at high tide in pursuit of crabs, flounder and smolts. Scale-shaped flints found in abundance almost certainly had been set in poles to harpoon these fish, together with myriads of eels moving down from Lough Neagh in autumn. Autumn too was the season for gathering hazelnuts: these were supplemented by crab-apple, goosegrass, vetches and water-lily seeds. In midwinter, wild pigs began their rutting, and male yearlings, driven out by the mature boars, were vulnerable then to hunting parties armed with flint-tipped spears and arrows. Flint had to be carried from as far away as the north coast beaches of Portrush and Downhill. At a tool-working area to the west of the hollow, flint cores were roughed out and fashioned into picks and axes, while the smaller blades struck from them were shaped into knives, arrowheads, hide-scrapers, awls and harpoon flakes.

But our view of the past must always be altered in the light of fresh evidence: in 2016 came radiocarbon proof that a bear's kneecap with cut marks, recovered from a cave in Co. Clare, had been butchered some 12,000 years ago. Palaeolithic (Old Stone Age) humans may have reached Ireland after all.

Since 1973, the remains of around twenty Mesolithic (Middle Stone Age) sites have been investigated across the country, though none compare with that at Mount Sandel. For at least 3,000 years these hunter-gatherers lived undisturbed in Ireland. Over the whole island, they may not have numbered more than two or three thousand. Certainly, they made little impression on the landscape. Then, from around 4000 BC, a dramatic transformation of the Irish economy began. Until then a small, scattered population had lived exclusively by foraging, trapping and hunting. Now they began to clear the land of trees to create pastures for domestic livestock and cultivation ridges for growing cereals. Most of these people seem to have been newcomers, but it may be that some of the original inhabitants had learned of these farming techniques, which had first been developed in Anatolia and other parts of the Middle East.

Intrepid family groups began to venture across the Irish Sea and the North Channel in dug-out canoes and skin-covered boats. The perils of crossing the sea in frail craft with frightened and thirsty horned beasts can be imagined.

On landing, the first task was to find a stand of elm, a reliable guide to fertile and easily worked soil. Perhaps because conditions were generally too wet in Britain and Ireland for burning the forests,

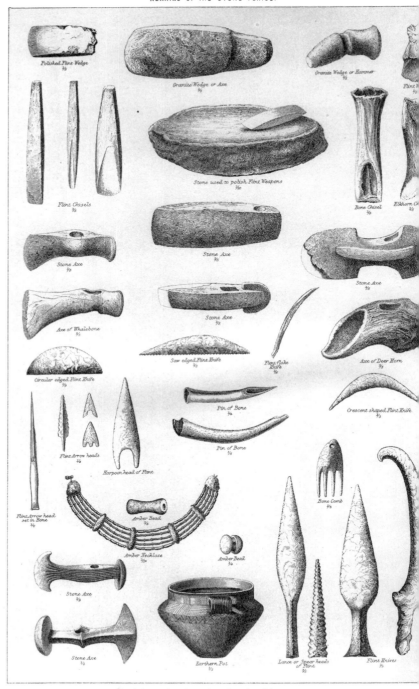

Polished Flint Wedge ⅔

Granite Wedge or Axe ⅖

Granite Wedge or Hammer ⅔

Flint W ½

Flint Chisels ⅔

Stone used to polish Flint Weapons ⅗

Bone Chisel ⅗

Elkhorn Ch ½

Stone Axe ½

Stone Axe ⅜

Stone Axe ⅜

Axe of Whalebone ½

Stone Axe ⅜

Axe of Deer Horn ⅔

Saw edged Flint Knife ⅜

Flint Flake Knife ⅘

Circular edged Flint Knife ⅜

Pin of Bone ¾

Crescent shaped Flint Knife ⅔

Flint Arrow heads ¾

Pin of Bone ½

Harpoon head of Flint

Bone Comb ⅔

Flint Arrow head set in Bone ¾

Amber Bead

Amber Necklace ⅓

Amber Bead ¾

Stone Axe ¼

Stone Axe ¼

Earthern Pot ⅖

Lance or Spear heads of Flint ⅔

Flint Knives ⅔

The relative proportion to the true size is given under each figure

Vintage engraving of Stone and Bronze Age artefacts

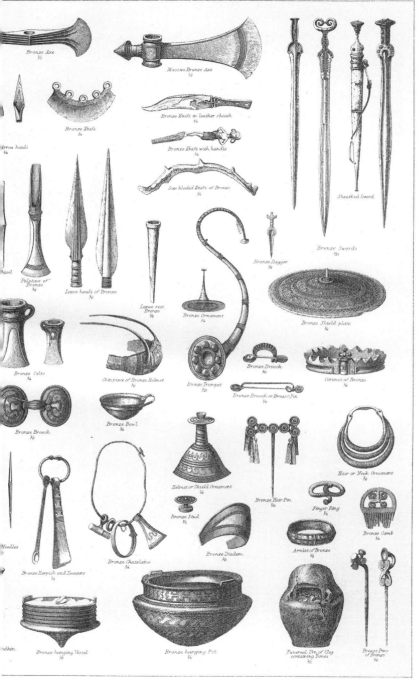

Bronze Axe
2/6

Massive Bronze Axe
3/6

Bronze Knife
3/4

Bronze Knife in leather sheath
4/4

Bronze Knife with handle

Saw bladed Knife of Bronze
3/4

Arrow heads
3/4

Palstave of Bronze
2/6

Lance heads of Bronze
2/6

Lance rest Bronze
2/6

Bronze Ornament
3/4

Bronze Dagger
2/6

Bronze Swords
3/21

Sheathed Sword.

Bronze Swords

Bronze Shield plate
2/6

Bronze Celts
2/4

Chin piece of Bronze Helmet
2/3

Bronze Trumpet
2/21

Bronze Brooch
3/6

Bronze Brooch or Breast Pin.

Coronet of Bronze
2/6

Bronze Brooch
2/6

Bronze Bowl
3/6

Helmet or Shield Ornament
2/6

Bronze Stud
3/3

Bronze Hair Pin
2/6

Finger Ring
2/4

Hair or Neck Ornament
3/6

Bronze Comb
3/4

Needles

Bronze Chatelaine
3/4

Bronze Diadem
2/6

Armlet of Bronze
2/6

Bronze Earpick and Tweezers
3/2

Bronze hanging Vessel
2/6

Bronze hanging Pot
2/6

Funeral Urn of Clay containing Bones
3/6

Breast Pins of Bronze
3/6

Bodkin

The relative proportion to the true size is given under each figure farmers preferred to spread out through the wood and girdle the trees with their stone axes, causing them to die back and open up the canopy. Meanwhile, the women and children put up shelters and gathered leaves, twigs and other fodder to carry the cattle and the sheep through their first critical winter. When the clearings lost their fertility, the farmers simply moved on to create new pastures. In the fourth millennium BC farming was helped by a significant improvement in the climate which allowed these Neolithic (New Stone Age) people tilling the soil to expect better harvests. The main crops were barley and emmer wheat, and, once cut with stone-edged sickles, the cereals were ground with rubbing stones on saddle querns and eaten as gruel or bread and perhaps converted into fermented drinks.

Archaeologists have recorded no fewer than 18,000 axes in Ireland fashioned from a wide variety of rock types including flint, mudstone, shale, schist and sandstone. The most highly prized stone was porcellanite, formed sixty million years earlier when hot Antrim lavas poured over clays to compress them into hard china-like stone. Specialist factories emerged at Tievebulliagh, Co. Antrim, and on Rathlin Island; from here polished porcellanite axe heads were traded as far away as Dorset and the Shetlands.

Megalithic monuments and the beginning of metalworking

. . .

JUST WEST OF SLIGO town on the top of Knocknarea mountain glistens a massive cairn visible from many miles around known as Queen Maeve's tomb. Over many years, a well-organised community struggled uphill with tens of thousands of great rocks to create this artificial mound as a monument to their dead. What is more, this enormous monument erected in the fourth millennium BC is no mere heap of stones: almost certainly it contains a carefully constructed passage grave which has yet to be excavated.

As Neolithic farmers removed much of Ireland's forest canopy, cleared the scrub, worked the ground with stone-edged adzes and wooden ploughs for crops of corn, and tended their herds, they created settled communities which grew in numbers and wealth. Firmly believing in the afterlife and laying claim to the lands they occupied, they venerated the bones of their ancestors. More than 1,200 megalithic monuments have been identified in Ireland.

The Carrowmore complex, on flat land looking up at Knocknarea, is the largest megalithic cemetery in the whole of Europe. To view the array of around eighty-five portal tombs, passage graves and chambered burial mounds is an awesome experience.

Court cairns, the earliest megalithic monuments, were probably temples of a kind, where farming communities paid respect to departed ancestors and invoked magical help to ensure good harvests. Portal tombs, or dolmens, are the most splendid and striking reminders of Ireland's Stone Age farmers, particularly when seen against the skyline. Built of three or more great upright stones, carrying a massive capstone sloping downwards towards the back, these above-ground graves were described incorrectly in the nineteenth century as 'druids' altars'. Capstones of enormous size, sometimes brought from a considerable distance, had to be placed on the stone uprights, presumably hauled up earthen or stone ramps by workers using oxen, ropes, timber sledges and rollers, and then lifted in stages by means of levers and platforms raised gradually to the required height.

The most awe-inspiring creations of Neolithic farmers in Ireland are the passage tombs, regarded as the first great achievements of monumental architecture in prehistoric Europe. The most magnificent are to be found in the huge necropolis in the Boyne valley, Co. Meath. This includes Dowth and Knowth but the finest, on top of a small hillock overlooking the Boyne, is Newgrange. Towards the end of the fourth millennium BC a great mound, just over 103 metres in diameter, was raised using some 200,000 tons of material from the river a kilometre away, faced all over with slabs of sparkling white quartz and surrounded by ninety-seven kerbstones, many of them elaborately carved. The twenty-four-metre passage rises gently to a burial chamber with three niches, each containing shallow stone basins. Archaeologists were astonished at the dryness of the passage and the chamber: the slabs forming the roof slope slightly downwards from the centre to prevent damp percolating down, and they had not only been caulked with sea sand and burnt soil but also etched with grooves to drain off rainwater.

It was at the winter solstice in 1968 that Professor Michael O'Kelly discovered the most renowned feature of Newgrange. He noticed that the sun, as it rose above the horizon to the south east at 8.58 a.m., cast a pencil-thin beam of light into the burial chamber, striking the triple-spiral motif carved in the deepest recess of the tomb. Seventeen minutes later it was gone. Only a highly organised and sophisticated society, equipped as it was with little more than stone, could have created such a powerfully moving way of delivering the message that the dead could look forward to a new life beyond, just as nature began a fresh period of growth after the depths of midwinter.

Passage tomb Brú na Bóinne

Knowledge of metalworking arrived in Ireland around 2500 BC. In 1962 the geologist John Jackson began to explore one of the very few prehistoric copper mines to survive in Europe, Mount Gabriel in west Cork. The miners had cut a total of twenty-five mineshafts into the hill, then lit fires as far along the shafts as they would stay alight, and finally thrown water onto the hot rock to shatter it. With the use of large cobbles collected from the sea shore, grooved to give anchorage to ropes, the broken rock was scooped out, smashed and made ready for the furnace. Jackson estimated that the prehistoric mines in this south-western corner of Ireland produced no fewer than 370 tonnes of finished copper. This copper was mixed first with arsenic, sometimes with lead, and then with tin (some found locally but most of it brought over from Cornwall) to make bronze. Ireland for a time was the leading producer – more than 2,000 flat bronze axes have been found here, more than in any other country in Europe.

EPISODE 4

The coming of the Celts

. . .

MOST EVOCATIVE OF A bygone culture shining across the centuries are the astonishingly rich finds of gold made in Ireland. Gold almost certainly was panned in the beds of streams flowing off ancient igneous rocks, particularly in the Mourne and Wicklow mountains. As the last millennium BC progressed, so the quantity and quality of gold objects in Ireland increased remarkably. The finds from this period are among the most elaborately decorated to be found anywhere in Europe, many of them in a style regarded today as distinctively Celtic.

The largest gold hoard to be found anywhere outside the eastern Mediterranean was unearthed close to the hill fort of Mooghaun in the 1850s. Known as the 'Great Clare Find', the 146 ornaments included a great number of penannular bracelets with expanded terminals, and dress fastenings so heavy that they must have been a burden to wear.

Another hoard discovered at Gorteenreagh, also in Co. Clare, included a gold lock-ring hair fastener so perfectly and intricately fashioned that modern jewellers are convinced it would be almost impossible to copy. It consists of two conical shapes and a tube with a neat slit into which locks of hair were enclosed. Only after microscopic examination was it discovered that the tiny concentric lines on the cones were made up of perfectly laid wires a mere third of a millimetre wide.

The quality of the gold-working was matched by that of the bronze-smiths. The craft of the bronze-worker was well illustrated by the discovery in the 1820s of a hoard of over 200 objects in a bog at Dowris in Co. Offaly. Dating from around 700 BC, it included twenty-six beautifully crafted bronze horns which can be blown either at the side or at the end to produce a powerful sound similar to that of an Australian didgeridoo. This hoard also contained fine swords, socketed axes, razors and a set of tools for a carpenter, including gouges, chisels and knives. Expertly crafted from riveted sheets of bronze is a great cauldron fitted with two large rings so that it could be suspended over a fire and then carried to a feast, fully laden and suspended from a pole on the shoulders of two strong bearers. A beautiful flesh hook, decorated with birds, found at Dunaverney, Co. Antrim, was no doubt for guests to fish out pieces of stewed meat from such cauldrons.

The archaeological finds from the last millennium BC are dominated by bronze weapons, including a fearsome eighty-centimetre-long rapier from Lissan in Co. Derry. A new and deadlier slashing sword also makes its appearance. This was a time of more intensive warfare. What caused people in Ireland to place so many precious objects, including heavy gold ornaments, deep in the soil? The answer seems to be that rapid change dislocated communities, bringing about circumstances they could not explain, so that they felt the need to appease the gods by ever more generous offerings.

The Celts were the first people north of the Alps to emerge into recorded history. Their distinctive culture is thought to have evolved during the second millennium BC between the east bank of the Rhine and Bohemia before spreading out from there. When did the Celts come to Ireland? A clear answer cannot be given because they do not seem to have formed a distinct race. Celtic civilisation may have been created by a people in central Europe, but it was primarily a culture – a language and a way of life – spread from one people to another. Archaeologists have searched in vain for evidence of dramatic invasions of Ireland, and now they prefer to think of a steady infiltration from Britain and the European mainland over the centuries. The first Celtic-speakers may have come to Ireland as early as 1000 BC. They were arriving in greater numbers from about 500 BC; equipped now with iron weapons, led by nobles on horseback or in chariots, and commanding the countryside from their hill forts, they brought the native peoples of Ireland under subjection.

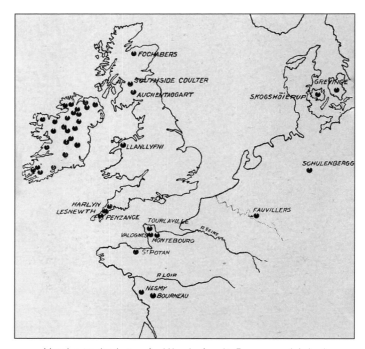

Map showing distribution of gold lunulae found in Europe – mostly Ireland

Like their continental counterparts, the Celtic elite in Ireland assuaged the anger of the gods by casting their valuables into sacred pools. One of these pools, adjacent to Emain Macha, the ancient capital of Ulster, yielded four large bronze horns magnificently decorated in the Celtic style known as La Tène after a site in Switzerland. First developed in central Europe, this imaginative art style, in contrast with the realism and natural beauty preferred by Greek and Roman artists, delighted in restless symbols and intricate curvilinear patterns. The earliest Irish examples of this art can be seen on bronze scabbards for iron swords from Lisnacrogher, Co. Antrim.

In hoards deliberately placed in rivers, lakes and pools after around 300 BC, bronze horse-bits are the commonest surviving metal artefacts. This shift demonstrates the crucial role of the horse in helping to keep the ruling caste in power.

Preparing for the Otherworld in pre-Christian Ireland

. . .

THE *LEBOR GABÁLA ÉRENN* ('The Book of the Taking of Ireland'), compiled in the eleventh century, but drawing on traditions going back several centuries earlier, was an elaborate attempt to reconcile ideas the Irish had of their remote origins with the Bible, in particular the Book of Genesis. According to this account, Ireland was successively inhabited by five blood-related invading groups: the first, led by Cessair, granddaughter of Noah; the second by Partholón; the third were the Fir Bolg from Scythia, who had to overcome evil monster spirits, the Fomorians; the fourth invasion was by the Tuatha Dé Danann, who had learned the arts of magic in the northern world; and the last conquest was achieved by the sons of Míl, the ruler of Spain. Their descendants, the Gaels, ruled Ireland since that time.

This confabulated pseudo-history was believed for centuries. By the beginning of the Christian era, the Irish – or at least the ruling elite – were referring to themselves as Gaels. And the *Lebor Gabála*, in its account of the Tuatha Dé Danann, does provide a very comprehensive description of the gods of the Irish before the coming of Christianity.

The Tuatha Dé Danann were to become the sídhe, who, when conquered, became invisible and lived in fairy mounds. Lir was one of their kings and the story of his children – changed into swans by his third wife, Aoife – is one of the most poignant in western literature. Lir's son, Manannán mac Lir, was god of the sea. The greatest of the gods was Dagda, who had beaten off the monster Fomorians when they attacked in a magical mist. The best-loved was Lug the Long-Handed, the god of sun and fertility. Medbh – who appears as Queen Mab in Shakespeare's plays – was the goddess of drunkenness.

Fionn and Tuatha Dé Danann

In Ireland the Celtic year began with *Samhain*, now Hallowe'en, when cattle had been brought in from their summer grazing; this was a time when the spirits flew free between the real world and the other world. *Imbolg*, the first day of February, marked the start of the lambing season; and the feast of *Bealtaine*, at the start of May, was for the purification of cattle, which were driven ceremoniously between two fires. *Lughnasa*, the first day of August, celebrated the harvest and paid homage to Lug, the sun god.

It is now becoming clear that the ancient capitals of Ireland were ritual rather than political sites. These include Emain Macha (or Navan Fort) near Armagh, the capital of Ulster; Cruachain (or Rathcroghan) in Co. Roscommon, the capital of Connacht; Dún Ailinne near Kilcullen, Co. Kildare, the capital of Leinster; and Tara in Co. Meath, long regarded as the capital of Ireland. It is clear that they were not constructed for military purposes as the ditch in each of the locations was placed *inside* rather than outside the great circular earthen enclosures. If defence was needed, it was against hostile spirits from the Otherworld.

At Emain Macha archaeologists found evidence that a great circular temple, 43 metres in diameter, had been built, probably by a whole community acting together. Held up by concentric rows of posts thicker than telegraph poles and steadied by horizontal planks, the roof had been covered by a cairn of stones enveloped with sods. Then the whole structure had been deliberately set on fire. No one knows why. Had this been a ritual to invoke the aid of the gods while the kingdom was under attack? Remains of a similar structure were found at Dún Ailinne, and it may have provided tiered seating for large numbers of devotees until it too was purposely destroyed.

No king of importance could hope to rule with authority unless fully initiated at one of these ancient sites. Lia Fáil, the Stone of Destiny, can still be seen in Tara – it was said to cry out in approval when the rightful king was inaugurated. Whether the Turoe Stone from Co. Galway was an oracle, a totem or a phallic symbol is impossible to say: a glacial erratic boulder, it is covered in swirling Celtic art motifs similar to those etched on metal objects.

There is good reason to believe that some of the most powerful kingdoms in Ireland at the beginning of the Christian era were carved out by warrior tribes driven west from Gaul and Britain by Roman expansion.

By the beginning of the fifth century, the situation had changed dramatically. The Roman Empire was reeling under the attack of German-speaking peoples from central and northern Europe. Legion after legion was withdrawn from outposts to defend Rome, itself weakened by civil dissensions. The time had now come for the Irish to play their part in collapsing this empire by striking eastwards across the sea.

Patrick the Briton

. . .

IN AD 82, GNAEUS Julius Agricola, governor of Britain, summoned his fleet into Solway Firth to take aboard his waiting cohorts. Ireland was directly across the sea and this land he meant to conquer – a climax to a dazzling career the Empire would not forget. Returned after a distinguished service as a governor in Gaul and a consul in Rome, Agricola swept all before him; in the fastnesses of Snowdonia he reduced the Ordovices to abject submission and then, pressing relentlessly into Caledonia, he reached the base of the Highlands and ordered the erection of a network of castella.

But Agricola's invasion was not to be: a legion of Germans stationed in Galloway mutinied and there was disturbing news of Pictish rebellion. Agricola was recalled and later the Romans retired behind Hadrian's Wall. Ireland would not become part of the Roman Empire after all.

Three hundred years later Roman rule in Britain was fast disintegrating. Towns and villas fell into decay, bathhouses were abandoned, the great sewers of York became blocked with excrement, and the once-thriving town of Winchester became completely deserted. From the north came the Picts, from the east the Angles, Saxons and Jutes and from the west the Irish. Irish raiders found rich pickings. In 1854 a hoard of Roman loot was found at Ballinrees, just west of Coleraine, including 1,500 silver coins, silver ingots and silver bars. Five hundred silver coins were unearthed near the Giant's Causeway, 300 more nearby at Bushmills, and in 1940 pieces of cut silver plate and four silver ingots were discovered at Balline in Co. Limerick. Coins dated these raids to the early fifth century.

Roman Britain in its death throes had become Christian. From there and from Gaul, Christianity had been brought by traders and others into the south of Ireland. We know this because in 431 Pope Celestine sent a churchman from Auxerre, Palladius Patricius, as a bishop to 'the Irish believing in Christ'. Unquestionably, however, the main credit for bringing Christianity to Ireland must go to the man we know as St Patrick, the author of the very first document in Irish history, his own autobiographical *Confessio*.

Patrick was not yet sixteen when he was seized by Irish pirates, from Bannavem Taburniae, a Romanised town somewhere in western Britain. Once in Ireland, he was sold as a slave and taken 200,000 paces – that is, 200 miles – westwards, probably to Tirawley in north Co. Mayo. There he herded sheep and cattle for six years. In his extreme loneliness, he turned to God for comfort:

> *The love of God and the fear of Him came to me more and more, and my faith increased, and my spirit was stirred, so that in one day I used to say up to a hundred prayers and at night as many, and I stayed in the forests and on the mountains, and before daylight I used to be roused to prayer in snow and frost and rain.*

One night, Patrick tells us, he heard a voice bidding him to return to his fatherland. A ship was waiting for him, he was told. Not doubting that this was God speaking to him, Patrick fled his master. For 200 miles he trudged alone along the cattle tracks until he came to the Irish Sea, where, indeed, a ship was making ready to sail. After much persuasion, the captain agreed to take him. Somehow Patrick found his home again. His parents joyfully embraced their long-lost son and pleaded with him not to leave them again. But Patrick could not forget the land which had enslaved him. One night in a dream Patrick tells us that he saw a man coming from Ireland with many letters. One he handed to Patrick was entitled *Vox Hiberniae*, the 'Voice of the Irish'. As he began to read he seemed to hear the people he had known in Ireland calling with one voice: 'We beg you, holy boy, to come and walk among us once again.' Many years later Patrick could still recall: 'It completely broke my heart, and I could read no more and woke up.' Patrick had no doubt now what he should do: he must return to Ireland and preach the Gospel there.

Assailed though they were by heathens from all sides, the Romanised Britons managed for long to maintain a vigorously evangelical church. And it was that church that gave Patrick full support to bring Christianity to the Irish. He took holy orders, was appointed Bishop of the Irish by the British Church and returned to Ireland.

Patrick's very humility frustrates inquiry: his writings give no clues about the location of his British home, or where he preached. He likely carried out his work mainly in the northern half of Ireland, for it is there that places traditionally associated with him are located, including Armagh, Templepatrick, Saul, Downpatrick, Lough Derg and Croagh Patrick.

Saint Patrick

The early Irish Church

. . .

The ruins of Clonmacnoise Cathedral

THE ANNALS OF ULSTER state that Patrick died on 17 March 492 in the 120th year of his age. This need not be taken seriously, and, indeed, his mission cannot be confidently dated: it was probably some time in the middle or late fifth century.

Patrick seems to have established a church along the lines of that which prevailed in the western Roman Empire: that is, churches with parishes grouped together in dioceses ruled by bishops and with boundaries similar to those of Irish kingdoms of the time. Ireland, however, had no towns to form the centre of parishes and no cities capable of being capitals of dioceses. Fairly soon after Patrick's death monasteries became the favoured type of Christian community in Ireland. Much of the inspiration came from the Coptic Christian monasteries which flourished in north Africa.

The earliest monastic foundations in Ireland were established by Finnian at Clonard and Ciarán at Clonmacnoise in the sixth century. Local kings vied with one another to be patrons of monasteries. Some monasteries soon became the nearest equivalent Ireland had to towns, with substantial populations, thriving markets, schools and even prisons. The best-known, however, became celebrated for their strict discipline and asceticism.

Eight miles out beyond the rugged Iveragh peninsula in south-west Kerry the lonely island of Skellig Michael, a pyramid of bare rock, rises to a peak 700 feet above the Atlantic Ocean. In winter, gales howl around its crags and gigantic waves thunder at the base of its cliffs. Even in summer, the sea is rarely calm, and it is not easy to make a landing. Only sea pinks and a few other hardy plants can survive in its thin soil. This is, perhaps, the most desolate place in Ireland, fit only for fish-hunting gannets and puffins. Yet nearly 1,500 years ago Skellig Rock was chosen by Irish monks as a site for their monastery, where they would leave behind the world of violence and the temptations of ambition and riches.

Lacking both timber and mortar, they used only the rock around them. On the brow of a 500-foot precipice, the monks placed pieces of hewn rock on the ground to form flat terraces which they surrounded with great drystone walls. Then, on the highest terrace, they erected six beehive-shaped cells nestling against the rock. So perfectly were these stones fitted together that even today the driving rain cannot penetrate the uncemented walls and corbelled roofs.

Inside the cells, where the monks studied and slept, the walls are carefully smoothed, with built-in stone cupboards and stone hooks for book satchels, and the floors are paved and drained. Two oratories, looking like upturned boats, built in much the same way as the cells and decorated with simple crosses, served as places of worship. In summer, when great shoals of mackerel broke the surface in pursuit of sprats, and when seabirds nested on the rock, the monks could survive on gulls' eggs, fish and herbs grown in the scanty soil of the monastery garden. During the winter gales they must have hungered, and no doubt some of the monks buried in the tiny graveyard died of starvation.

The greatest Irish monasteries, such as Monasterboice in Co. Louth and Clonmacnoise in Co. Offaly, were placed on fertile lands, where, patronised by kings, they became centres of wealth as well as famous centres of craftsmanship and scholarship. Even though Ireland had never been a Roman province and Latin was for everyone a foreign language, Irish monasteries played a pivotal role in preserving and celebrating the civilisation of the classical world now overwhelmed by Germanic conquerors.

The main purpose of the monastic life was worship by constant prayer, psalms and songs of praise. Part of each day was spent in private prayer and part in the scriptorium – the thirst for scholarship seems to have been as strong as that for the simple life. Manuscripts from early Christian Ireland are frequently embellished with little hymns or poems in praise of nature, often written in the margins, such as this one:

> *A hedge of trees is all around;*
> *The blackbird's praise I shall not hide;*
> *Above my book so smoothly lined*
> *The birds are singing far and wide.*
> *In a green cloak of bushy boughs*
> *The cuckoo pipes his melodies –*
> *Be good to me, God, on Judgment Day! –*
> *How well I write beneath the trees!*

Rather than using parchment, the Irish preferred the more expensive skins of newborn calves, which, after being tanned and carefully scraped free of hair, were turned into smooth and almost luminous vellum. Monks cut their own goose quills and prepared inks from carefully collected pigments. One cut himself, probably sharpening his quill, and drew a black circle around the blot of blood on the page with this note: 'Blood from the finger of Melaghlin.'

Kings, nobles, 'men of art' and commoners

. . .

MANY IRISH PEOPLE CLAIM to be descended from kings. It is not altogether preposterous. From the beginning of the Christian era to the coming of the Normans in the twelfth century there were probably no fewer than 150 kings in Ireland at any given date – a remarkably high number when the population was probably no more than half a million.

Each king ruled over a tribal kingdom, a population group which formed a distinct political entity known as a *tuath*. The family group containing those who were *rígdamnaí*, literally 'king material', was limited to the *derbfine*, which means 'certain family'; even so, this was a very large group which included first cousins and extended over four generations. The reality was that in any kingdom a man might make himself king so long as he was popular enough and powerful enough to do so. Certainly, dynasties were constantly rising and falling.

Once a king was chosen by the high-born, he was not crowned but inaugurated in a ceremony usually held on an ancient Neolithic or Bronze Age site, such as Tara in Meath or Carnfree in Roscommon. The site had to include a special slab (similar to the Scottish Stone of Scone) or flagstone chair and a sacred tree or *doire*, a grove of oak trees. Typically, a golden shoe was thrown over the king's head and then a senior noble would circle the seated ruler several times, place a hazel wand of office in his hand and slip the shoe onto one foot.

Equal in status to the warrior nobility were the *filí*, the poets. The honour of a king or a nobleman could be destroyed by the satire of a poet, and this was much feared – in old Irish tales a satire could bring the victim's face up in blisters. Poets were members of a highly privileged caste known as the *áes dána*, the 'men of art', which also included judges, jurists, bards, metalworkers and genealogists. The status of noblemen depended on the number of clients they could maintain, in addition to lands and property. They formed the warrior class, travelling to the battlefield on horseback or by chariot. It was the custom of kings and nobles to send their children to be fostered by others, partly to promote good relations with neighbours. Girls were sent away between the ages of seven and fourteen, and boys

between seven and seventeen – powerful bonds were established between foster parents and their charges.

Below the *nemed*, the 'sacred' classes of kings, men of the arts and the nobility, were the *sóer*, the 'free', who were high-ranking commoners, and the *dóer*, the unfree, who were utterly dependent on those above them for access to land. Manual labour was despised

Vintage engraving from 1864 of a crannóg. Crannógs were used as dwellings over five millennia from the European Neolithic period

by the aristocracy – a king could lose his honour-price if seen with an axe or a spade – and so the functioning of the economy depended heavily on farmers with many obligations.

In modern Irish *baile* means a town, but in earlier times this word, which has left its mark on so many of our placenames, and is anglicised as 'bally', simply meant a settlement. The settlement pattern was entirely dispersed and rural, and the economy depended almost entirely on farming. Ireland's landscape is thickly scattered with the remains of thousands of ring forts, farmsteads surrounded by circular banks and ditches. In rocky areas, where the fort was known as a *caiseal* or *cathair*, the wall was made of unmortared stone without a surrounding ditch. The word *ráth* referred to a ring fort with an earthen bank surrounded by a ditch, and the term *lios* was applied to the enclosed space inside. These elements appear in placenames in their tens of thousands. Examples include *Cahirsiveen*, 'little Saibh's fort'; *Cashelreagh*, 'grey fort'; *Rathfriland*, 'Fraoile's fort'; and *Listowel*, 'Tuathal's fort'.

The earthen and stone circular banks and walls would have kept out wolves and would-be cattle thieves and marauders, but not a determined attack. These were simply the homes of extended families, and the enclosures – with room for around six houses – served as farmyards for chickens and pigs and for activities such as butter-churning. A feature of later ring forts was an underground ventilated passage leading to a carefully drained chamber, known to archaeologists as a 'souterrain'. These were not only cool stores for food and precious seedcorn but also temporary hiding places if the homestead was attacked.

The remains of some two thousand lake dwellings have been identified in Ireland. Known as 'crannógs', these artificial islands were used as secure places for metalworkers to practise their craft and they may also have served as the equivalent of holiday homes for the wealthy. A king or noble, as a member of an elite military caste, usually lived above or apart from commoners in a ring fort built for defence on a carefully chosen site known as a *dún* – a word incorporated into numerous placenames such as *Dunseverick*, 'Sobhairce's fort'.

'Not the work of men but of angels'

. . .

IN EARLY CHRISTIAN IRELAND, the forts of kings and their aristocratic relatives might seem to have been the greatest centres of wealth and prestige, but they were not – the monasteries were pre-eminent. These ecclesiastical settlements became for a time some of the most dynamic centres of scholarship and art in the western world.

The earliest surviving Irish manuscript is a copy of the Psalms, known as the *Cathach* (the 'Battler') because it was later carried into battle as a talisman by the O'Donnells. An ancient tradition, which may well be true, attributes the writing of the *Cathach* to Colmcille himself. And most of the great illuminated Irish manuscripts were written and decorated in monasteries founded by him. The Irish developed their own unique insular half-uncial, majuscule and minuscule script and specialised in enlarged capital letters at the beginning of paragraphs. In time these capital letters increased in size and elaboration. Scribes often tried to relieve this arduous work by scribbling in the margins, for example: 'Alas! My hand! O my breast, Holy Virgin! This page is difficult.'

But this scribe seems to have recovered a few pages later when he tells us: 'The third hour. Time for dinner!'

Other scribes wrote verse:

> *My hand is weary with writing,*
> *My sharp quill is not steady,*
> *My slender-beaked pen juts forth*
> *A black draught of dark-blue ink.*

A stream of the wisdom of blessed God
Springs from my fair-brown shapely hand:
On the page it squirts its draught
Of the ink of the green-skinned holly.

The greatest achievements of early Christian Ireland are the magnificent illuminated Gospels and other sacred texts. The *Book of Durrow*, completed around 670, was the first to include a so-called carpet page: an abstract design based on intricate Celtic interlacing. The high point of manuscript illumination was reached in the *Book of Kells*, which combines strong compositions with astonishingly detailed, almost microscopic ornament. The most admired page combines the sacred *chi-rho* monogram with images of Christ, the Resurrection and the Eucharist; and the stately rounded script is punctuated with scenes such as cats pursuing mice, an otter seizing a fish, a cock with hens, and a greyhound hunting. It has a good claim to be the most beautiful book executed during the first millennium. Overseas, Gospels and commentaries almost as accomplished can be found in greatest number in the monastery founded by St Gall in Switzerland, carried there by Irish pilgrims or written there by Irish scribes. After examining the *Book of Kildare*, now lost, Gerald of Wales came to the conclusion that it was 'not the work of men but of angels'.

The greatest Irish monasteries developed into sophisticated communities served by, among others, specialist craftsmen. These men produced superlative metalwork pieces of extraordinary refinement and delicacy. These were liturgical vessels and reliquaries, that is, containers for holy bells, bishops' staffs and a wide range of saints' relics. These include the Ardagh Chalice, the Cross of Cong and, found as recently as 1980, the altar service unearthed at Derrynaflan in Co. Tipperary, including an outstandingly beautiful chalice.

The most distinctive reminders of early Christian Ireland are the high crosses characterised by a ring of stone that connects the arms to the upright. Erected in the precincts of monasteries, they depicted not only the crucifixion but also a wide range of episodes from the Old and New Testaments. The one at Kells, Co. Meath, may have been put up to give thanks for the safe transfer to that site of the monastic community of Iona, which had fallen prey to Viking attack.

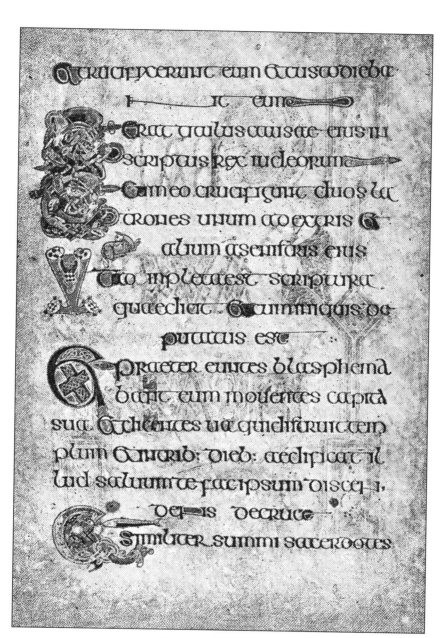

A page from the Book of Kells

For more than a century the kingdom of Dál Riata flourished on both sides of the North Channel: on the one side of the kingdom, the basalt cliffs of Antrim rose dramatically from the sea, bristling with hill forts, and the island of Rathlin; and on the other the Mull of Kintyre, the many islands of the Inner Hebrides and, adorned with mountains in season purple with heather, the peninsulas of Argyll thrusting into the sea. By the middle of the sixth century, the Dál Riata kings had made Dunadd, in the heart of Argyll, their capital. The language spoken on both sides of this narrow sea was Gaelic.

The Gaelic rulers of Dál Riata steadily expanded their territory and their speech at the expense of their neighbours: Picts to the north and east; the Angles of the kingdom of Northumbria then expanding northwards to the Firth of Forth; and the Britons of Strathclyde. The Strathclyde Britons were Christians, but the Argyll Gaels, the Picts and the Angles had their own gods. At the end of the fifth century, Ireland possessed a flourishing Christian Church. It was not long before the new beliefs were being brought across from the north of Ireland to Argyll. The man who did most to launch that mission was an Uí Néill prince of Ulster, Colmcille or, in Latin, Columba, 'dove of the church'.

Colmcille, Aidan, Columbanus, wandering Irish and marauding Vikings

. . .

AN UÍ NÉILL PRINCE born at Gartan in Donegal, Colmcille studied to become a monk under Finnian at Moville in Co. Down and at Clonard on the Boyne, before returning to build his own monastery at Derry in 546. It seems that Colmcille was forced to flee across the North Channel after becoming embroiled in a dynastic dispute. Conall mac Comgaill, the Dál Riata king residing at his capital of Dunadd, welcomed Colmcille, guaranteeing his protection and granting him the island of Iona. Here on this Hebridean island, Colmcille built a monastery capable of housing 150 monks, scholars and novices, around AD 563. Iona in time would become the most famous centre of Christian learning in the Celtic world, producing the finest illuminated manuscripts – almost certainly the *Book of Durrow* and the *Book of Kells* were completed here before being carried to Ireland.

Colmcille's main achievement was the spreading of Christianity to his fellow Gaelic speakers in Argyll. In addition, he pioneered the mission to the Picts. After his death, Iona became the powerhouse from which the Gospel was brought to the many in Britain who had not heard it before. Oswald, son of Aethelfrith, King of Northumbria, took refuge in Iona when his father had been overthrown and killed. There Aidan, an Irish monk, deeply impressed Oswald with his piety and energy. Oswald returned to Northumbria and, after defeating his enemies, took for himself the crown his father had once worn. Aidan received the gift of Lindisfarne and on this island a great monastic foundation thrived, modelled on Iona, becoming the dynamic centre of the mission to these pagan Angles.

Saint Columbanus

Some Irish monks simply put out to sea and let the wind take them away. This is how the Irish came to be the very first humans to set foot in Iceland. One monk there, describing the midnight sun, reported that it was so bright he could see the lice on his hair shirt.

As a centre of learning and Christian zeal, Bangor in north Down rivalled Iona. It was principally from here that the great Irish mission to the European mainland was launched. Towards the end of the sixth century, by the ruined fort of Annegray in the Vosges mountains, Irish pilgrims halted after travelling more than 900 miles from Bangor. Here under the direction of their leader, Columbanus, they built three monasteries. In his forthright condemnation of the worldliness of the Frankish Church, Columbanus aroused the hostility of Theoderic, King of Burgundy. Forced to move on, the Irish monks struck overland to the Rhine, where they made their way upstream. This inspired Columbanus to write his 'boat song':

> Lo, little bark on twin-horned Rhine
> From forests hewn to skim the brine.
> Heave, lads, and let the echoes ring.
>
> The tempests howl, the storms dismay,
> But manly strength can win the day
> Heave, lads, and let the echoes ring.

> *The king of virtues vowed a prize*
> *For him who wins, for him who tries.*
> *Think, lads, of Christ and echo him.*

When they reached Lake Constance, they preached to the Germans, who had not heard the Gospel before, and founded a monastery at Bregenz. The restless Columbanus was eager to travel on, but Gall, one of the Bangor monks, stayed to become the local patron saint – a church, a town and a canton in Switzerland are called St Gallen to this day. Columbanus pressed on to northern Italy to found another monastery at Bobbio, where his tomb can still be seen. He inspired a great flood of Irish pilgrims and scholars to make their way to the European mainland for decades to come.

For almost a thousand years, unlike almost every other part of Europe, Ireland was free from large-scale invasion. Then, in the year 795, Rathlin Island was attacked. Within the next few years, a succession of undefended monasteries along the coast fell victim to Viking raids.

> *There was an astonishing and awfully great oppression over all Erinn, throughout its breadth, by powerful azure Norsemen, and by fierce hard-hearted Danes, during a lengthened period, and for a long time, for the space of eight score and ten years ...*

So wrote the author of *Cogadh Gaedhel re Gallaibh* ('Wars of Irish with Foreigners') at the beginning of his long history of the impact of the Viking raids on his country. So frequent and devastating were the assaults that one monk wrote in the margin of his manuscript a poem in thanks for the storm raging outside:

> *Fierce and wild is the wind tonight,*
> *It tosses the tresses of the sea to white*
> *On such a night I take my ease;*
> *Fierce Northmen only course the quiet seas.*

Churches and monasteries suffered most in the early attacks; the raiders were attracted to them, not only because of precious liturgical vessels and reliquaries, but also by their rich stores of butter and corn.

'There came great sea-belched shoals of foreigners': Ireland and the Vikings

. . .

ONCE THE FRANKISH EMPEROR Charlemagne had broken up the fleets of Frisian pirates in the North Sea, nothing formidable stood in the way of the Vikings, leaving them masters of the north Atlantic. Their longships were well designed to cope with the hazards of the ocean: built of seasoned overlapping oak planks, riveted with iron, and bound to the ribs with tough pine roots, their hulls could not only flex to the swell but also, with their shallow draught, negotiate treacherous mud banks at the mouths of rivers. Since the records were written by monks, the Northmen were viewed as black-hearted barbarians by the chroniclers:

> Although there were an hundred hard-steeled iron heads on one neck, and an hundred sharp, ready, cool, never-rusting, brazen tongues on each head, and an hundred garrulous, loud, unceasing voices from each tongue, they could not recount, or narrate, or enumerate, or tell, what all the Gaedhil suffered in common, both men and women, laity and clergy, old and young, noble and ignoble, of hardship and of injury, and of oppression, in every house, from these valiant, wrathful, foreign, purely pagan people.

Ruled by a disorganised multiplicity of kings frequently in conflict with one another, the Irish were unable to put up a united resistance to the Vikings. In addition, these raiders – most of them Norse rather than Danes – were more formidably armed than the Irish, their helmets being fitted with protective nose pieces, their torsos covered in flexible coats of mail, and their weaponry comprising fearsome battleaxes and long slashing swords edged with superbly welded hard steel. Shallows and waterfalls proved no protection – the invaders simply carried their longships past such obstructions to navigable water upstream.

A major fresh assault was launched in 821 when great numbers of women were seized at Howth and even the seemingly impregnable Skellig Rock was attacked. In 837, two formidable fleets, each made up of sixty ships, penetrated the Liffey and Boyne rivers. The *Book of Leinster* recorded this campaigning and, in particular, the exploits of one Viking leader, Turgeis:

> There came a great royal fleet into the north of Ireland with Turgeis. This Turgeis assumed the sovereignty of the foreigners of Ireland. A fleet of them took possession of Lough Neagh. Another fleet took possession of Louth. Another on Lough Ree.
>
> Moreover, Armagh was plundered by them three times in the same month, and Turgeis himself took the abbacy of Armagh and ... broke the Shrine of Patrick.

It seemed that no part of Ireland was safe from the Vikings. Some of these Northmen, indeed, had decided to make Ireland their home.

In the year 841 the Vikings entered the Liffey estuary, as they had so often before; but this time they had come not to raid but to stay. By the black pool – in Irish *Dubh Linn* – formed where the Poddle stream met the Liffey, they pulled their longships ashore onto a dry bank, covered them, lashed them down, and erected a stockade around their vessels for protection. Here a ridge of well-drained ground provided an obvious place for the Norse to overwinter and build a stronghold. This is where Dublin Castle now stands. With the coming of every summer, more bands of Northmen arrived and settled there, making it the principal colony of the Vikings in Ireland.

In 902 the Viking settlers under the command of Ivar the Boneless were driven out of Dublin by the Irish; but they returned twelve years later, led by Ivar's grandsons, Ragnall and Sitric the Squinty. The whole country 'became filled with immense floods and countless sea-vomiting of ships, boats and fleets'. Dublin was recovered and, indeed, all along the southern and eastern coasts the Vikings converted their temporary ship fortresses into Ireland's first towns. Limerick, on the Shannon estuary, and Waterford, where the Barrow, Nore and Suir rivers meet to join the sea, became great cities. Dublin, however, was always pre-eminent: here Vikings settled the countryside around the city and the Irish called the area *Fine Gall*, 'foreign people'.

These men from the north never conquered all of Ireland – indeed, their invasions seem to have encouraged several native Irish rulers to make the high kingship a reality. In 967 Limerick was sacked by the men of the neighbouring kingdom of Dál Cais. Then under the command of their leader, Brian, they seized control of the whole of Munster. After many campaigns and battles, the other kingdoms of Ireland yielded one by one. Everywhere the advancing warlord was known as Brian Boru, 'Brian of the Tributes'. When Máel Mórda, King of Leinster, and Sitric Silkenbeard, King of Dublin, submitted in 999, Brian Boru was acknowledged as High King of Ireland – the first high king ever to win the support of every part of the island. For almost fifteen years Brian Boru was the unchallenged high king. But he had made enemies. Brian had won his crown not by birth, but by the sword.

The opposing of the landing of the Danes under Turgesius on the shores of the Liffey

Brian Boru and the Battle of Clontarf

. . .

NOTHING IRKED MÁEL MÓRDA, King of Leinster, more than a journey to pay homage to Brian at his palace at Kincora. Brian had made Máel Mórda's sister Gormflaith his queen, only to cast her aside for another. Finally, insulted by Brian's arrogant son Murchad during a game of chess, the King of Leinster could stand it no longer. He rode off without so much as bidding farewell to the high king, back to his fort at Naas. And when Brian sent a messenger after him to call him back, Máel Mórda lashed at the fellow with his yew horse switch, smashing his skull to pieces.

There was no turning back now. Brian had sworn revenge, and Máel Mórda would no longer submit Leinster to Brian's authority. Sitric Silkenbeard too resented the many humiliating defeats he had suffered at Brian's hands and the loss of his city's independence. Dublin was the mightiest Viking city in Ireland. It had become a Viking kingdom even before Denmark, Norway and Sweden had kings. To throw off Brian's yoke would be a real prize.

That very year, 1013, had not King Sven of Denmark conquered all of England? Might not the Northmen win a kingdom to match it in Ireland? The King of Dublin and the King of Leinster knew they could not win without help. Longships – one of them with Sitric aboard – left Dublin to sail across the Irish Sea and to the Hebrides and beyond. After many months they returned with firm offers of support.

Good Friday, 23 April 1014: on this day the fate not only of Dublin but of all Ireland would be decided, and, whatever the outcome, this conflict would be long remembered in the island's annals and

BRIAN BOROIHME.
MONARCH OF IRELAND AND HERO OF CLONTARF.
A. D. 1027.

Brian Boru

the sagas of the Northmen. Looking east towards Howth from the fortified earthen wall along the southern Liffey shore, Sitric Silkenbeard could see silhouetted against the rising sun the massed prows of longships stretching round into the bay. His heart leapt to see these Vikings he had summoned fall in behind their captains on the foreshore. There were, it was said, fighting men from as far away as Norway and France; King Brodar of the Isle of Man, with his long black hair tucked into his belt; and Earl Sigurd the Fat of the Orkneys.

This day, along with King Máel Mórda and all his men of Leinster, these Northmen would do battle not only with Irishmen from a host of kingdoms but also with Brian's Viking subjects from Limerick and Waterford. This would not be a simple battle between Irishmen and Northmen: Irish would fight Irish, and Vikings would fight Vikings.

As Sitric's warriors set out for Dubhghall's Bridge, built to span the deepest channel of the Liffey at Áth Cliath, the 'ford of hurdles', the King of Dublin remained behind to command the city's defence. Brian too would not be a combatant, for he was now over seventy years old; as he prayed in his tent for victory his son Murchad led out a mighty host – the men of Munster, the Norse of Limerick and Waterford, Ospak of Man, and Connacht allies. The Dublin army, advancing north east, crossed the Tolka stream and drew up in formation at Clontarf with their backs to the sea to stand beside their allies from overseas.

Challenges by champions to engage in single combat began the battle; then, to the sound of horrible war cries, the two sides closed in:

> *And there was fought between them a battle furious, bloody, repulsive, crimson, gory, boisterous, manly, rough, fierce, unmerciful, hostile, on both sides; and they began to hew and cleave, and stab, and cut, to slaughter, to mutilate each other ...*

Never before had so great a battle been fought on Irish soil. Never before had so many men of noble birth lost their lives in one engagement in Ireland: among them were Murchad, Earl Sigurd, the Mormaer of Mar, Máel Mórda, Brodar of Man, and the two kings leading the Connacht forces. Late in the afternoon, the Leinster-Norse army began to fall back to Dubhghall's Bridge and into the advancing tide, and here there was a fearful slaughter:

They retreated therefore to the sea, like a herd of cows in heat, from sun, and from gadflies and from insects; and they were pursued closely, rapidly and lightly; and the foreigners were drowned in great numbers in the sea, and they lay in heaps and hundreds ...

Long after, tales of the battle were recited by northern firesides; Valkyries were seen weaving a web of battle with swords on a loom of death; and in the Icelandic *Njal's Saga* Earl Gilli spoke of his vision before the battle:

> *I have been where warriors wrestled,*
> *High in Erin sang the sword,*
> *Boss to boss met many bucklers;*
> *Steel rang sharp on rattling helm;*
> *I can tell of all their struggle;*
> *Sigurd fell in flight of spears;*
> *Brian fell, but kept his kingdom*
> *Ere he lost one drop of blood.*

The assassination of Brian Boru at the moment of victory made certain that, for a long time to come, all Ireland would not be ruled by one man. Brian had made the high kingship a reality, and now the provincial kings were locked in a violent and inconclusive contest to become the ruler of the whole island. Brian's death also ensured that the Vikings would stay. Indeed, their towns and cities continued to grow, and the Northmen did much to promote the modernisation of Ireland by drawing the country more closely into European trade networks. The Viking settlers had become Christian and Sitric Silkenbeard himself built Dublin's first cathedral, Christ Church, in 1038. It was probably constructed in wood.

Meanwhile, so fierce was the warring of the Irish kings to control the whole island that one annalist declared that they were making Ireland a 'trembling sod'. The country was being left open for another invasion: that of the Normans.

'At the creek of Baginbun, Ireland was lost and won'

. . .

GRANTED TO VIKINGS IN 911 in return for a promise of peace, Normandy in time became a powerful state and, in 1066, led by their Duke William, the Normans defeated Harold of England at Hastings. The conquest of England was ruthlessly completed within a few years, and soon Norman barons were penetrating south Wales and southern Scotland. Other Normans carved out a kingdom for themselves in southern Italy and Sicily, while the descendants of William the Conqueror extended their dominions in France.

Meanwhile, in Ireland, a dreary wasting warfare continued year after year as kings struggled with each other for dominance. In 1166 the King of Bréifne, Tiernan O'Rourke, with the full support of his high King, Rory O'Connor, drove Dermot MacMurrough out of his kingdom of Leinster. Taking refuge in England, Dermot laid plans to recover his kingdom. He called on his friend Robert Fitzharding, the reeve of Bristol. Fitzharding advised him to seek out his king, Henry II, by now the most powerful monarch in western Europe. Dermot travelled to Aquitaine and, according to *The Song of Dermot and the Earl*, addressed Henry as follows:

> *Of Ireland I was born a lord, in Ireland acknowledged king;*
> *But wrongfully my own people have cast me out of my kingdom.*
> *To you I come to make plaint, good sire,*
> *In the presence of the barons of your empire.*
> *Your liege-man I shall become henceforth all the days of my life,*
> *On condition that you be my helper ...*

Henry listened sympathetically, for Dermot had championed his claim to the English throne at a difficult time in the past.

On a clear day, Norman barons in south-west Wales could see the mountains of Wexford and Wicklow across the sea, seeming to beckon them on to further conquest. Now they could go by invitation and eagerly pledge their support to Dermot in return for promises of land. To the greatest of them, Richard fitz Gilbert de Clare, Lord of Strigoil, better known as 'Strongbow', MacMurrough pledged the hand of his daughter Aoife in marriage, and the kingdom of Leinster when Dermot himself died.

In August 1167, Dermot slipped back to Leinster with a small force of Flemings under Richard fitz Godebert of Rhos. O'Connor and O'Rourke allowed themselves to be bought off with 100 ounces of gold. Then in May 1169, 300 fighting men, commanded by Robert fitz Stephen, Hervey de Montmorency and Maurice de Prendergast, sailed over from Milford Haven. Landing at Bannow Bay, they advanced on the Viking town of Wexford and forced its submission. Early in May 1170, reinforcements commanded by Raymond 'le Gros' fitz Gerald arrived in an inlet eight miles to the east of Waterford city. This place is still known as Baginbun, named after two ships which carried over the invaders, *La Bague* and *La Bonne*, and immortalised in the rhyme:

> At the creek of Baginbun
> Ireland was lost and won.

A momentous era in the history of the island had begun.

Strongbow set sail soon after with an imposing flotilla and came ashore close to Waterford. Joined by Raymond le Gros, he lay siege to this Viking city. Gerald of Wales informs us:

> They were twice vigorously repulsed by the citizens. Then Raymond noticed a small building which hung down from the town wall on the outside by a beam. He quickly sent in armed men to cut down the aforesaid beam. The building immediately collapsed, and with it a considerable part of the wall. The invaders eagerly effected an entry, rushed into the city and won a most bloody victory, large numbers of the citizens being slaughtered in the streets.

The siege of Waterford by Strongbow in 1170

At the moment of victory Dermot MacMurrough arrived, and after the rulers of Waterford, both called Sitric, were executed in Reginald's Tower, his daughter Aoife was married to Strongbow amidst the ruins of the city.

The next objective was Dublin. Here the high king, Rory O'Connor, had assembled a formidable army outside the walls at the urgent request of Earl Hasculf, the city's ruler. Hasculf guarded the approaches along the coast at Bray and the Scalp, while from the plain of Clondalkin Rory kept watch over Slí Cualann, the road on the western side of the Wicklow Mountains. Dermot knew his own kingdom, however, and brought his allies across the thickly wooded plateau from Glenmacnass to Sally Gap, and from there over the flank of Kippure Mountain to Rathfarnham.

Seeing the impressive array of mailed horsemen and archers emerge from the woods, Hasculf sent out Laurence O'Toole, the Archbishop of Dublin, to seek terms. The Norman adventurers had come too far to parley now. With Milo de Cogan and Raymond le Gros in the van, Strongbow's men made a furious assault on the walls, overran the city and butchered many citizens.

The first time an English monarch sets foot in Ireland

. . .

STRONGBOW HAD SEIZED WATERFORD and Dublin, and Dermot MacMurrough had been restored to his kingdom of Leinster; but neither Hasculf, Earl of Dublin, nor Rory O'Connor, High King of Ireland, were prepared to accept this new state of affairs. During the winter of 1170–1, the newcomers repaired Dublin city's defences and built a motte castle surrounded by a deep ditch. Then, in the spring of 1171, the whole Norman enterprise was threatened with disaster. Hearing that Dermot was dying in Ferns, Strongbow sped southwards to claim the kingdom pledged to him, only to find that the Leinstermen, rallying to Murtagh MacMurrough, had risen in revolt against their new overlords.

Earl Hasculf now returned with sixty longships filled with warriors from the Northern Isles, led by John the Wode, a famous berserker fighter. At the mouth of the Liffey, the Northmen leapt from their vessels to advance in a phalanx on the city walls. They were, in the words of Gerald of Wales,

> *warlike figures, clad in mail in every part of their body after the Danish manner. Some wore long coats of mail, others iron plates skilfully knitted together, and they had round, red shields protected by iron round the edge. These men, whose iron will matched their armour, drew up their ranks and made an attack on the walls at the eastern gate.*

At the first onset a knight's hip bone, protected though it was by an iron cuirass, was cut away with one blow of a Viking battleaxe. Milo de Cogan, appointed governor of Dublin by Strongbow, was forced

47

to retreat behind the wall; his brother Richard and his men, however, made an unobserved sortie through the southern gate and rounded on the attackers' rear.

The Northmen now faced a new enemy. Mounted knights – protected by chainmail from head to toe, carrying kite-shaped leather shields, secure on high-fronted saddles and with their feet firmly placed in stirrups – were able to charge the foe directly with long lances. In support were Welsh longbowmen and Flemish foot soldiers with crossbows shooting mail-piercing arrows. The Norse were put to flight; John the Wode was slain by Walter de Riddlesford; and Hasculf was dragged back from the shore.

> *His life was spared [recorded Gerald of Wales] with a view to ransom, and he was in the court, in Milo's presence, when in everyone's hearing he made the following angry assertion: 'This is only our first attempt. But if only I am spared, this will be followed by other expeditions on a far larger scale, and having a different outcome from this one.' When they heard him say this he was immediately beheaded on Milo's orders, and these arrogant words cost him that life which he had been mercifully granted only a short while before.*

Next, the Normans had to face a great Gaelic host led by Rory O'Connor with his men of Connacht, O'Rourke of Bréifne, O'Carroll from Ulster, and Murtagh MacMurrough with his Leinster kinsmen. With no knowledge of siege engines, the high king counted on starvation to bring the invaders to submission, and with the help of thirty longships from Man and the Isles, he very nearly succeeded. A daring stroke was needed to extricate the garrison from its desperate position. Shortly after noon, on an early September day in 1171, picked fighting men burst out of Dublin, the van of twenty knights led by Raymond le Gros, followed by Milo de Cogan's company of thirty knights, with Strongbow in the rear commanding forty knights. Crossing Dubhgall's Bridge and taking a circular route over the Tolka, they fell on the Irish camp so suddenly that Rory, bathing in the river at Castleknock, barely escaped with his life. Hundreds of the Irish were slain, and the foreigners now had secure possession of Dublin.

Henry authorises Dermot to levy forces

Henry II, the most powerful monarch in western Europe, ruler of England, Normandy, Brittany, Anjou, Aquitaine, and much of Wales, viewed Strongbow's victories with deep misgiving. The defeat of the high king presented him with a spectre: an independent Norman state which could threaten his empire from the west. Henry prepared a great expedition for Ireland, though the cares of his vast dominions lay heavy on his shoulders. There was another reason for removing himself from his usual sphere of activity: he was deeply implicated in the murder of Thomas Becket, Archbishop of Canterbury, and cardinal legates had arrived in Normandy to put embarrassing questions to the king concerning the atrocity.

On St Luke's Day, 18 October 1171, 400 ships entered Waterford haven, and King Henry's progress from there to Dublin was one of the finest triumphs of his long reign. So great was the royal retinue and baggage that camp had to be made outside the city walls at the Thingmote, a forty-foot-high man-made hill where the Vikings held their assemblies. On this spot, a great hall was built of stripped willow rods. Here Henry held court and received the submission of a queue of Irish kings, acknowledging his new title as Lord of Ireland.

Creating the Lordship
of Ireland

. . .

WHEN IRISH KINGS LINED up to make their submission to an alien ruler, Henry II, acknowledging him as Lord of Ireland, they may have had little understanding of feudal terminology and of the obligations involved in giving fealty to a liege lord. At the same time, Henry did not attempt to detach Irish princes from their duty to their high king, Rory O'Connor. Henry II possessed a great asset: back in 1155 Pope Adrian IV had granted Ireland to Henry. It just so happened that Adrian, born Nicholas Breakspear, was the only Englishman to have been elected pope. As the chronicler John of Salisbury explained: 'He did this in virtue of the long-established right, reputed to derive from the donation of Constantine, whereby all islands are considered to belong to the Roman Church.'

Actually, Henry's main purpose in coming to Ireland may have been to clip Strongbow's wings: perhaps he feared that the earl intended to set up a Norman state in Ireland. The city of Dublin the king gave to the men of Bristol who had fitted out his great expedition. He put a strict limit on the borders of Strongbow's possession of Leinster by granting the fertile land of Meath to Hugh de Lacy, provided he could conquer it. For himself, Henry took the title of 'Lord of Ireland' – with the unwritten assumption that the lordship covered only the territory possessed by the Norman newcomers.

Soon after Henry II returned to England, Irish kings quickly forgot the submissions they had made. Nor did the newcomers have any intention of remaining confined to the lands they had already seized. Hugh de Lacy made a successful advance into Meath, defeating and killing Tiernan O'Rourke, the one-eyed King of Bréifne, who had attempted to hold him back. There was no concerted Gaelic resistance to the Norman newcomers. Indeed, Dermot MacCarthy, King of Desmond, and Donal O'Brien, King of Thomond, were such inveterate enemies that they were both prepared, when it suited them, to fight alongside the Norman adventurers. Milo de Cogan made a successful raid into Connacht in 1177 at the invitation of one of Rory O'Connor's sons, Murchad – when Milo left, the high king had Murchad blinded to punish him for his perfidy.

The Normans thrust into the south west and conquered most of Desmond. The year 1177 also witnessed the invasion of Ulster. Early in February, John de Courcy, a knight from Cumbria, took twenty-two mailed horsemen and around three hundred foot soldiers out of Dublin northwards over the Moyry Pass and then eastwards to Downpatrick, the ancient kingdom of Dál Fiatach. So unexpected was this Norman incursion that the local king, Rory MacDonleavy, fled with all his people. Invoking his authority as over-king of the Ulaid, MacDonleavy returned with a great host only to have it routed by the banks of the River Quoile. Over the next few years, de Courcy seized control of the coastlands of Down and Antrim. The sea was his essential lifeline, made more secure when he married Affreca, daughter of Godred, King of Man, which gave him the use of a formidable fleet. For a quarter of a century, he ruled his Ulster lands with as much independence as a warlord. And like all the Norman adventurers, he kept his conquests secure by building castles.

Even though they were already going out of fashion in England, motte castles were erected in every part of Ireland occupied by the first Norman invaders. A motte was a fortification erected on top of an artificial mound; the steeply sided, roughly circular mound was partly constructed with soil from its surrounding ditch but raised higher by soil brought in from further afield, carefully sloped inward to provide stability. A few had an additional base court, or 'bailey', such as Dromore in Co. Down, particularly if they were intended to house permanent garrisons.

Once a territory had been pacified, it was secured by stone castles. The site had to be chosen carefully, with solid rock as a stable base for preference. The largest of all was de Lacy's Trim Castle, though it may not have been complete before this Lord of Meath was murdered in 1186 on the orders of an Irishman known as 'the Fox'. At its centre was a massive 'donjon', square in shape, to which was added a square tower at each of the four corners. The main defences were curtain walls which formed a D-shape along the banks of the River Boyne, from which water was diverted to make a water-filled ditch around the walls. The largest keep in Ireland was erected by de Courcy at Carrickfergus on a tongue of rock jutting into Belfast Lough. Behind a curtain wall, masons built this massive rectangular tower with walls nine feet thick from local basalt, red sandstone from Whiteabbey, and cream Cultra limestone shipped across the lough, to rise ninety feet above the rock.

Trim Castle

John, Lord of Ireland: 'dreading the fury of the king'

. . .

WHEN HE WAS PARCELLING out responsibilities to his untrustworthy sons in 1177, Henry II decided to make his youngest son, John, Lord of Ireland. Since John was then only ten, the lordship had to be administered by a royal governor – as it was ever after. In 1185 John was sent to visit his lordship; when greeted after landing at Waterford by Irish kings and lords, John and his retinue 'treated them with contempt and derision', his tutor, Gerald of Wales, recorded, 'and showing them scant respect, pulled some of them about by their beards, which were large and flowing according to the native custom ... So with one accord they plotted to resist.'

Henry II died in 1189; his son Henry was already dead; Geoffrey had been fatally wounded during a tournament in Paris; and Richard the Lionheart succeeded his father. After a colourful career on crusade and in foreign captivity, Richard died in 1199, meaning John was now not only Lord of Ireland but King of England. John proved to be a vengeful and capricious monarch who trusted no one. King John ignominiously lost possession of Normandy, and this made him all the more determined to tighten his control in Ireland. In particular, he became jealous of Norman barons who had become rich and powerful at the expense of the Gaelic Irish. John authorised the son of Hugh de Lacy, also called Hugh, to drive John de Courcy out of his conquests in Antrim and Down. De Lacy was made Earl of Ulster but it was not long before he got on the wrong side of his king by allying himself with his kinsman, William de Braose, Lord of Limerick.

King John

De Braose became John's sworn enemy. Not only had he fallen behind in his payments to the Crown, but, worse still, his wife, Matilda de Saint-Valéry, had denied the king her son as a hostage, saying to the royal messenger: 'I will not deliver up my son to your lord, King John, for he basely murdered his nephew Arthur, when he should have kept him in honourable custody.' As John prepared a great expedition to break the power of his overmighty subject, de Braose took refuge in Ulster with de Lacy. On 20 June 1210, the king disembarked near Waterford with 7,000 knights, archers and foot soldiers. It was the mightiest army yet seen in Ireland.

Nine days after disembarking at Waterford, King John was in Dublin, his force increased by feudal levies from Munster and Leinster. The king marched north and was joined in Meath by Cathal Crobhderg O'Connor, who had succeeded his brother Rory as King of Connacht. The *Annals of Inishfallen* record:

When Hugh de Lacy had discovered that the king was going to the north, he burned his own castles and he himself fled to Carrickfergus, leaving the chiefs of his people burning, levelling and destroying the castles and dreading the fury of the king ... When the king saw this disrespect offered him, he marched from Drogheda to Carlingford.

To avoid a likely ambush in the Moyry Pass, the king transported his army over Carlingford Lough with a bridge made of boats and hundreds of pontoons brought from Dorset, Somerset and York. Then, while his men marched by the coast by Kilkeel and Annalong, the king himself sailed to Ardglass in Lecale and rested there in Jordan de Saukville's castle. Dundrum Castle looked impregnable with its great round keep recently constructed by de Lacy. John had brought with him an intimidating array of siege engines, however, and it fell in the middle of July. Soon afterwards siege was laid to Carrickfergus by land and by sea, and in a short time the castle surrendered.

King John stayed at Carrickfergus for ten days, making many payments, including £2 12s 6d for repairs to the castle. He ordered the Bishop of Norwich to have galleys built at Antrim to patrol Lough Neagh, paid sixty shillings to mariners from Bayonne, and left for England in August.

And what happened to de Broase and de Lacy? They both escaped to France, but Matilda de Broase and her son William were captured at sea, then cast into prison and there, by the king's orders, starved to death. After many years fighting in the crusade against the Cathars in southern France, de Lacy returned to be given back his earldom in Ulster in the reign of Henry III.

On his departure, King John had the satisfaction of knowing that not a baron, king or chieftain would defy his authority. Even Cathal Crobhderg of Connacht paid fealty as his liege subject. Meanwhile, John had ordered the building of Dublin Castle: 'a strong castle there with good ditches and strong walls in a suitable place for the governance and, if need be, the defence of the town'. Begun in 1210 and finished in 1228, Dublin Castle swiftly became the administrative heart of the lordship.

The feudal transformation
of Ireland

. . .

THE ENGLISH CROWN'S LORDSHIP of Ireland was ruled from Dublin Castle. Here taxes, rents from royal demesnes, fines and other profits of justice were accounted for at the exchequer – which an illustration of the time shows was, indeed, a chequer board – staffed by a treasurer, the chancellor and barons of the exchequer. The royal governor acted as the viceroy, chaired meetings of the council, and called up leading barons to provide military support when required. The common law of England became the law of the lordship of Ireland, and it was administered by the royal governor, travelling justices and the sheriffs. The process of creating counties had begun: the county was the equivalent of a shire in England, and here the sheriff had responsibility, with the power to call out a posse of local men if needed.

The number of counties increased steadily in the thirteenth century, a time when the frontiers of the English lordship of Ireland were being extended deep into Gaelic territory. By the late 1200s around two-thirds of Ireland had been conquered. The high point of expansion was the conquest of Connacht. The province's last great king, Cathal Crobhderg, had died in 1224 and in the confusion which followed a Tipperary baron, Richard de Burgo, put together a great invasion force in 1235. The war was taken to the Atlantic Ocean, and naval engagements involving O'Flahertys and O'Malleys were at their fiercest around the numerous islands of Clew Bay. After ravaging Murrisk and Achill Island in north Mayo, the invaders advanced northwards and inland to make an assault on the island fortress of the Rock on Lough Key in Roscommon.

The Rock was taken and the power of the O'Connors was broken. Five baronies were set aside for Henry III and, possessor of twenty-five baronies, de Burgo became Lord of Connacht. He built a great castle at Loughrea and made it his principal manor. His ally, Maurice FitzGerald, founded Sligo town and, around another de Burgo castle, the town of Galway began to grow, attracting Anglo-Norman merchant families, the fourteen most prominent becoming known as the 'Tribes of Galway'.

Ports founded by the Vikings, especially Dublin, Waterford, Cork and Limerick, prospered under the rule of the English Crown. Other successful Norman ports included Drogheda, founded by Hugh de Lacy in the 1180s; Dundalk, laid out by the de Verdons; and Carrickfergus, begun by John de Courcy and then developed as a royal town thereafter.

When Strongbow died in 1176, the only heir to his possessions in Leinster was his daughter Isabella. On coming of age in 1189, she wed William the Marshal, one of the most powerful barons in the land and owner of vast estates in Normandy, England, Wales and – now, thanks to his marriage – Ireland. When King John died in 1216, Marshal (who had adopted his title as a surname) was chosen to be regent until Henry III came of age. All this time he worked hard and often ruthlessly to promote the economic development of his Leinster lands.

Marshal made Kilkenny the capital of his lordship of Leinster, and large towns grew up around his castles of Carlow and Ferns. His prize project was New Ross, a deep-water port he developed just below where the Barrow joins the Nore. New Ross soon became a great trading centre, outstripping Wexford and Waterford and rivalling Dublin. Between 1275 and 1279, for example, New Ross exported no fewer than 1,871,207 fleeces and 623,402 hides.

By the end of the thirteenth century, by far the most powerful lord in Ireland was Richard de Burgo, who was not only Lord of Connacht and in possession of great estates in Leinster and Munster, but also had been given the de Lacy lands in the north to become the Earl of Ulster. This man, who had in his possession almost half the land of Ireland, gave fealty to Edward I, Lord of Ireland and King of England. This meant that de Burgo was obliged to provide military service whenever called upon by the king. It was this feudal duty which was to draw him inexorably into the affairs of Scotland.

In January 1296, de Burgo – known as the 'Red Earl' – commanded a fleet across the North Channel conveying twenty-eight barons and an army of over 3,000 men to campaign against William Wallace, the man leading the Scots resisting Edward's attempt to conquer them. The Red Earl led another expedition to Scotland in 1298. Wallace was

defeated and condemned to a grisly death. Then on 27 March 1306, Robert the Bruce, Earl of Carrick, had himself crowned at Scone. Edward II, succeeding his father, commanded de Burgo to help him secure the English conquest of Scotland by waging war on this upstart. An acute problem for the Red Earl was that he had earlier married his daughter Elizabeth to the enemy, the man who was now Robert, King of Scots.

The English Crown's lordship of Ireland was ruled from Dublin Castle. This image is of Irish rebels' heads on spikes at Dublin Castle

When Edward Bruce 'caused the whole of Ireland to tremble'

...

ONE REASON WHY THE lordship of Ireland was gravely weakened in the final decades of the thirteenth century was that Edward I waged endless wars. While he campaigned in Gascony, fought the Scots and conquered north Wales, encircling it with great castles, the king had constantly called his Irish vassals to his side, imposed heavy emergency war taxes on them, seized grain without paying for it, and even had sections of his Welsh castles prefabricated in Dublin and shipped across the Irish Sea to Anglesey.

His son, Edward II, was then ignominiously routed by the Scots at Bannockburn in 1314. Robert Bruce, the victor, knew that the English king had drawn heavily on his Irish lordship to prosecute the war, and was determined to destroy it. King Robert knew Ireland well: he had taken refuge on Rathlin in 1294 and 1306, and in 1302 he had married Elizabeth, daughter of Richard de Burgo, the 'Red Earl' of Ulster and Lord of Connacht.

It was to his brother Edward that Robert Bruce entrusted the invasion of Ireland. As described by an Irish annalist, a formidable Scots expeditionary force disembarked at Larne on 26 May 1315:

> Edward came to Ireland, landing on the coast of north Ulster with the men of three hundred ships, and his warlike slaughtering army caused the whole of Ireland to tremble, both Gael and Foreigner. He began by harrying the choicest part of Ulster, burning Rathmore in Moylinny, and Dundalk, and killing their inhabitants. He then burned Ardee and took the hostages and lordship of the whole

province without opposition, and all the Gaels of Ireland called him King of Ireland.

When news of the landing of the Scots arrived, the royal governor, Edmund Butler, was in Munster, and the Red Earl was in Connacht, attending to his vast estates there. Butler advanced northwards to defend Dublin, while de Burgo made his way to meet the Scots head on.

The two armies finally met in battle by the Kellswater at Connor. There on 10 September the Scots spearmen completely overwhelmed the earl's feudal host. Close to Connor, the royal castle of Carrickfergus held out. The garrison was reduced to eating hides as the Scots attempted to starve the castle into submission. A parley was arranged in June 1316; the defenders then treacherously seized the Scots negotiators, and later eight of these men were killed and eaten by the garrison. After a siege lasting more than a year, Carrickfergus surrendered to Bruce in September 1316.

Meanwhile, Edward Bruce was sweeping all before him: he defeated de Lacy in Meath in December 1315, before crushing the royal governor's army at Ardscull, Co. Kildare, in January. On 1 May 1316 Edward had himself crowned King of Ireland at Dundalk, and his brother, King Robert, joined him in December. After inflicting another defeat on the Red Earl, the two brothers advanced on Dublin. The frantic citizens demolished St Saviour's Priory and brought its stone across the River Liffey to build a wall along the quays. Further supplies of stone were obtained from St Mary's Abbey, where the citizens had locked up the Red Earl after he had taken refuge in the city, just in case he would be tempted to join King Robert, his daughter's husband. The bridge of Dublin was torn down, and, by direction of the mayor, dwellings outside the walls were set on fire. Lacking siege engines and seeing the desperate measures taken, the Scots turned back.

The Bruce invasion was beginning to fail. Above all, the Scots were being weakened by hunger as a terrible famine took hold in the country. The Bruce brothers rampaged across the country, plundering as far south as Limerick. There was little left to seize during a winter that was even harsher than the one before it. The *Laud Annals* assert that

> [*The Scots*] *were so destroyed with hunger that they raised the bodies of the dead from the cemeteries ... and their women devoured their own children from hunger. They were reduced to eating one another, so that out of 10,000 there remained only about 300 who escaped the vengeance of God.*

Hunger was to stalk the land many times in the decades that followed the failure of this great Scottish enterprise.

In July 1318, John of Athy, admiral of Edward II's fleet, captured Thomas Dun, who had organised transportation for the Scots across the North Channel. His supply lines cut, Edward Bruce was now on the defensive. Edward marched south from Ulster, only to meet a formidable army under the command of John de Bermingham at the hill of Faughart near Dundalk. There, Edward Bruce, who had invaded three years before and crowned himself King of Ireland only a few miles away two years before, was defeated and killed. Not only the English rejoiced at his death – the *Annals of Connacht* contain this arresting entry for the year 1318:

Edward Bruce, he who was the common ruin of the Gaels and Foreigners of Ireland, was by the Foreigners of Ireland killed at Dundalk by dint of fierce fighting. And never was there a better deed done for the Irish than this, since the beginning of the world and the banishing of the Fomorians from Ireland. For in this Bruce's time, for three years and a half, falsehood and famine and homicide filled the country, and undoubtedly men ate each other in Ireland.

The Bruce invasion had led to the devastation of much of the island, but it was the English colony there that had suffered most. Acute food shortages made it very tempting for the Gaelic Irish to burst out of their impoverished lands to plunder and seek to recover the fertile plains their forebears had lost to the Normans. Their attacks became ever more successful after the colony had been ravaged by the Black Death.

Carrickfergus Castle, a twelfth century Norman fortress north of Belfast

Pandemic:
The Black Death

. . .

THE BLACK DEATH ARRIVED in western Europe in the year 1347. This fearful bacillus appeared in three main forms of plague: bubonic, pneumonic and septicaemic. Some forms were transmitted by fleas carried principally by black rats, and, when the rats were killed by this disease, the fleas sought other hosts including human beings. People infected by the commonest form suffered painful swellings or buboes in the groin, armpits and neck. Symptoms included sudden chills, hallucination and delirium. Between 50 and 80 per cent of victims died within a week.

The Black Death made its first appearance in Ireland in the prosperous Co. Dublin port of Howth in late July 1348. Soon the disease was raging in Dublin, Drogheda and Dundalk, and during the autumn it spread inland to the manors of Louth, Meath and Co. Dublin. Waterford was hit next, and traders took the disease up the River Nore to Kilkenny. Here Friar Clyn was keeping a chronicle, and he recorded the arrival of the plague:

> *More people in the world have died in such a short time of plague than has been heard of since the beginning of time. The pestilence was so contagious that whosoever touched the sick and the dead was immediately infected and died, so that penitent and confessor were carried to the grave. That pestilence deprived of human inhabitants villages and cities, so that there was scarcely found a man to dwell therein.*

Friar Clyn tells us that the arrival of the Black Death prompted a pilgrimage to *Teach Moling*, the house of St Moling, on the River Barrow in Co. Carlow:

> *1348: In this year particularly in the months of September and October there came together from diverse parts of Ireland, bishops and prelates, churchmen and religious, lords and others to the pilgrimage at* Teach Moling, *in troops and multitudes ...*
>
> *Some came from feelings of devotion, but others, and they the majority, from dread of the plague, which then grew very rife.*

By Christmas Day 1348, 50 per cent of all the Franciscan friars of Drogheda had died of the plague. In the following months, the Black Death reaped a terrible harvest in Kilkenny. Friar Clyn continued:

> *Many died of boils and abscesses and pustules which erupted on their shins or under their armpits; others died frantic with pain in their head and others spitting blood. This plague was at its height in Kilkenny during Lent; for on the sixth day of March eight of the Friars Preachers died. There was hardly a house in which only one had died, but as a rule man and wife with their children and all the family went the common way of death.*

The striking feature of the Black Death in Ireland is that it raged principally in the ports and towns. In short, the English colony was much more severely affected than the Gaelic Irish living in the countryside. The Irish annals, never slow to mention disasters, made only very brief references to the Black Death. The *Annals of Ulster* has only one reference, specifically mentioning one area in Roscommon:

> *1349: The great plague of the general disease that was throughout Ireland prevailed in Moylurg this year so that great destruction of people was inflicted therein. Matthew, son of Cathal O'Rourke, died thereof.*

Clothes infected by the Black Death being burnt in medieval Europe, circa 1340.
The Black Death was thought to have been an outbreak of the bubonic plague,
which killed up to half the population of Europe. An illustration from the
'Romance of Alexander' in the Bodleian Library, Oxford

Meanwhile, Friar Clyn knew his end was near:

> *I, Brother Clyn of the Friars Minor of Kilkenny, have written in this book the notable events which befell in my time. So that notable deeds shall not be lost from the memory of future generations, I, seeing many ills, waiting for death till it come, have committed to writing what I have truly heard; and lest the writing perish with the writer, I leave parchment for continuing the work, if haply any man of the race of Adam escape this pestilence and continue the work which I have begun.*

Then, beneath a blot of ink, is written in another hand: 'Here, it seems, the author died.'

On Christmas Eve 1350 one young man wrote this prayer:

> *The second year after the coming of the plague into Ireland. And I am Hugh, son of Conor Mac Aodhagáin; under the safeguard of the King of Heaven and earth who is here tonight I place myself and may He put this great Plague past me and past my friends and may we be once more in joy and happiness. Amen. Pater Noster.*

He survived, but on most of the manors of the lordship of Ireland, many did not. We do not know how many victims there were, except for Colemanstown in the royal manor of Newcastle Lyons, Co. Dublin, where 84 per cent of the tenants were, it was reported, 'cut off by the late pestilence'. Certainly, there were many manors with vacant farms. This weakened colony in Ireland was therefore less able to defend itself against the native Irish, now employing mercenaries from the Western Isles of Scotland.

King Art, King Richard and the Pale

. . .

THE ABILITY OF GAELIC lords to win back lost territory in the late Middle Ages is in part explained by the employment of *gallóglaigh*, which literally means 'young foreign warriors'. The word *gallóglaigh* was anglicised by the colonists in Ireland as 'gallowglasses'. Gallowglasses were fighters of mixed Viking-Gaelic blood, who after the King of Scots had broken any remaining power the King of Norway had in the Hebrides in 1263, sought employment for their arms in Ireland, and in greater numbers during the following century.

In spring these clansmen from the Western Isles would plant their seed oats, and then gather their weapons and armour to row and sail their galleys across the North Channel to Ulster, there to offer their services to the highest bidder. For protection in battle, they wore quilted linen garments waterproofed with wax or pitch well rubbed in, and then given a covering of deer skin. Most had a metal helmet known as a 'bascinet' and some had a full coat of mail, an 'actoun' or 'habergeon', which had to be worn over a thick coat to prevent the rivets from digging into the flesh. Their standard fighting kit was either a single-handed or double-handed axe, a firmly held spear and a short bow. Their style of combat was to fire their arrows first and jettison their bows to charge, each protected by a round shield (either a buckler or the larger targe). One royal governor, Sir Anthony St Leger, observed that 'these sorte of men be those that doo not lightly abandon the field, but byde the brunte to the deathe'.

When the summer season of fighting was over, these Scottish warriors – the survivors, at any rate – received their pay, mostly in the form of butter, beef and live cattle, and sailed back to the Isles in time to reap, thresh and winnow their harvests. In time, however, these gallowglasses made a new home in Ireland.

Three branches of the MacSweeneys were granted extensive territories in the O'Donnell lordship of Tír Conaill. Other gallowglasses who settled in Ulster included the MacCabes, energetic campaigners south of the province; the MacRorys; the MacSheehys; the MacDowells descended from Alexander mac Dubhghaill (Dubhgall means a 'black-haired foreigner', i.e. a Danish Viking); and the MacDonnells, descendants of the legendary Viking Lord of the Isles, Somerled. The most important branch of the MacDonnells settled in the Glens of Antrim, in time to play a pivotal role in shaping Ulster's future.

Art MacMurrough-Kavanagh, King of Leinster

During the fourteenth and fifteenth centuries, the English lordship of Ireland contracted dramatically. In 1333 William de Burgo, the young Earl of Ulster and Lord of Connacht – one of the greatest landowners in western Europe – was murdered by his tenants near Shankill church outside Belfast. Known as the 'Brown Earl', William had only a two-year-old baby girl, Elizabeth, as his heir. The de Burgo lordship rapidly disintegrated thereafter.

Descendants of the first Norman conquerors were going native. Increasingly isolated from the heart of the English lordship in Dublin, they adopted the Irish language and dress, married into native Gaelic ruling families, engaged Irish harpers and poets, and gained the confidence to throw off their feudal allegiance to the English Crown.

In 1385 members of the Irish Great Council, predicting that Gaelic lords would overrun most of the island, made this appeal: 'because of the weakness and poverty of the English lieges, they are not able or know how to find or think of other remedy except the coming of our king, our lord, in his own person'. Finally, in 1394, Richard II agreed to come. Setting off from Milford Haven, the English king landed at Waterford with 10,000 men – by far the largest army yet prepared for Ireland.

The greatest single threat was Art MacMurrough Kavanagh, who had won recognition from his people as King of Leinster. King Richard ringed the Wicklow and Blackstairs mountains with heavily armed positions, ravaged the foothills to deny King Art supplies and completed his ring of steel by closely patrolling the coastline with his castellated ships. The French chronicler Froissart recorded that as a result 'the Irishmen advised themselves and came to obeisance'. Art and eighty other chieftains made submission. After nine months in Ireland, Richard II returned triumphantly to England, convinced he had saved the Irish lordship from destruction.

In June 1398, Roger Mortimer, Richard's royal governor, was killed by the Irish in a skirmish near Carlow. It demonstrated that the great expedition the king had led to Ireland at such immense cost had been for nothing. One by one Irish lords threw aside the oaths of loyalty they had made to Richard in person. Art once again assumed the title 'King of Leinster'. In despair, Richard decided to come to Ireland again in 1399. Ill-prepared and under-resourced, the expedition at once began to fail. When the Duke of Lancaster raised a successful rebellion in England, Richard had to hasten back – only to be made prisoner and thrown into the Tower of London, whence he was eventually taken away and murdered.

In 1427, the author of *The Little Book on English Policy* pointed out that 'the wylde Yrishe' had regained so much of the lordship of Ireland that

> *Our grounde there is a little cornere*
> *To all Yrelande in treue comparison.*

Henry VI was informed by his Irish council that the royal writ only ran in an area around Dublin 'scarcely thirty miles in length and twenty miles in breadth'.

The council was referring to the 'Pale'. The Dublin government had erected paling, put up fortifications, dug trenches, given grants towards the building of castles, appointed guards to hold the bridges, and assigned watchmen – paid by a tax called 'smokesilver' – to light beacons when danger threatened. The Pale ran from Dundalk in the north, inland to Naas in Co. Kildare, and then back to the coast just eight miles south of Dublin at Bray. Other coastal towns such as Waterford, Cork and Galway also attempted to remain loyal to the English Crown. They included Carrickfergus, described in 1468 as 'a garrison of war ... surrounded by Irish and Scots, without succour of the English for sixty miles'. And on the main gate of Galway was inscribed: 'From the fury of the O'Flahertys, good Lord deliver us.'

The truth was – most of Ireland was beyond the Pale.

The rebellion of
Silken Thomas

...

Silken Thomas

AS LONG AS ENGLAND was dislocated by the Wars of the Roses, both the Gaelic lords and the warlords of Norman origin in Ireland were secure in their virtual independence. They only had each other to fear. A stopgap solution for the English Crown was to turn to a great lord in Ireland to shoulder the burden of government. Then, in 1485, a new era began with the victory of the Lancastrian

Henry Tudor at the Battle of Bosworth. The Wars of the Roses were over. How would the new Tudor monarch, Henry VII, govern Ireland?

The royal governor since 1478 had been Garret Mór FitzGerald, the eighth Earl of Kildare, possessor of great estates adjoining the Pale. For most of his reign, Henry VII was content to let the 'Great Earl' of Kildare rule on his behalf. The earl – extracting great sums of protection money from lesser lords – covered all his expenses to such an extent that Henry was able to withdraw his army from Ireland altogether.

When the Great Earl died in 1513 of a gunshot wound while fighting the O'Mores, he was virtually the ruler of Ireland. Henry VIII, who had succeeded his father in 1509, had no hesitation in appointing his son, the ninth earl, known to the Irish as Garret Óg, as his governor. But Garret Óg was not the man his father had been, and the days of the Kildare hegemony were now numbered.

The earl was proving himself to be an overmighty subject. For example, he quarrelled unendingly and ferociously with the Butlers of Ormond – for long the king's faithful supporters – and led an expedition into Ulster without royal permission. Garret Óg was summoned to London but, as he travelled – like his father before him – he was dying of a gunshot wound he had received fighting the Irish in Leinster. 'The Earl of Kildare is here sick both in body and brain by the shot of an arquebus', the Spanish ambassador reported to Emperor Charles V.

Before travelling to England, the earl had appointed his eldest son – so well known for his love of finery that he was called 'Silken Thomas' – as deputy governor in his place. Hearing of his father's death in London, Silken Thomas at once concluded Garret Óg had been executed. He melodramatically entered Dublin with 1,000 men on 11 June 1534. Then he rode to St Mary's Abbey, surrendered the sword of state, resigned his office, and renounced his allegiance to the king before a terrified council. The *Annals of the Four Masters* chronicled the great rebellion which now began to convulse the island:

> *The Archbishop of Dublin came by his death through him, for he had been opposed to his father; many others were slain along with him. He took Dublin from Newgate outwards, and … totally*

plundered and devastated Fingall from Three Rock Mountain to
Drogheda, and made all Meath tremble beneath his feet.

Silken Thomas, by now the tenth Earl of Kildare, forged an alliance with Conor O'Brien, the Lord of Thomond, who in turn was seeking Spanish aid. Thomas was also sure of the support of his father's cousin, Conn Bacach O'Neill of Tír Eóghain, but Piers Butler, Earl of Ormond, remained loyal to King Henry. All that Silken Thomas got from Emperor Charles V was some gunpowder and shot from a Spanish vessel putting in at Dingle in Kerry. The rebels failed to take Dublin Castle, and then in October, Sir William Skeffington landed in Dublin with the largest English army Ireland had seen in over a century. One by one the earl's allies made their peace. For six days in March 1535, cannon battered Thomas's main stronghold, Maynooth Castle in Co. Kildare. When it fell the earl surrendered to the marshal of Henry VIII's Irish army, Leonard Grey, and was taken to London. There the Lord Chancellor expressed his amazement that

> *so arrant and cankered a traitor should come into the king's sight,*
> *free and out of ward. If this be intended, that he have mercy, I*
> *marvel much, that divers of the king's council in Ireland have told*
> *the king, afore this time, that there should never be good peace and*
> *order in Ireland, till the blood of the Geraldines were wholly extinct.*

Henry VIII was a suspicious and ruthless monarch who would brook no opposition from over-powerful subjects. Now, early in 1537, he had no hesitation. Silken Thomas, along with five of his uncles, was condemned to a traitor's death. The Grey Friars in London recorded their end:

> *The 3rd day of February the Lord Fytzgaarad with hys five unkelles*
> *of Ireland ... were draune from the Tower in to Tyborne, and there*
> *alle hanged and quartered, save the Lord Thomas for he was but*
> *hongyd and heeded and his body buryd at the Crost Freeres in the*
> *qwrere, and the quarters with their heddes set up about the cittie.*

Turbulence under the Tudors

. . .

THROUGHOUT THE MIDDLE AGES all the people who lived in Ireland, natives and colonists alike, were Christians, and all, of course, were Catholics. There were some differences, however. In the English-controlled lordship, the Church was organised in much the same way as in France and England. In the areas beyond the reach of the English – more than half the island – the Church was still run in the old Irish way. Above all, in Gaelic areas, the rule of celibacy was everywhere ignored.

There is no doubt that the Church throughout Ireland enjoyed strong and warm support. Gaelic lords, particularly in Ulster, went out of their way to fund the building of friaries. The friars, especially the Franciscans, were extremely popular because they were dedicated to a simple communal life, open-air preaching and pastoral work among the people. Donegal friary was founded in 1474 by Finola O'Connor, wife of the Lord of Tír Conaill; Bonamargy friary was built in 1500 by Rory MacQuillan, Lord of the Route; and others sprang up at Larne, Massereene, Lambeg, Sligo, and all over what the English described as the 'land of war'.

This friary-building boom was in full swing in the 1530s when Henry VIII dissolved the monasteries in England. Soon afterwards he decided to get rid of the monasteries in Ireland as well.

When the papacy refused to allow Henry VIII to divorce Catherine of Aragon in order to marry Anne Boleyn, the king severed the English Church from Rome and declared himself to be the head of that church. In May 1536 a parliament in Dublin agreed to accept Henry VIII as the supreme head of the Irish Church:

to repress and extirpate all errors, heresies and other enormities and abuses, heretofore used in the same: be it enacted by authority of this present parliament that the king our sovereign lord, his heirs and successors shall ... be accepted, taken, and reputed the only supreme head in earth of the whole church of Ireland.

There is no doubt that Irish nobles, knights and burgesses attending this parliament were deeply unhappy about this break with the Roman Church. But too many of them feared for their lives, having been involved so recently, however indirectly, in the rebellion of Silken Thomas FitzGerald: they, therefore, passed the legislation as the king wished. The task of enforcing the act was given to Archbishop Browne of Dublin, who sent out this instruction to the clergy:

I exhort you all, that ye deface the said Bishop of Rome in all your books, where he is named pope, and that ye shall have from henceforth no trust in him, nor in his bulls or pardons, which, beforetime, with his juggling, casts of binding and loosing, he sold you for your money and also that ye fear not his great thunder claps of excommunication, for they cannot hurt you.

The Irish clergy, including those most loyal to the Crown, were aghast. Ireland was experiencing the first impact of a profound upheaval in western Christianity – the Reformation.

Portrait of Mary I of England, Queen of England and Ireland from July 1553 until her death

Henry VIII found aggressive campaigning in Ireland too heavy a financial burden. In a long letter, the king sketched out an alternative approach 'to bring Irish captains to further obedience' and to recover royal lands; he suggested 'circumspect and politic ways, which thing must as yet rather be practised by sober ways, politic drifts, and amiable persuasions'.

Sir Anthony St Leger, appointed chief governor in 1540, was a firm believer in 'amiable persuasions'. His scheme was known as 'surrender and regrant'. Henceforth, Gaelic lords were to be invited to hold their lands by English feudal law from the king: they would drop their traditional Irish titles and give up their lands to the king, receiving them back immediately with English titles. It was a scheme that was to enjoy a remarkable amount of initial success. One of the first to respond was Conn Bacach O'Neill of Tír Eóghain, who travelled to London in 1542 to receive his new title of the Earl of Tyrone. One by one, nearly all the lords submitted and received English titles. Murrough O'Brien became Earl of Thomond; Ulick MacWilliam Burke of Connacht became Earl of Clanricarde; Dermot MacCarthy, Lord of Muskerry, got a knighthood; and so on.

In 1541 the Irish parliament gave Henry VIII the title 'King of Ireland'. No great protest followed. But stresses and strains returned to Ireland when Henry VIII died in 1547. The Lord Protectors of his ten-year-old son, now Edward VI, introduced the *Book of Common Prayer*, destroyed shrines and acted pugnaciously to impose the Reformation on Ireland. Mary, who succeeded Edward after his early death in 1553, immediately restored the Catholic religion, to the relief of the great majority. But Mary gave her full support to those at court who thought that tough military action was the only lesson that the rebellious Gaelic Irish would understand. O'Mores, O'Dempseys and O'Connors in the midlands were crushed and their lands were 'planted' with loyal subjects: Leix became 'Queen's County' and Offaly was titled 'King's County' after Mary's husband, King Philip of Spain.

In 1558 Mary died without an heir. Her successor was Elizabeth I. It was during Elizabeth's long reign that Ireland was to be conquered from end to end by the English for the first time. To do that she had to concentrate on subjugating the most Gaelic part of Ireland, the province of Ulster.

Shane the Proud

. . .

BY FAR THE MOST powerful man in Ulster was Shane O'Neill of Tyrone. Brutal, vindictive and drunken, Shane had driven his aged father, Conn Bacach, into the Pale, where he died soon after. Conn, who was created the first Earl of Tyrone in 1542, had nominated Matthew, another son, as his heir, and this had been accepted in London. The problem was that the earl had married several times and had innumerable offspring. By Gaelic law, each one of his sons could compete to succeed him. In a fierce succession dispute, Shane had come out on top. He had murdered his half-brother Matthew, whom he claimed – probably correctly – to have been Conn's illegitimate son by a blacksmith's wife.

To his own people, he was *Seán an Díomais*, Shane the Proud: arrogant, ruthless and wily, he was without rival in Tyrone. He aspired to dominate the Antrim Scots, the Clandeboye O'Neills and the O'Donnells of Tír Conaill. By 1560 so many Scottish mercenaries had entered his service that the viceroy, Sir William Fitzwilliam, sent a desperate appeal to the English government: 'Send us over men that we may fight ere we die.'

Though Queen Elizabeth refused to recognise Shane as Earl of Tyrone, at first she seemed to hope the problem would somehow go away. Then Shane swept south and launched an attack on the Pale. After that, in May 1561, he moved west against Calvagh O'Donnell, Lord of Tír Conaill. Calvagh's wife, Catherine, seems to have become infatuated with Shane; certainly, she led Calvagh into a trap while he was besieging a rebellious kinsman in Glenveagh. The O'Donnell chief was bound in chains, and Catherine became Shane's mistress, only to be abused cruelly and cast aside soon after.

Queen Elizabeth

The problem for Elizabeth was that Calvagh was at that time supposed to be an ally of the English Crown. She sent over the Earl of Sussex as her viceroy. The earl forged his way into Ulster, only to find that Shane O'Neill had pulled back into the forests with his cattle. Cut off by floods and running out of supplies, Sussex had no choice but to make a humiliating retreat. In desperation, the earl concocted a plan to poison Shane, with a contingency scheme – which he frankly explained to the queen – to murder the poisoner should he fail. Nothing came of this plan. The queen felt she had no recourse but to make her peace with Shane, and to this end, she invited him to London.

On 3 January 1562 Shane entered London, accompanied by the Earls of Kildare and Ormond, and with an escort of fifty gallowglasses. Bare-headed, with hair flowing onto their shoulders, wearing short tunics, heavy cloaks, and linen vests dyed saffron-yellow with urine, the warriors drew crowds of onlookers as large as those that had turned out to gape at Native Americans and Chinese in the city a short time before.

The next day at Greenwich, in the presence of ambassadors and all the court, Shane threw himself to the floor before Elizabeth. Then rising to his knees, he made a passionate speech in Irish, punctuated by howls which caused great astonishment. 'For lack of education and civility I have offended ...', he began, the words of his speech being translated into English by the Earl of Kildare. Elizabeth eventually agreed to recognise Shane as 'captain' of Tyrone on condition that he kept the peace for the next six months.

Almost as soon as he was back in Ulster, Shane O'Neill was making devastating raids on his neighbours. A punitive expedition to Ulster led by the Earl of Sussex in 1563 failed to bring O'Neill to heel. To complete his domination of all of Ulster, Shane then prepared to strike at the MacDonnells of Antrim.

As Shane bore down on the Glens in 1565, the Scots set their beacons ablaze on Fair Head and the high ground behind Torr Head. The men of Kintyre seized their weapons and manned their galleys, but it was already too late. Sorley Boy MacDonnell, who had been leading the defence of the Glens, fell back to join his brother James, and together they made a desperate last stand by the slopes of Knocklayd. Shane overwhelmed the Scots, as he triumphantly reported in a letter written in Latin and sent to Dublin Castle:

> God, best and greatest, and for the welfare of her Majesty the Queen, gave us the victory against them. James and his brother Sorley were taken prisoners, besides many of the Scottish nobility were captured, and great numbers of their men killed, amounting in all to six or seven hundred.

James died of his wounds, Dunseverick fell, Ballycastle was taken, and – after Shane threatened to starve Sorley Boy to death – Dunluce capitulated. O'Neill had all Ulster in thrall, as he exultantly declared in a letter to Sir Henry Sidney:

I am in blood and power better than the best of them. My ancestors were Kings of Ulster, Ulster was theirs, and shall be mine. And for O'Donnell, he shall never come into his country if I can keep him out of it, nor Bagenal into the Newry, nor the Earl of Kildare into Lecale. They are mine; with this sword I won them, with this sword I will keep them. This is my answer.

The queen was horrified that such slaughter had been claimed on her behalf, and she wrote to Sir Henry Sidney, her new Lord Deputy, to ask how 'such a cankred dangerous rebel' might be 'utterly extirped'.

In the end, it was Shane's neighbours in Ulster who brought about his downfall. In 1567 as the O'Neills crossed the River Swilly at Farsetmore they met a furious onslaught of O'Donnells and MacSweeneys. Shane's warriors retreated into the advancing tide, there to be drowned or cut down. O'Neill himself fled eastward to take refuge with the MacDonnells in the Glens. It was an extraordinary decision, but perhaps Shane hoped that by openly associating with Sorley Boy he could buy protection. The MacDonnells prepared a feast at Glenshesk in an apparent mood of reconciliation. They 'fell to quaffing' – as one report put it – and a quarrel broke out, during which O'Neill was hacked to death. Shane's head was sent 'pickled in a pipkin' to Sidney, who placed it on a spike over Dublin Castle gate-arch. But many more campaigns would have to be fought before Ulster would be subdued.

'Warring against a she-tyrant': holy war in Ulster and Munster

. . .

THE KILLING OF SHANE O'Neill did little to increase English power in Ulster. Elizabeth did not feel she had money to spare for more expensive military expeditions. Perhaps private enterprise could achieve something there? The queen approved a scheme put forward by one of her privy councillors, Sir Thomas Smith, to 'plant' or colonise the eastern part of the province. The expedition was led by his son, also called Thomas; it was doomed from the outset. Only around a hundred prospective colonists disembarked at Strangford village in August 1572. Very soon the English were surrounded by Sir Brian McPhelim O'Neill, Lord of Clandeboye. Smith was killed by his Irish servants the following year, and his body was boiled and fed to dogs. By then a more ambitious enterprise was already under way.

Walter Devereux, Earl of Essex, was so certain of success that he mortgaged most of his great estates in England and Wales to raise the £10,000 he thought was needed. When he landed at Carrickfergus Sir Brian McPhelim thought it politic not to quarrel with such a powerful English noble; as Essex reported, 'I took him by the hand, as a sign of his restitution to her Highness's service'. Sir Brian invited Essex to a feast in Belfast Castle. At the end of the feast, however, as the annals record,

> *as they were agreeably drinking and making merry, Brian, his brother, and his wife, were seized upon by the earl, and all his people put unsparingly to the sword – men, women, youths, and maidens – in Brian's own presence. Brian was afterwards sent to Dublin, together with his wife and brother, where they were cut in quarters.*

Elizabeth and her attendants out hawking. Woodcut from
George Turbevile or Turbeville *Booke of Faulconrie* 1575

Essex also authorised a ferocious attack on the MacDonnells. An assault fleet led by Francis Drake – already famous for seizing a Spanish treasure convoy – disembarked on Rathlin Island on the morning of 22 July 1575. The men 'did with valiant minds leap to land', Essex reported, 'and charged them so hotly, chasing them to a castle which they had of very great strength'. The castle surrendered on condition the lives of those besieged would be spared. But the 'soldiers ... made request to have the killing of them, which they all did ... there were slain out of the castle of all sorts 200 ... they be occupied still in killing'.

Despite this apparent victory, Essex was running out of men and money. He pulled back in despair to Dublin, where in September 1576, rather suddenly, he died of dysentery. He was thirty-six years old. By then it was Munster, not Ulster, which was causing Elizabeth the greatest anxiety.

Gerald FitzGerald, the fifteenth Earl of Desmond, constantly defied the Queen, principally because he was appalled by the Crown's establishment of a Protestant church in Ireland. He was arrested in 1567 and spent the next five years languishing in the Tower of London. In his absence, the two men managing his estates, his cousin James FitzMaurice FitzGerald and his brother Sir John of Desmond, prepared resistance and broke out in rebellion in 1569. But the colonel commanding Elizabeth's forces, Sir Humphrey Gilbert, crushed the rebellion with a savagery unusual even for that time. In six weeks he took twenty-three castles and in each one slaughtered all those inside – men, women and children. As every defeated rebel made abject surrender, he had to walk down a grisly corridor of severed heads.

The Earl of Desmond, allowed back to Ireland in 1573, soon made it clear that he would not tolerate further erosion of his traditional power by Protestant heretics. Meanwhile, James FitzMaurice obtained an audience with Pope Gregory XIII in Rome and put together an expedition composed of Italians and Portuguese veterans. FitzMaurice's manifesto proclaimed: 'For the defence of the Catholic religion against the heretics ... we are warring against a she-tyrant who has deservedly lost her royal power by refusing to listen to Christ in the person of her vicar'. The expedition put in at Smerwick harbour in Co. Kerry on 18 July 1579. Here they built a fort which became known as *Dún an Óir*, the 'fort of gold'. Then the Pope sent Spaniards and more Italians who joined their compatriots at Smerwick in September 1580.

Soon after, Lord Deputy Grey closed in with an overwhelming force. The garrison surrendered, thinking quarter had been given. 'And then', the Lord Deputy chillingly reported to the queen, 'put I in certain bands, who straightway fell to execution. There were 600 slain.' The rebellion raged on futilely: John of Desmond was killed in 1582 and the Earl of Desmond the following year. The Lord Deputy's secretary, Edmund Spenser, who had witnessed the massacre at Smerwick, now described the suffering of the ordinary people in Munster:

> *Out of every corner of the woods and glens they came creeping forth upon their hands, for their legs would not bear them; they looked like anatomies of death, they spake like ghosts crying out of their graves; they did eat of the dead carrions, happy were they if they could find them, yea, and one another soon after ...*

The wreck of the Armada

. . .

WALTER RALEIGH, A CAPTAIN who had superintended the slaughter at Smerwick, was one of many who argued that now was the time to colonise the confiscated estates of the Earl of Desmond and his adherents. A hasty survey was made in 1584, and finally, the decision was taken to settle people of English birth on the confiscated lands. The lands were divided into portions of between 4,000 and 12,000 acres, each to be granted to an 'undertaker', that is, a man who undertook to bring in a specified number of families to work the land – no Gaelic Irish tenants were permitted. Demand was strong, and eventually, thirty-five undertakers were successful in getting estates. It was not long, however, before the Plantation of Munster began to run into trouble. Not enough ordinary English farming families came over, and those who did were fatally exposed to the turbulent conditions following the outbreak of war between England and Spain.

In 1588 Philip II of Spain, the most powerful monarch in the world, sent north against England his supposedly invincible Armada. But from the time the Armada entered the English Channel, the Spanish king's dream of conquest was turning to dust. Raked by English cannon fire and scattered by fireships, the Spanish fleet could do no other than take flight up the North Sea, around the Orkneys and westwards deep into the Atlantic. In the mountainous seas stirred up by autumn gales some Armada vessels were driven inexorably towards the western shores of Ireland. Eating only ship's biscuit riddled with weevils and parched by lack of fresh water, the crews were exhausted and ill, and many were dying.

In Dublin Castle, orders given to Sir William Fitzwilliam, Queen Elizabeth's Lord Deputy, were clear: put to the sword any Spaniard who stepped ashore.

Fighting between the English fleet and the Spanish Armada

Twenty-four men survived the wreck of a frigate in Tralee Bay, only to be seized and hanged there by the orders of Lady Denny. In Blasket Sound the *Nuestre Señora de la Rosa* split open on a hidden reef; all 700 on board drowned save for one man. Don Pedro de Mendoza landed at Clare Island off the Mayo coast, but he and his crew of a hundred were butchered there by the O'Malley chief. Don Luis de Córdoba came ashore at Galway harbour. All his men were hanged or shot, with the exception of Don Luis, who was held for ransom.

On 14 September *La Trinidad Valencera* sought shelter in the lee of the Inishowen peninsula. One of the greatest ships of the Armada, the vessel had been shipping water in the wild south-westerly storm. The ship cast anchor and the Commander of the Regiment of Naples, Don Alonso de Luzon, sent a cockboat ashore 'whereupon they found four or five savages who bade them welcome'. The 'savages' were O'Dohertys who did what they could for the stricken Spanish. Then without warning *La Trinidad Valencera* sank; forty men who were below decks were drowned. Don Alonso made up his mind to cross the Foyle and seek the help of the MacDonnells of the Glens. With barely the strength to make the journey, this mixed band of Spaniards, Neapolitans, Greeks and Dalmatians set out with banners flying only to be confronted at Galliagh, close to Derry, by Irish soldiers in English pay. Exhausted, they gave up their weapons only to be stripped naked and at first light taken into a field. There almost two hundred of them were butchered.

Don Alonso Martínez de Leiva de Rioja, Knight of Santiago, Commander of Alcuéscar, was general-in-chief of the land forces of the Armada entrusted with the conquest of England. When his ship *Sancta Maria Rata Encoronada* foundered in Blacksod Bay, de Leiva attempted to sail north to neutral Scotland, only to be forced to go ashore in Loughros More Bay. Although his leg had been broken against the capstan, the commander rallied the survivors to cross a mountain pass to join three other Spanish vessels at Killybegs. Here only one Spanish ship remained afloat, the *Girona*, a three-masted galleass. De Leiva resolved to sail for Scotland. About 1,300 Spaniards crowded aboard at the end of October. But a northerly gale smashed her rudder and blew the vessel onto the north Antrim coast. Close to the Giant's Causeway the ship struck a long basalt reef and split apart. Only nine men survived.

A survivor of the Armada, commenting on this loss of life, wrote: 'The gentlemen were so many that a list of their names would fill a quire of paper.' That survivor was Captain Francisco de Cuéllar. He had been on board the *Lavia*, one of three ships wrecked on sandbanks at Streedagh in Sligo Bay. The secretary to the Irish Council reported to London: 'At my late being in Sligo I numbered in one strand of less than five miles in length above 1,000 dead corpses of men which the sea had driven upon the shore.' The queen's troops cut down hundreds more who had come ashore alive.

Protected by the MacClancys and O'Rourkes in Leitrim, de Cuéllar survived to write an account of his ordeal to Philip II.

'The wild Irish are barbarous and most filthy in their diet'

. . .

THE SPANISH ARMADA CASTAWAY Captain Francisco de Cuéllar lived with the Irish in the far north west of Ireland for almost a year. Though he was grateful for their kindness to him, he and other Spaniards without hesitation described the Irish as savages:

> The custom of these savages is to live as brute beasts in the mountains, which are very rugged in that part of Ireland where we lost ourselves. They are great walkers, and inured to toil. The men are all large-bodied, and of handsome features and limbs; and as active as the roe-deer. The most of the women are very beautiful, but badly got up. They do not eat oftener than once a day, and this is at night; and that which they usually eat is butter with oaten bread. They drink sour milk, for they have no other drink; they don't drink water, although it is the best in the world. On feast days they eat some flesh half-cooked without bread or salt, as that is their custom.

Edmund Campion, an English scholar subsequently executed as a Jesuit traitor, commented on what was on the menu of the Irish:

> Shamrocks, watercresses, roots and other herbs they feed upon, oatmeal and butter they cram together. They drink whey, milk and beef-broth, flesh they devour without bread, corn such as they have they keep for their horses.

There is no doubt that cattle were at the heart of the Gaelic farming economy and that dairy produce formed the most important part of the diet. Oats had a much better chance of ripening than wheat, particularly in the wetter parts of the north and the west. On one occasion the O'Donnells fell upon Shane O'Neill's warriors while they were holding out their helmets to be served raw oatmeal with molten butter poured over it. Fresh milk was generally too precious to be drunk in any quantity, but buttermilk was widely consumed. Fynes Moryson, secretary to Lord Deputy Mountjoy, wrote that the people 'esteem for a great dainty sour curds, vulgarly called Bonaclabbe'. This was *bainne clabair*, or bonnyclabber: clotted milk.

An Irish banquet, 1581.
An illustration from *A Short History of the English People* by John Richard Green

Blood was sometimes drawn from below the ears of living cattle or horses and mixed with butter to form a jelly. Moryson adds, 'No meat they fancy so much as pork, the fatter the better.'

By this time wine was imported by the Gaelic lords in exchange for hides or, for example in Tír Conaill, as payment by Spaniards for the right to fish. Malted oats and barley could not only be brewed to make ale but were now often distilled to make *uisce beathadh*, whiskey, the 'water of life', much favoured by English commanders for medicinal purposes. Sir Josias Bodley found priests in eastern Ulster pouring 'usquebaugh down their throats by day and by night'.

As the sixteenth century drew to a close, few Englishmen travelled all parts of Ireland as much as the Lord Deputy's secretary, Fynes Moryson. It should be remembered that his uncomplimentary accounts were written about the Irish who were constantly on the move as the forces of Queen Elizabeth were closing in on them:

> The wild Irish, inhabiting many and large provinces, are barbarous and most filthy in their diet. They scum the seething pot with an handful of straw, and strain their milk taken from the cow through a like handful of straw, none of the cleanest, and so cleanse, or rather more defile the pot and milk. They devour great morsels of meat unsalted, and they eat commonly swine's flesh, seldom mutton, and all these pieces of flesh they seethe in a hollow tree, lapped in a raw cow's hide, and so set over the fire, and therewith swallow whole lumps of filthy butter.

Moryson, like other English observers, mentions the liking the Irish had for shamrock – almost certainly this was wood sorrel (known to some today as 'Sour Sally'), rightly regarded as a piquant enhancement to a good, fresh salad:

> They willingly eat the herb shamrock, being of a sharp taste, which as they run and are chased to and fro, they snatch like beasts out of the ditches ... They drink milk like nectar, warmed with a stone first cast into the fire, or else beef-broth mingled with milk; but when they come to any market town to sell a cow or a horse, they never return home, till they have drunk the price in Spanish wine (which they call the King of Spain's Daughter), or in Irish 'usquebaugh' till they have out-slept two or three days' drunkenness. And not only the common sort, but even the lords and their wives, the more they want this drink at home, the more they swallow it when they come to it, till they be as drunk as beggars.

As more and more of the island fell under their control, the English found much about its people to both attract and repel them.

'A fit house for an outlaw, a meet bed for a rebel, and an apt cloak for a thief'

. . .

THE SPANISH ARMADA CASTAWAY Captain Francisco de Cuéllar found the Irish men who protected him handsome and fine-limbed and was constantly encountering Irish girls 'beautiful in the extreme'. He was not, however, impressed by how the Irish dressed:

> *They clothe themselves, according to their habit, with tight trousers and short loose coats of very coarse goat's hair. They cover themselves with blankets, and wear their hair down to their eyes.*

The 'goat's hair' was probably coarse sheep's wool, and 'blankets' were the mantles which were the most distinctive item of Irish dress. The mantle was an enveloping outer woollen cloak. These rectangular garments were worn by everyone in Ireland, young and old, rich and poor. The most popular mantles had a tufted or curled nap raised with the aid of a teasel seedhead. These tufts on the inside of the mantle helped with insulation and were treated with a mixture of honey and vinegar to stop them from uncurling. Tightly woven mantles were remarkably waterproof; when they were issued to English soldiers in Ireland in 1600, it was argued that

> *Being never so wet, [the mantles] will presently with a little shaking and wringing be presently dry; for want of which the soldiers, lying abroad, marching and keeping watch and ward in cold and wet in winter time, die in the Irish ague and in flux pitifully.*

English writer, poet and soldier Edmund Spenser described the mantle as

> *a fit house for an outlaw, a meet bed for a rebel, and an apt cloke for a thief. First the outlaw, being for his many crimes and villainies banished from the towns and houses of honest men and wandering in waste places, far from danger of law, maketh his mantle his house, and under it covereth himself from the wrath of heaven, from the offence of the earth, and from the fight of men. When it raineth, it is his pent-house, when it bloweth it is his tent, when it freezeth, it is his tabernacle. In summer he can wear it loose; in winter, he can wrap it close; at all times he can use it; never heavy, never cumbersome.*
>
> *Likewise for a rebel it is serviceable: for in his war he maketh when he still flieth from his foe, and lurketh in the thick woods, it is his bed, yea, and almost his household stuff ... Yea, and oftentimes their mantle serveth them, when they are near driven, being wrapped about their left arm, in stead of a shield; for it is hard to cut through with a sword, besides, it is light to bear, light to throw away, and being (as they commonly are) naked, it is to them all in all.*

The better-off made some attempt to keep up with the latest Spanish, Flemish and English fashions, and Edmund Campion was only one of many who observed the love that Irish men had for voluminous shirts and hanging sleeves:

> *Linen shirts the rich do wear for wantonness and bravery, with wide hanging sleeves pleated, thirty yards are little enough for one of them. They have now left their saffron, and learn to wash their shirts, four or five times in a year. Proud they are of long crisped glibs, and do nourish the same with all their cunning: to crop the front thereof they take it for a notable piece of villainy.*

A 'glib' was a thick roll of hair at the forehead; a law of 1537 specifically forbade the English in Ireland to wear their hair in this fashion.

A lady's gown, dating from the late sixteenth century, was found in remarkably good condition in a bog in Co. Tipperary. Beautifully tailored, it has a very low U-shaped neckline with an opening down the front to a low waist which appears to be pointed over the stomach. The extraordinarily heavy ankle-length full skirt is made of twenty-three triangular pieces of cloth sewn together, measuring no fewer than 22½ feet at the bottom. There are ninety-two folds formed by welts sewn at intervals. The dress also has a small stand collar at the back of the neck.

Irish women seem to have been quite happy to expose their breasts in full in polite society. Nor were they ashamed to be naked, as a Czech nobleman discovered in 1601. Just what Jaroslav z Donína was doing in what is now Co. Londonderry in the middle of a devastating rebellion is impossible to say. Anyway, he encountered sixteen high-born women, all naked, with 'which strange sight his eyes being dazzled, they led him into the house' to converse politely in Latin in front of the fire. Joining them, the Lord O'Cahan threw all his clothes off and was surprised that the Bohemian baron was too bashful to do likewise.

As the sixteenth century was drawing to a close, outsiders were learning a great deal more about the country which the English, for the first time, were conquering from end to end.

A drawing by Albrecht Dürer in 1521 shows four men.
The man in the middle wears a mantle with a shaggy lining. The two younger men on the right wear jackets with wide sleeves. All men wear *léinte* (the linen shirts)

Granuaile: the Pirate Queen of Connacht

...

DURING THE FIFTEENTH CENTURY, nearly all of the province of Connacht had fallen out of the control of the English Crown. Descendants of the Norman conquerors of earlier times had gone native, married local girls, and adopted Gaelic customs and surnames. But the tide turned in the sixteenth century. Some lords were prepared to accept knighthoods and other English titles. Other nobles were alarmed as growing English power eroded their independence. One of these was Granuaile, Gráinne O'Malley. The O'Malleys dominated the entire coastlands and islands of Mayo and maintained a formidable fleet of galleys. In 1546, at the age of sixteen, Gráinne was married to Donal O'Flaherty, head of another strong seafaring family based in Connemara.

Her husband Donal got the nickname 'the Cock', and she was in turn called 'the Hen'. When Donal was murdered by the Joyces of eastern Connemara, she fought back with fury. The castle on an island in Lough Corrib she defended with such determination became known as 'Hen's Castle', the name it still bears today.

From then on Gráinne's main opponents were English. She led another defence of Hen's Castle and forced the Crown forces to retire after she ordered the lead from the roof to be torn off, melted down and then poured onto the heads of her assailants. In 1566 she married Risdeárd-an-Iarainn Burke, or, as the English called him, 'Richard-the-Iron'. This marriage alliance created an alarming challenge to royal authority.

Gráinne O'Malley secured the release of captured
relatives in her audience with Queen Elizabeth in 1593

In an attempt to strengthen royal control in the province, Sir Edward Fitton was appointed the first Lord President of Connacht in 1569. Once he had smashed up as many holy images in churches as he could find, Fitton decided to curb the power of Richard-the-Iron and his wife. In 1574 he advanced on their main fortress, Rockfleet Castle at the head of an inlet in Clew Bay. Here Gráinne had a long chain from her favourite ship tied to her bedpost every night in case anyone would be tempted to steal the vessel.

After a three-week siege, the English were forced to withdraw with heavy losses. Then Gráinne travelled to Galway to talk terms with Lord Deputy Sir Henry Sidney. He was fascinated to meet this 'famous feminine sea captain called Grany Imallye ... a notorious woman in all the coasts of Ireland'. Failing to keep the peace she had made with Sidney, she was imprisoned in Dublin Castle.

Released on condition of good behaviour, Gráinne knew she needed her wits about her if she was to survive the inexorable extension of English royal power. Sir Richard Bingham, appointed the new Lord President in 1584, was proving himself a merciless governor. One by one, the great lords of the province submitted. He unveiled his ambitious 'Composition of Connacht' which included a prohibition on keeping armed men.

Gráinne O'Malley was among those who refused to be reconciled to the new regime. Bingham decided he had no choice but to deal in person with this proud woman. After hanging in public seventy men from leading Connacht families for breaking terms of the Composition, Bingham advanced northwards from Galway in February 1586. Gráinne was now on her own: her husband had died four years earlier. But with the help of her son-in-law, Richard Burke of Achill, known as the 'Devil's Hook', Gráinne successfully defended her fortress on an island on Lough Mask, called Hag's Castle. White-capped waves stirred up by a storm foiled Bingham's attack by boats.

Eventually, she was brought to heel and she travelled to Dublin in 1588 to obtain a pardon from the Lord Deputy. The Devil's Hook acted as a guarantor of Gráinne's good behaviour. Foolish man. Her continued piracy caused Bingham to write to the queen's secretary 'to gyve your honour Knowledge of her naughty disposicion towards the state'. He condemned her as 'a notable traitoress and nurse to all the rebellions in the Province for forty years'.

In 1593 Gráinne decided to counter Bingham's criticisms and appeal to Elizabeth herself. The queen summoned her to London. Gráinne captained one of her galleys and sailed to meet her. She steered out of Clew Bay into the Atlantic, south beyond Connemara and the Aran Islands, and on round the Blaskets and the wild headlands of Kerry. Then she directed her ship past Cape Clear eastwards, down the English Channel and into the Thames estuary.

There is no detailed account of the meeting at Greenwich between the pirate queen and Queen Elizabeth. Clearly, Gráinne got much of what she wanted, for afterwards, Elizabeth informed Bingham, 'for the pity to be had of this aged woman ... yield to her some maintenance ... And this we do write in her favour as she showeth herself dutiful ... She hath confessed the same with assured promises by oath.'

Bingham very much doubted that Gráinne would behave herself in future, and he was right. She was to join forces with the Gaelic lords of Ulster in a great rebellion which would convulse Ireland from end to end.

The Nine Years' War begins

. . .

IN 1590 LORD DEPUTY Sir William Fitzwilliam led a punitive expedition against Hugh Roe MacMahon, the principal Gaelic lord of Monaghan, and hanged him. Then MacMahon's extensive lands were divided and apportioned to other family members. Not one of the new owners of these Co. Monaghan estates would be strong enough to threaten rebellion – indeed, each was happy to pay taxes and give allegiance in return for a secure title to farms which each could pass on by English law to an eldest son. The Master of the Ordnance concluded that this sort of division was the 'soundest and surest way to bring Ireland to due obedience'.

Sir Henry Bagenal, the queen's marshal, with lands centred on Newry, agreed. Now he sought the break-up of all the great Gaelic lordships of Ulster: 'The chiefest, or rather the only means to reduce these barbarous people to obedience is to disunite them as all may be enforced to depend upon the queen'.

Hugh O'Neill, the Earl of Tyrone, viewed these developments with alarm. Given a good education in the Pale near Dublin, he had been expected to promote the interests of the Crown in the heart of Ulster. The earl, however, was proving rather more independent than expected. In 1592 he organised the dramatic escape of the young Red Hugh O'Donnell from Dublin Castle to bring him back to his lordship of Tír Conaill. Then in 1593, Tyrone rode alongside Marshal Bagenal to besiege Enniskillen Castle: here Hugh Maguire, threatened with the partition of his Fermanagh lordship, was holding out having risen in rebellion. At Enniskillen, the earl found that Red Hugh was helping Hugh Maguire. Suddenly O'Neill changed sides.

Joining O'Donnells and Maguires, on 7 August 1594 the earl routed a relief force bringing up food provisions and munitions to the marshal's forces at a ford over the River Arney – known thereafter as 'The Battle of the Biscuits', from provisions abandoned in flight.

The great rebellion, led by the Gaelic lords of Ulster and known later as the Nine Years' War, had begun. On 13 June 1595 at Clontibret, O'Neill, O'Donnell and Maguire overwhelmed a column taking supplies to Monaghan Fort. Sir Edward York, in command of the cavalry, ruefully observed that Tyrone commanded a highly professional force, admitting 'that in no place whatsoever had he served in all his life he never saw more readier or perfecter shot'. Soon after it was estimated that Hugh O'Neill commanded no fewer than 1,000 horsemen, 1,000 pikemen and 4,000 foot soldiers shouldering modern firearms. He had brought together the squabbling ruling families of Gaelic Ulster under his command. Meanwhile, Red Hugh, the earl's most loyal ally, carried the revolt successfully into Connacht and took Sligo Castle.

Hugh O'Neill
circa 1595

At the same time, the earl knew that he could only triumph in the end by seeking allies overseas. At war again against England, Philip II of Spain was eager to help. Don Alonso de Cobos, landing at Killybegs with munitions and relics from the Pope, walked forty miles to Lifford to meet the Gaelic lords. He took away with him a letter to the Prince of the Asturias, son of the King of Spain; sealed and signed by O'Neill and O'Donnell, it asked him to 'aid in his clemency this most excellent and just cause, that of asserting Catholic liberty and of freeing the country from the rod of tyrannical evil'.

> *I protest to God, the state of the scurvy fort of Blackwater, which cannot long be held, doth more touch my heart than all the spoils that ever were made by traitors on mine own lands. The fort was always falling, and never victualled but once (by myself) without an army.*

So wrote the Earl of Ormonde, advising that the fort be pulled down. His advice was ignored. The Crown's military strategy was to build forts in hostile territory: in the end, this was a tactic that worked well. But now – as more and more Gaelic lords across the island joined Tyrone's rebellion – too many were dangerously exposed and none more so than Blackwater Fort in Tír Eóghain. This had been built on the orders of Lord Deputy Thomas Burgh, who had described it as 'my first child ... an eyesore in the heart of O'Neill's country'. Now the 150 men in the garrison were starving. Fresh English troops arrived in Dublin in July 1598. Marshal Bagenal agreed to use these soldiers to bring food and ammunition to the Blackwater Fort. He led northwards 300 cavalry and 4,000 foot soldiers – the largest army to have entered Ulster for many years.

Hugh O'Neill had long prepared for this opportunity. For months his men had been engaged in digging a deep trench a mile long between two treacherous bogs. His plan was to draw the Crown forces towards this trench into a carefully laid ambush. An epic battle was about to begin.

'We spare none of what quality or sex soever'

. . .

IN 1598 THE QUEEN'S marshal, Sir Henry Bagenal, led a great army into Tír Eóghain to bring relief to the garrison of Blackwater Fort. On 14 August, as the commander thrust across the country, his army was assailed by caliver and musket shot from the woods, where the Irish were safe from the English cavalry. Pack-horses and four cannons dragged by bullocks held up regiments marching behind, widely separating English troops at the front who were advancing into an elaborate trap laid by Hugh O'Neill, Earl of Tyrone. Then a heavy cannon stuck fast in the bed of a stream oozing from a bog – the yellow ford which was to give the battle its name. Bagenal rode back to help pull the gun out, but when he raised his visor he was shot in the face and fell, mortally wounded. The Irish closed in as the English fled back wildly to the mêlée at the ford. This defeat became a disaster when a soldier, refilling his powder horn, exploded two barrels of gunpowder with his slow-burning match.

The Battle of the Yellow Ford was almost certainly the most crushing defeat the English had ever suffered at the hands of the Irish. News of the victory spread rapidly. In the far south the Munster Plantation – that is, the colony of English promoted by Elizabeth – completely collapsed. When her Irish Council thought of considering a peace offer from O'Neill, the queen was appalled, writing that 'this foul error to our dishonour' would only lead to 'the increasing of the traitor's insolency'.

Elizabeth had no longer any wish to talk. The Battle of the Yellow Ford convinced her that she must empty her coffers, if need be, to defeat this rebellion. Over the winter of 1598–9, troops were levied on an unprecedented scale across England. As these regiments raised in the shires crossed the Irish Sea, another 2,000 men were transferred from the Netherlands to the island. By early 1599, there were at least 17,000 English troops in Ireland.

The Earl of Essex was chosen to command this army, the like of which had never been seen in Ireland before. This was a mistake. 'By God, I will defeat Tyrone in the field,' Essex boasted; but instead of directly confronting the Gaelic lords of the north, he campaigned against their allies in the south to no great effect. As reports of aimless expeditions were brought to Elizabeth, one courtier observed: 'She walks much in her privy chamber, and stamps her feet at ill news, and thrusts her rusty sword at times into the arras in great rage.'

Worse was to follow. When Essex finally marched northwards, he made a truce with O'Neill. When she heard of it, Elizabeth was outraged: she described the truce as 'a quick end to a slow proceeding'. Without permission, Essex abandoned his command and raced back to England. The queen chose a new commander, one capable of turning the tide.

Charles Blount, Lord Mountjoy, appointed Lord Deputy of Ireland in January 1600, very soon inspired his men with greater success than any other English commander before him, and he appeared to be fearless in battle – at different times his horse was shot under him, his greyhound running beside him was shot dead, and his chaplain, one of his secretaries, and a gentleman of his chamber were killed close by him.

Since 1594, the Gaelic lords of Ulster had won so many victories that Queen Elizabeth had come close to losing Ireland altogether. Now Mountjoy planned to break this rebellion by starving the people. He preferred to fight in winter when it was more difficult for the Irish to hide in the leafless woods, and when their stores of corn and butter could be burnt, and their cattle down from their summer pastures could be more easily slaughtered.

Leading a naval assault into Lough Foyle, Sir Henry Docwra made a secure base in the monastic ruins of Derry, thus driving a wedge between the O'Donnells in Tír Conaill and the O'Neills in Tír Eóghain. Docwra invaded the MacSweeney lordship of Fanad, destroying 'houses and corn, whereupon winter approaching ensured the death of most of his people'. Sir Arthur Chichester, using

Carrickfergus as his base, crossed Lough Neagh to create havoc on the western shores. In May 1601 he reported to Mountjoy:

> We have killed, burnt and spoiled all along the lough within four miles of Dungannon ... in which journeys we have killed above one hundred people of all sorts, besides such as were burnt, how many I know not. We spare none of what quality or sex soever, and it hath bred much terror in the people ...

Charles Blount

Mountjoy himself broke through the defences of the Moyry Pass and, according to his secretary, 'destroyed the rebels' corn about Armagh ... this course causing famine, being the only way to reduce or root out the rebels'.

At this point, Philip III of Spain sent an armada to Ireland. Sailing out from Lisbon with half a million ducats and 4,500 men, Don Juan del Águila landed at Kinsale in Co. Cork. His admiral insisted on taking the ships away. Finding himself surrounded by the English, Águila dashed off a frantic appeal to O'Neill and O'Donnell, calling on them to march south to join him.

The Battle of
Christmas Eve

. . .

IN SEPTEMBER 1601, FROM Kinsale, a walled town on the Bandon river estuary in west Cork, Don Juan del Águila sent a messenger northwards with this message for the Gaelic lords of Ulster:

> *I was confident your Excellencies would have come. I beseech you so to do, with as much speed, and as well furnished as you possibly may ... I will give the enemy their hands full from the town, and their first fury resisted, all is ended.*

Fewer than 4,000 in number, the Spaniards could do little more than sit tight and wait for Hugh O'Neill, Red Hugh O'Donnell and their allies to march south. Lord Deputy Mountjoy was soon in control: his army surrounded Kinsale, digging trenches as deep as a lance-length, and building platforms from which cannons pounded the town continuously. Queen Elizabeth's vessels captured forts in the estuary downstream as reinforcements raised in the English shires came ashore nearby at Oysterhaven.

O'Neill was reluctant to leave the fastness of Ulster, but O'Donnell insisted that they had no choice but to march south. *The Annals of the Four Masters* records:

> *The resolution they came to, with one mind and one intention was that each lord should proceed without dallying or delaying, to aid and assist the Spaniards ... O'Donnell was the first prepared*

to go on this expedition. As for O'Neill, he left a week after All Hallowtide.

Sir George Carew, the Lord President of Munster, advanced north to block Red Hugh's approach in Co. Tipperary. But O'Donnell gave him the slip by taking his men over a treacherous bog which had frozen hard overnight in the Slieve Felim Mountains. O'Neill took an easterly route and ravaged the counties around Dublin to weaken the Lord Deputy's supply lines.

The Irish from the north and the west had covered over 300 miles in the depths of a bitterly cold winter, wading river after river, often up to the chest, and drew up to Kinsale in good order, camping to the north of the English entrenchments. Another small Spanish force, led by Don Pedro de Zubiaur, had driven back a squadron of English naval vessels and landed further south at Castlehaven. These Spaniards joined the Ulstermen at Kinsale with O'Sullivans, O'Driscolls and MacCarthys.

The Spanish in Kinsale, the English besieging them, and the Irish surrounding the English, all suffered terrible losses from hunger, disease and the wet and the cold. Men on watch dropped dead during the night. The Lord Deputy's secretary wrote:

> *And it was most true, that our men daily died by dozens, so as the sick and runaways considered, we were grown as weak as at our first setting down.*

It was admitted that the English lost some 6,000 men in this way during the siege. The Spanish made a fierce sally from the town and spiked two of the English heavy guns. But the cost in lives was high, and the men were weak from lack of food. The English too made an assault but failed to breach Kinsale's walls. Del Águila's desperate appeal to the Irish to attack without delay was foiled when his message was intercepted by the English. On 23 December O'Neill finally agreed to Red Hugh's pleadings that the Irish, numbering around 6,000, should launch a full-scale attack on the English lines at dawn on Christmas Eve. The Lord Deputy's secretary recalled:

Drawing of the Siege and Battle of Kinsale by George Carew

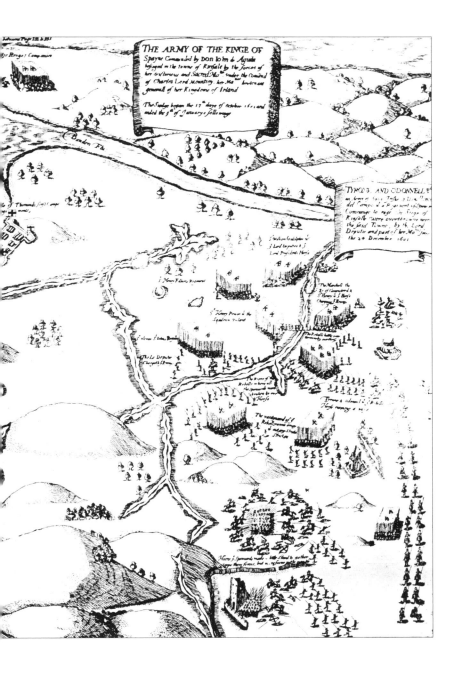

All the night was clear with lightning (as in the former nights were great lightnings with thunder) to the astonishment of many. This night our horsemen set to watch, to their seeming did see lamps burn at the points of their spears in the midst of these lightning flashes. Suddenly one of the Lord President's horsemen called the Lord Deputy at his door, and told him, that Tyrone's army was come up very near to our camp.

The horseman had seen the slow-burning fuses of the Irish handguns glowing in the dark. Red Hugh's army lost its way in the half-light, and Hugh O'Neill, against the advice of the Spanish officers, halted behind boggy ground. Vital time was lost as the three massive Irish armies finally made a coordinated advance. Dawn had come when Mountjoy ordered his captains to charge the Irish with their cavalry. O'Neill saw his great army scattered and slaughtered. Mountjoy's secretary's account concludes:

The Irish not used to fight in plain ground, and something amazed with the blowing up of a gunpowder bag (they having upon the like fright defeated the English at Blackwater), but most discouraged to see their horse fly, being all chiefs and gentlemen, were suddenly routed, and our men followed the execution.

It was all over before the Spanish realised what had happened, and their sally from the town came too late.

This was the most terrible defeat the Gaelic Irish had ever suffered in the entire history of their conflict with the English. In less than two years all of Ireland from end to end would be conquered by the English Crown for the very first time.

The Treaty of Mellifont

. . .

Tyrones false Submiſsion afterwards rebelling.

Hugh O'Neill makes a formal submission to the English after the suppression of his Irish rebellion

THE ANNALS OF THE *Four Masters* recognised that the victory of Lord Deputy Mountjoy over Hugh O'Neill, Red Hugh O'Donnell and the Spanish at Kinsale on Christmas Eve 1601 was a catastrophe from which Gaelic Ireland would never recover:

> *Manifest was the displeasure of God, and misfortune to the Irish of fine Fodhla. ... Immense and countless was the loss in that place; for the prowess and valour, prosperity and affluence, nobleness and chivalry, dignity and renown, bravery and protection, devotion and pure religion, of the island, were lost in this engagement.*

Red Hugh sailed for Spain; twice he was given an audience with Philip III, but the king was unwilling to provide further aid to the Irish. The Tír Conaill chief died at Simancas in August 1602, poisoned, it was said, by an English spy. Hugh O'Neill, the Earl of Tyrone, tried to negotiate a compromise peace, but Queen Elizabeth would not hear of it. She instructed her Lord Deputy:

> We do now require you very earnestly to be very wary in taking the submissions of these rebels. Next we do require you, even whilst the iron is hot, so to strike, as this may not only prove a good summer's journey, but may deserve the title of that action which is the war's conclusion. For furtherance whereof we have spared no charge.

The concluding months of this great rebellion of the northern Gaelic lords were among the most terrible. Docwra, busy rounding up rebels around Ballyshannon, reported that those who

> came into my hands alive ... I caused the soldiers to hew in pieces with their swords. ... The axe is now at the root of the tree, and I may well say, the neck of the rebellion as good as utterly broken.

The Lord Deputy was in the heart of Tyrone, where he took the opportunity to smash the ancient inauguration chair of the O'Neills as well as to destroy the harvest. A terrible man-made famine now began to sweep across Ulster, as Mountjoy's secretary, Fynes Moryson, recorded:

> Now because I have often made mention formerly of our destroying the rebels' corn, and using all means to famish them, let me by two or three examples show the miserable estate to which the rebels were thereby brought. Sir Arthur Chichester and the other commanders saw a most horrible spectacle of three children (whereof the eldest was not above ten years old), all eating and gnawing with their teeth the entrails of their mother, upon whose flesh they had fed twenty days past, and having eaten all from the feet upward to the bare bones, roasting it continually by a slow fire, were now coming to the eating of her said entrails in like sort roasted, yet not divided from the body, being as yet raw ...

No spectacle was more frequent in the ditches of towns, and especially in wasted countries, than to see multitudes of these poor people dead with their mouths all coloured green by eating nettles, docks, and all things they could rend above ground.

Queen Elizabeth at last relented and instructed her Lord Deputy to offer a pardon. The Earl of Tyrone, who had been desperately fighting a rearguard action in the forests of Glenconkeyne, eagerly accepted the offer of safe conduct. This was brought to him by his old friend Sir Garret Moore, who took him to his estate of Mellifont Abbey in March 1603 to meet Lord Mountjoy face to face. O'Neill was astonished at the lenient terms offered to him. What was the explanation? The answer was that Mountjoy knew what the earl did not know: that the old queen had died just a few days previously. James VI of Scotland was now James I of England, Scotland, Wales and Ireland. No one, particularly Mountjoy, knew what his policy would be.

Provided he renounced the title of The O'Neill and handed the Church lands of Ulster to the Crown, the earl was allowed to retain his lordship over most of his traditional territory. On 2 June 1603 Hugh O'Neill and the newly elected Lord of Tír Conaill, Rory O'Donnell, left Ireland in the company of Lord Deputy Mountjoy. After narrowly avoiding shipwreck, they arrived in England, where the Gaelic lords were pelted with stones and mud by women who had lost their menfolk in the Irish wars. They were well received by King James I, and O'Donnell was created the Earl of Tyrconnell. This generous pardon infuriated those English officers who had risked their lives campaigning in Ireland. One of them wrote angrily:

I have lived ... to see that damnable rebel Tyrone brought to England, honoured and well liked ... How I did labour after that knave's destruction! I adventured perils by sea and land, was near starving, ate horse flesh in Munster, and all to quell that man, who now smileth in peace at those who did hazard their lives to destroy him: and now doth dare us old commanders with his presence and protection.

However, he and other men who had served the Crown were soon to have the satisfaction of seeing these proud Gaelic lords lose all that they had.

Borderers: 'A fractious and naughty people'

. . .

DURING THE FIRST DAYS following the death of Queen Elizabeth, riders broke out from the Borders all along the frontier between Scotland and England, slaughtering, looting, burning, and driving deep into Cumbria and Northumbria in search of plunder. This would be remembered as the 'Ill Week'.

For centuries this wild border country, the 'Debatable Land', had been lawless and violent. Riding nimble unshod ponies, known as 'hobblers', wearing steel helmets and jacks – quilted coats of stout leather sewn with plates of metal or horn – and armed with lances, bills, cutting swords and heavy handguns known as 'dags', these border reivers brought their reign of terror to a climax in the sixteenth century. Gavin Dunbar, Archbishop of Glasgow, excommunicated them in what must be the longest curse in history, running to over 1,500 words:

> *I denounce, proclaimis, and declares all and sindry the committaris of the said saikles murthris, slauchteris ... theiftis and spulezeis, oppinly apon day licht and under silence of nicht ...*
>
> *I curse thair heid and all the haris of thair heid; I curse thair face ... thair mouth, thair neise, thair toung, thair teith, thair crag, thair schulderis, thair breast, thair hert, thair stomok, thair bak, thair armes, thair leggis, thair handis, thair feit, and everilk part of thair body, frae the top of thair heid to the soill of thair feit, befoir and behind, within and without ...*

I condemn thaim perpetualie to the deip pit of hell, to remain with Lucifer and all his fallowis, and thair bodies to the gallowis ... first to be hangit, syne revin and ruggit with doggis, swine, and utheris wyld beists ...'

It did no good. From Nithsdale, Annandale, Eskdale, Ewesdale, Liddesdale, Teviotdale and Tweeddale the reivers continued to feud with one another and inflict slaughter, destruction and misery on their more peaceful neighbours. But, in the spring of 1603, James VI of Scotland became also James I of England. The Borders, which he referred to as the 'Middle Shires' of his kingdom, must be thoroughly pacified. A special force, known as the Armed Guard, set up in Dumfries, began the purging process by sending thirty-two Elliots, Armstrongs, Johnstons and Battys to the gallows and outlawing 140 more. 'Hard trot' pursuits were launched repeatedly from both sides of the border. Mass hangings followed in Dumfries and Carlisle. The pacification would take seven bloody years.

The most recalcitrant reivers, the Grahams of Eskdale, Leven and Sark, paid a particularly heavy price. The Border Commission, set up by the King in 1605, with special instructions to deal with 'the malefactors of the name of Graham', confiscated the lands of 150 of them, relentlessly carrying out orders to hunt them down forthwith, burn their homes and expel their families. The king later gave special immunity to Sir William Cranston, head of the commission, for executing outlaws without trial.

Then, to the government's astonishment, Sir Ralph Sidley, a landowner in Co. Roscommon, offered to settle the Grahams on his estate. King James was delighted and compelled local property owners to subscribe to a fund to transport large numbers of them there. In September 1606, after a 'prosperous voyage' to Dublin, they made their way to the west of Ireland. Sidley pocketed most of the money raised. Soon the Grahams were complaining that they could not understand the language, that the land was waste and that 'we ... cannot get a penny to buy meat and drink withal'. They scattered and drifted north to Ulster. As Lord Deputy Sir Arthur Chichester reported:

They are now dispersed, and when they shall be placed upon any land together, the next country will find them ill neighbours, for they are a fractious and naughty people.

The Right Hon:le Right Wise and Valiant ARTHUR LO: CHICHESTER, LO: Baron of Belfast Lo: High Treasurer of Ireland and some times Lo: Deputy of that Kingdom a:ii yeare & upward. One of the Privy Counsell in ENGLAND.

Sir Arthur Chichester

But once the plantation of Ulster got under way, undertakers were eager to entice as many British as they could to become their tenants in order to fulfil the conditions of their patents. Meanwhile, more Borderers arrived in Ulster, fleeing from harsh justice and repression in their homeland. Fearful of arrest, many went as far west as they could, to Donegal and Fermanagh, to find landlords who would take them on as tenants. Though their family had served the Crown for generations in organising 'hard trot' pursuits of the reivers, Fermanagh undertakers Sir John and Alexander Home gladly settled them on their estates.

Few Borderers became members of the landed class, but they arrived in Ulster in great numbers to become diligent farmers. A perusal of Ulster's telephone directories would reveal how many Border surnames there are. The commonest are Johnston (the leading surname in Fermanagh until the census of 2001), Maxwell, Beattie, Elliot, Armstrong, Scott, Kerr, Graham, Crozier, Irvine, Bell, Crichton, Douglas, Robson, Nixon, Young, Davison, Tait, Burns, Dixon, Trotter, Oliver, Rutherford, Little, Carruthers, Carlisle, Storey, Noble, Forster, Hall, Turnbull, Routledge, and Pringle – and those are only from the Scottish side of the border.

The Flight of the Earls

. . .

ENGLISH OFFICERS WHO HAD done so much to conquer the whole island of Ireland were infuriated by generous pardons given in 1603 to the defeated Gaelic lords of Ulster. They felt as veterans they should have been rewarded with lands confiscated from traitors.

Their moment arrived when James I appointed one of their number, Sir Arthur Chichester, as his Lord Deputy in 1605. Chichester set out to make life as uncomfortable as possible for the northern lords. The authority of Hugh O'Neill, Earl of Tyrone, was whittled away, so that, Chichester reported, 'the law of England, and the Ministers thereof, were shackles, and handlocks unto him, and the garrisons planted in his country were as pricks in his side'. Red Hugh O'Donnell had died in Spain. His brother, Rory O'Donnell, was made the Earl of Tyrconnell by King James; but Chichester was making his position impossible. It was ruled that O'Boyles, MacSweeneys and others did not have to pay the earl rent. Other fertile lands were being assigned to clergy and fortress commanders. Left only with a poor mountainous patrimony, Tyrconnell was 'very meanly followed'.

The Flight of the Earl of Tyrone, 1607

On 25 August 1607, a vessel sailed into Lough Swilly and anchored off Rathmullan. It had been brought in great secrecy from Nantes by Cúchonnacht Maguire of Fermanagh. At nightfall, a man came ashore with Spanish ducats to bring news to Tyrconnell of the ship's arrival. O'Neill was in Co. Louth. When told of Maguire's ship, he hastened north, gathering up as many members of his family as he could.

They crowded aboard the vessel, the cream of Ulster's Gaelic aristocracy; but in the haste of leaving, many, including Tyrone's son Conn, were left behind. Then, as the earls themselves reported to Philip III of Spain, at noon on Friday 4 September,

> *leaving their horses on the shore with no one to hold their bridles,*
> *they went aboard a ship to the number of about one hundred*
> *persons, including soldiers, women and principal gentlemen.*

Tadhg Ó Cianáin, who sailed with the earls, tells us that they planned to sail straight for Spain, but 'They were at sea for thirteen days with excessive storm and dangerous bad weather', forcing them to change course for France. After landing at the mouth of the River Seine, they were allowed to move on to Spanish Flanders. Here Archduke Albert and his wife, the Infanta Isabel, treated these Irish as heroes, as champions of the faith against the heretics. Their long war against Queen Elizabeth had seemed like a struggle of David against Goliath.

But Philip III of Spain had recently agreed peace terms with the King of England, Scotland and Ireland, James I. Philip could not harbour these fugitives. With some reluctance, Pope Pius V agreed to put them up in Rome. The journey south was arduous and, when crossing the Alps, one of O'Neill's horses, carrying most of their cash, Ó Cianáin recorded, 'fell down the face, of the high, frozen, snowy cliff which was in front of the bridge ... the money decided to remain blocking the violent, deep, destructive torrent'. 'His Holiness', an ambassador informed Philip, 'will give them nothing, or very little, because the apostolic treasury is very low and His Holiness is not very liberal.' And so it proved.

While adjusting to their cramped and poorly furnished accommodation in Rome, the earls got news of a fresh insurrection in Ulster. Sir Cahir O'Doherty had changed sides to join the English towards the end of the Nine Years' War. When that rebellion had ended in 1603, he had been restored to his lordship of Inishowen in north Donegal. Meanwhile James I decided that Derry should become a city and appointed Sir George Paulet as its governor. Paulet was contemptuous of the native Irish and in an argument punched O'Doherty in the face. The Lord of Inishowen, *The Annals of the Four Masters* records, 'would rather have suffered death than live to brook such insult and dishonour'.

O'Doherty began his rebellion by seizing Culmore Fort on 18 April 1608 and the following night attacked Derry, reducing it to ashes. Factions of MacSweeneys, O'Hanlons and O'Cahans joined the uprising. Then Chichester brought the full weight of the royal army down on the rebels. In the wild country of north Donegal, O'Doherty was cornered near Kilmacrenan and killed at the Rock of Doon. As the rebellion was being stamped out, James was sprucing up his ambitious scheme for Ulster's future.

In Rome during July, the Irish decided they needed relief from the summer heat of Rome by going to Ostia on the coast – a bad idea for, as Ó Cianáin explained, 'that particular place is one of the worst and most unhealthy for climate in all Italy'. Fever ravaged the company and, Ó Cianáin continued, 'so many of the choicest descendants of Míl Easpáinne died suddenly, one after another, in a foreign and strange land'. Tyronnell was one of the first to die and, after Cúchonnacht Maguire also died of fever in Genoa, the only prominent Irish noble to survive fever was the Earl of Tyrone himself.

A bizarre beginning:
planting Down and Antrim

. . .

A DUBLIN CASTLE OFFICIAL wrote to James I: 'The undutiful departure of the Earls of Tyrone, Tyrconnell and Maguire offers good occasion for a plantation'. It certainly did. The Lord Deputy, Sir Arthur Chichester, urged the king to seize the moment:

> *If His Majesty will, during their absence, assume the countries into his possession, divide the lands ... and will bestow the rest upon servitors and men of worth here, and withal bring in colonies of civil people of England and Scotland ... the country will ever after be happily settled.*

James responded enthusiastically. The lands of the fugitive northern lords were confiscated, and the king threw himself with enormous enthusiasm into a grand project which he named 'the Plantation of Ulster'. In any case, the king already had encouraging indications in Down and Antrim that the colonisation of the rest of the province could well be a triumphant success.

Back in 1603, at the close of the Nine Years' War, Conn MacNeill O'Neill, Lord of Upper Clandeboye and the Great Ards, held a party in Castlereagh. On the third day he – unsurprisingly – ran out of wine and sent retainers into the village of Belfast to get more. These men, 'they being very drunk', became involved in an altercation leading to the death of a couple of English soldiers. Conn was flung into a dungeon in Carrickfergus Castle.

Sir Hugh Montgomery, sixth Laird of Braidstane in Scotland, came to his aid. First, he sent over a cousin to win the heart of the jailer's daughter. This man 'ply'd his oar so well that in a few nights he had certain proofs of his bride's cordial love', the Montgomery Manuscripts assure us. Lady O'Neill also played her part by smuggling in rope to her husband Conn in two big cheeses, 'the meat being neatly taken out, and filled with cords, well packed in, and the holes handsomely made up again'. Then the jailer's daughter opened the dungeon cell and Conn O'Neill lowered himself down the rope to a waiting boat to be taken across the sea to Largs and freedom.

Montgomery had served James for many years as a secret agent in both England and Ireland. Without too much difficulty the king was persuaded to give Conn a pardon on condition that he gave one-third of his lordship to Sir Hugh and another third to Sir James Hamilton, another Scot due to be rewarded for his secret service in London and Dublin.

In this bizarre way began the most successful scheme of 'plantation', that is, colonisation, of any part of Ireland in the seventeenth century. The triple division was agreed upon in April 1605. Conn was probably fortunate to emerge from these tortuous dealings with sixty townlands, centred on Castlereagh. Hamilton's estates were in north Down around Bangor and Holywood and on the western shores of Strangford Lough. Montgomery got much of the Ards peninsula and made Newtownards his base.

Carrickfergus Castle, a twelfth century Norman fortress north of Belfast, Northern Ireland

Great numbers of Scots crossed over from Ayr and other parts of the Scottish Lowlands to begin a new life in Co. Down. The harbour built at Donaghadee became very busy: here arrived 'a constant flux of passengers daily coming over' ignoring 'evil report of wolves and woodkerns'. With proper ploughing, and fertilised with seaweed gathered from the shore, the soil gave bountiful harvests in 1606 and 1607. After that, the tempo of migration across the North Channel was raised further.

Sir Randal Arannach MacSorley MacDonnell, Lord of the Glynns and the Route, was to be as successful a promoter of British colonisation in Ulster as Montgomery and Hamilton. This is all the more extraordinary because not only could he speak no English, but also he made no secret of the fact that he was a devout Catholic. He had played a pivotal role in defeating the English at the Yellow Ford in 1598 and had been among those routed at Kinsale in 1601. What saved him was that in the past he had rendered James good service in the Western Isles against unruly subjects. Now Sir Randal strove hard to retain the king's favour by inviting Presbyterian Scots to cross over and become tenants on his estates. Lowland Scots were ready to accept: many had been driven out of Lewis in a disastrous attempt by the king to 'plant' the Outer Hebrides. James was so pleased with the tide of colonisation which ensued that he raised MacDonnell to the peerage as the Earl of Antrim in 1620.

Meanwhile, the Lord Deputy, granted lands in Carrickfergus and Lower Clandeboye, was settling army veterans on his estates. They included Captain Hugh Clotworthy at Massereene, Captain Roger Langford at Muckamore, Sir Fulke Conway at Killultagh, Ensign John Dalway in east Antrim and Sir Moses Hill in the Lagan valley. Chichester himself ordered the firing of over a million bricks to build a mansion and a town in Belfast.

As Chichester was extinguishing the last embers of O'Doherty's rebellion, James I confiscated six entire counties in Ulster. The Lord Deputy was now given a fresh task: that of putting into effect the king's greatly revised plan for his Plantation of Ulster.

The Plantation of Ulster

. . .

THE SUMMER ASSIZES OF 1608 confiscated virtually all the territory of Ulster west of the River Bann for King James I. English and Scots were already busily colonising the counties of Antrim and Down. The lands of Co. Monaghan had been redistributed in Queen Elizabeth's day. Out of the nine counties of the northern province, that left six to be included in the 'Plantation of Ulster': Armagh, Tyrone, Fermanagh, Cavan and counties then named Tyrconnell and Coleraine. This colonising project, the king explained to his Lord Deputy, would be a civilising enterprise which would 'establish the true religion of Christ among men ... almost lost in superstition'. Besides, a plantation would pacify Ulster and secure the province against the risk of further native rebellion and foreign invasion.

The first thing to be done was to make a detailed survey of the vast territory to be colonised. 'To avoid His Majesty's further charge', the decision was made not to attempt to measure the land but to conduct an inquiry. The traditional Irish local land divisions caused much confusion. The basic units were the *townlands*, called *tates* in Co. Fermanagh, *polls* in Co. Cavan, and *ballyboes* elsewhere. Each townland was supposed to be enough to support one extended family: small and compact on good land, and more extensive in mountainous and boggy areas. Groups of townlands made up larger divisions known as *ballybetaghs* and *quarters*. The commissioners making the inquiry found it all very perplexing. In the end, they decided to make grants based on the ancient land divisions, keeping the Irish names in an anglicised form. Tattyreagh, for example, means the 'grey townland'.

In April 1610, a detailed brochure was published in London. Readers of what became known as the 'Printed Book' could find

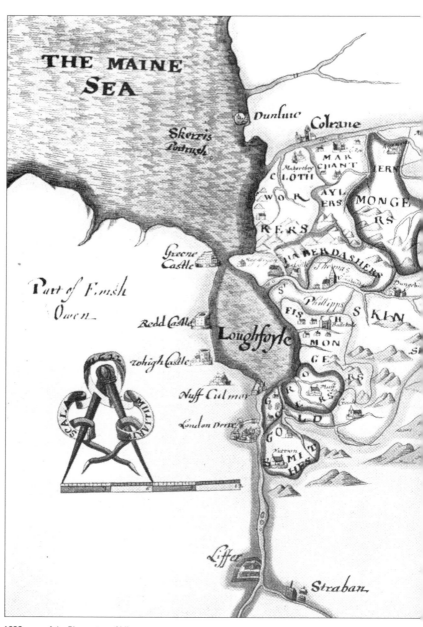

THE MAINE SEA

Dunluce
Colrane
Skerris
Portrush
MAR CHANT
Maherebay
CLOTH
WOR
AYL ERS
MONGE RS
KERS
Greene Castle
Macdonges
HABERDASHERS
Thomas
Part of Finish Owen
St
Phillipps
SKIN
Redd Castle
FIS H
MON
Loughfoyle
GE
whigh Castle
Nuff
RS
Nuff Cidmor
G
D
London Derix
GO
Natron
SMIT HS

SCALA MILITARI

Liffer
Straban

1622 map of the Plantation of Ulster

126

The Cuntie of Antrm

Toome

Part of Lough Neagh

Part of the Countie
of
Tyrone.

A GNNERALL PLAT
of the lands Belonginge to the
Cittie of london as they are deuided
and set out to the:12:Companies as the
doe Butt and Bound ech vpon othe
the perticuler platts where of do
followe more at large Described

out all the terms and conditions of the plantation. The confiscated land of each county was divided into 'precincts', often based on the existing structure of baronies, and each precinct was subdivided into large, middle and small estates, or 'proportions'. It soon became clear that separation was the essence of the scheme.

The largest group of colonists, known as 'undertakers', had to clear their estates completely of native Irish inhabitants. Undertakers had to be English or 'inland' Scots who had taken the Oath of Supremacy – that is, they had to be Protestants – and, having removed the natives, they had to 'undertake' to colonise their estates with British Protestants. Indeed, it was during the Ulster plantation that the term 'British' came into general use – officials got tired of constantly saying 'English, Scots, Welsh and Manxmen'. The undertakers paid rent of £5 6s 8d annually to the king for every thousand acres. In all, they received over a quarter of the confiscated land.

Another group of grantees were termed 'servitors'. They were councillors of state, captains and lieutenants with military commands and other servants of the Crown, and, between them, they were assigned about one-fifth of the plantation lands. They did not have to remove the native Irish, but they enjoyed reduced rents if they brought in British colonists. Their estates were not merely rewards for past service to the Crown: servitors were expected to play a key role in the defence of the plantation.

Between one-quarter and one-fifth of the confiscated lands were allocated to what were described as the 'deserving' native Irish. This was less generous than it seemed because a number of these grants were for the lifetime only of those named in them.

The leading planters of all categories had to build towns, parish churches, schools and forts. The Church of Ireland received over a thousand townlands. Trinity College Dublin, founded in the reign of Elizabeth, was also given generous grants.

It was not long before noblemen, adventurers, gentlemen and courtiers began applying to the king for lands in Ulster. King James issued a special proclamation for Scotland, urging his original subjects to become planters:

... yit, his sacred Maiestie, out of his vnspeikable love and tender affectioun towards his Maiesties antient and native subiectis of this kingdome hes bene pleasit to mak chose of thame to be Partinairis with his saidis subiectis of England, in the distribution foirsaid ...

The great migration to Ulster had begun, drawn from every class of British society. Some were noblemen like the Earl of Abercorn and the Earl of Ochiltree from Scotland, who responded to a personal appeal from King James to take estates in Co. Tyrone 'for a countenance and a strength to the rest'. Others were former army commanders who had helped to conquer this province: men like Sir Basil Brooke with the proportion of Edenacarnan in Donegal; Sir Richard Wingfield, who had led the victorious cavalry charge at the Battle of Kinsale, and who was granted the proportion of Benburb in Co. Tyrone; and the king's Lord Deputy, Sir Arthur Chichester, who received the proportion of Dungannon to add to his vast estates in Inishowen and Co. Antrim.

All of these planters brought over relatives, neighbours, trusted comrades-in-arms, stonemasons, carpenters, thatchers, labourers and tenant farmers. In the initial stages of the plantation, the estates granted to Englishmen were occupied by colonists who were mostly English. For example, in north Armagh, the Brownlow brothers from Nottinghamshire and other undertakers from Staffordshire enticed over many of their English tenants. They included families from the Vale of Evesham who carried over apple tree saplings, ensuring that in time Armagh would be known as the 'Orchard County'. No fewer than four members of the Cunningham family from Wigtownshire got estates in Co. Donegal.

'Great things move slowly'

...

Dulace Castle

BY THE LATE SUMMER of 1610, forty-four of the fifty-nine Scottish undertakers granted 'proportions' or estates in the Plantation of Ulster had arrived. Many were shocked to find that the countryside was still ravaged by the recent wars. Everywhere buildings were in ruin and there was scarcely one church with a roof intact. Both Alexander and John Achmutie, court servants from

Edinburgh, after just a few days' visit, sold their proportions in the Tullyhunco precinct in Cavan to the purveyor of the king's mines in Scotland, Sir James Craig. George Smailholm from Leith took one look at his estate in Fermanagh and went straight home, never to return. Lord Burley, with a neighbouring proportion by Lough Erne, nevertheless, was pleased with his.

The nine chief undertakers in charge of each precinct had the first choice of land, and they picked estates with fertile soil and close to rivers and loughs for easy access. Though his proportion in the precinct of Strabane included much mountainous land, the Earl of Abercorn had fertile ground on the east bank of the Foyle easily reached from the sea. The king also lent him the services of twenty-five men from the army to help him get started. Scots from Wigtownshire, given estates in the precinct of Boylagh and Banagh in Co. Donegal, had to cope with thin acid soil blasted by storms – the chief undertaker there, Sir Robert McClelland, made sure he got an estate well protected from the Atlantic. However, his neighbours in the Scottish precinct of Raphoe had better land, convenient to safe anchorages in Lough Swilly and Lough Foyle.

Because they were arriving in the late summer and the autumn, the planters had to bring enough food with them to tide their tenants over the winter. The devastated lands of Ulster could not supply them and so cattle and grain had to be brought in at great cost from Scotland. This was a considerable burden on Scottish undertakers because they appear to have brought over more families than the English. Undertakers had to erect fortified castles (known as bawns) and their tenants had first to build homes for themselves. The land needed to be ploughed for next year's crop and, breaking the condition of their grants that they were to remove *all* the natives from their proportions, Scots were not slow to let the humbler Irish stay on and employ them surreptitiously as labourers to help them with building and farming.

Meanwhile King James, rather unreasonably, was fretting that his Plantation of Ulster was falling behind schedule. Lord Deputy Sir Arthur Chichester assured him in October that 'great things move slowly'. The king ordered all undertakers to be present in Ireland by 1 May 1611 on pain of forfeiture. It proved an empty threat. So, in the summer of 1611, Sir George Carew, a former Lord President of Munster, was sent over to head a commission of inquiry. In his rather perfunctory survey report, he indicated that seventeen Scottish undertakers had yet to make an appearance. Appalled by this, the king commissioned another survey in 1613, this time supervised by Sir Josias Bodley, director-general of fortifications in Ireland and brother of the founder of the Bodleian Library in Oxford. Bodley did a thorough job. Work had not yet started on sixteen Scottish proportions, it is true, but progress on twenty-five of them was encouraging. Still bitterly disappointed, the king made fresh threats, but he shrank from outright confiscation and contented himself with imposing fines.

His Majesty was especially infuriated by the continued presence of the Irish on undertakers' proportions: he raged that the clearing of natives was 'the fundamental reason' for the plantation. In the previous century, when James was arranging the colonisation of some of the Hebrides by Lowlanders, he had demanded a very clear separation between planters and Islanders. Included in the 'Articlis to be contracted amongst the Societie of the Lewis', published in 1598, was a clause stating that no 'marriage or uther particular freindschip to be any of the societies, without the consent of the hail, with any Hyland man'. The plantation of Lewis had to be aborted due to attacks by 'bludie and wiket Hieland men'.

He should have been pleased with Bodley's findings. All over Ulster, new fortifications were springing up, many of them in the Scots baronial style. Striking examples can be found in Co. Fermanagh, for example. They include Tully Castle, Castle Balfour, Crom Castle, Monea Castle and Aghalane Castle. Around 2,200 British males had settled in the six counties of the plantation. What is more, unlike most of the English colonising Virginia at the same time, the British men had brought their womenfolk with them. From Bodley's report, it can be calculated that 490 families, totalling around 1,700 adults, had settled on the Scottish proportions alone. Yet another survey, headed by Captain Nicholas Pynnar in 1619, indicated that the number of British adults settled in the six counties had risen to 4,420. Pynnar did not distinguish between English and

Scots, but the British population on Scottish estates had more than doubled between 1613 and 1619.

And more colonists were still coming over from Scotland – so many, indeed, that the Scottish Secretary of State complained that the 'cuntrey people of the common sorte do flock over in so greit nowmeris that muche landis ar lastin [lying] waste for lacke of tennentis'.

The English colonists had more capital, but the Scots were the most determined. Sir William Alexander observed: 'Scotland by reason of her populousnesse being constrained to disburden her selfe (like the painfull Bees) did every yeere send forth swarmes.'

Some parts of Ulster, however, were not attracting swarms of planters. For this reason, King James now turned to the city of London.

London companies and 'the scum of both nations'

. . .

THE PART OF ULSTER which proved to be least attractive to planters was what was then called the county of Coleraine. Sir Thomas Phillips, given Church lands at Coleraine, explained to the king that colonisers were dangerously exposed to the native Irish, seething with resentment at the loss of their ancient territory. Elsewhere former Gaelic warriors – known as woodkerne – lurked in the forests, living as bandits.

The solution, Sir Thomas suggested, was to persuade the merchants of London to colonise this wild county. The king was delighted by this proposal. The city merchants were not so sure. The Fishmongers declared: 'It were best never to entermeddle at al in this busyness ... for that it will be exceeding chargeable'. To entice the companies, James granted them not only the entire county of Coleraine, but also the barony of Loughinsholin with its great forest of Glenconkeyne, as well a slice of Tyrconnell including Derry, and another slice of Co. Antrim to give more land to the town of Coleraine. The reduced county of Tyrconnell was renamed Co. Donegal.

The newly enlarged county was named Londonderry. City agents marked out ground for the newly founded city of Londonderry. Work began with a will on the construction of massive walls surrounding the very last walled city to be built in western Europe. On 17 December 1613 aldermen and freemen of the city of London crowded into the Guildhall, full of expectation. This day there would be a draw for the twelve proportions of Co. Londonderry. The fifty-five livery companies arranged themselves into twelve associations. The Goldsmiths, for example, joined with the Cordwainers,

Paintstainers and Armourers. Called to order, a hush descended on the packed guildhall as the City Swordbearer, with great pomp and ceremony, conducted the draw. By the luck of the draw, the Grocers, Fishmongers and Goldsmiths got the most fertile proportions. The Drapers and the Skinners were particularly disappointed: their estates included much land which was both difficult to access and infertile.

The London companies found it easier to attract planters from Scotland than from their own city. In 1637 more than half the inhabitants of the walled city of Londonderry were Scots. Sir Robert McClelland leased 23,000 acres in the Haberdashers' proportion east of the River Roe and persuaded many Scots, particularly from his county of Kirkcudbrightshire, to become his tenants there. By 1641 perhaps as many as 100,000 Scots and 20,000 English had settled in Ulster.

Bough Samuel – the Border Reivers – British School, nineteenth century

Indeed, the great migration of Scots to Ulster was well under way, drawn from every class of society. The Reverend Andrew Stewart of Donaghadee claimed that 'from Scotland came many, and from England not a few, yet all of them generally the scum of both nations, who, for debt or breaking and fleeing from justice, or seeking shelter, came thither'.

Though it is true that the Irish Council ordered the imprisonment of vagrant and criminal Scots 'pestring and disturbing the northern plantations of this kingdome', Stewart's assessment was excessively jaundiced. By the end of King James I's reign in 1625 there were no fewer than 8,000 Scots capable of bearing arms in Ulster. Many Scots were now also settling on estates held by English servitors and undertakers.

From smouldering resentment to a failed plot

. . .

HUGH O'NEILL, EARL of Tyrone, died in Rome in 1616. All hope of help from overseas had gone. Nevertheless, with no security of tenure, with their burdensome rents set by informal arrangements from year to year, and with their status severely reduced, the natives still yearned for a return to the old order. What is more, these Gaelic Irish were confronted by alien planters adhering to a variety of Protestantism far distant from their own Catholicism. The Puritan beliefs of the colonists were held not only by the Calvinist Presbyterians but also by the leading bishops of the Established Church, including the Scots George Montgomery, John Todd, James Spottiswood, James Dundas and Andrew Knox. Franciscans increased their numbers threefold between 1623 and 1639 and instilled a new zeal amongst native Irish Catholics. The uncompromising spirit of the Counter-Reformation faced the inflexible determination of the Puritan settlers. Hostility, suspicion and uncertainty created a dangerously unstable atmosphere in the province.

All over Ulster, with the exception of a few parishes in Antrim and Down, the native Irish everywhere outnumbered the British newcomers. The undertakers had not cleared the native Irish from their estates as they were required to do. The colonists could not possibly farm their lands without the Gaelic Irish; they were too useful as labourers and as tenants prepared to pay high rent to avoid eviction.

In the forests lurked the woodkerne, landless men and former soldiers of O'Neill, who threatened the settlements. Many were rounded up and shipped to Sweden to fight for King Gustav Adolph. The greater threat, however, was the smouldering resentment of the native Irish who worked and farmed with the colonists.

Tully Castle in Co. Fermanagh, built for the Scottish planter Sir John Hume

Those Irish who had been granted estates in the plantation, or otherwise had been able to hold on to their lands, had to adapt to a much-altered regime. Many proved unable to cope. They had to find ready cash to pay regular rents to the king's sheriffs; for marriage portions for female children; for the education of male heirs by attending university or the Inns of Court in London; and for fines, especially for failing to attend Protestant church services. This was a big change from depending on a largely subsistence economy in which livestock were a commonly accepted currency. The incoming British often ruthlessly exploited the frequent inability of Gaelic landowners to understand the newly introduced legal system and to manage their estates in the English way. The result was that most of the native Irish had to borrow, mortgaging land for ready money. This land was then usually lost because debts could not be repaid.

Conn O'Neill, Lord of Castlereagh, at one time the Lord of Upper Clandeboye, sold all his townlands, one by one. The Magennises in Iveagh in Co. Down lost possession of half their estates by 1641 and much of the land remaining to them was hopelessly encumbered by debt. By that time many native Gaelic gentlemen in Ulster, including those who had got land grants as 'deserving Irish', were fast becoming desperate. In Tyrone Sir Phelim O'Neill had mortgaged his estates for more than £13,000.

From the lowliest to the highest, the Gaelic Irish were looking for an opportunity to throw off the burdens that weighed so heavily upon them.

The *Eagle Wing* and the Black Oath

. . .

Thomas Wentworth, first Earl of Strafford (1593–1641),
English statesman and leading adviser to Charles I

WHEN CHARLES I HAD come to the throne in 1625, he had
not shared his father's enthusiasm for the Ulster Plantation. The
king sought only to increase his personal power, and for this he
needed money which did not have to be sanctioned by parliament.
In 1633 Thomas Wentworth was sent to Ireland as the king's trusted
Lord Deputy to raise funds for the royal coffers. Imperious and
indefatigable, Wentworth soon alienated every interest group in

Ireland. A Commission for Defective Titles sent ripples of alarm through the landed classes, including the British planters in Ulster.

As during the previous reign, Catholics of property had to pay heavy fines for refusing to attend Protestant churches. But Charles was also determined to enforce High Church conformity on Protestants in Ireland, and Wentworth was his willing agent. This immediately led to severe tension in Ulster. The Reformation had been a striking success in the Lowlands of Scotland. The variety of Protestantism brought there by John Knox was a Calvinist doctrine, Presbyterianism, opposed to formal liturgy and the rule of bishops. The Scottish parliament ratified the break with Rome in 1560 and the Presbyterian Church became the established Kirk of Scotland.

Most of the Scots colonising Ulster in the seventeenth century were Presbyterians. They had brought their ministers with them but as yet there was no Presbyterian Church there. During the reign of James I, those ministers were accepted and funded as clergy of the Church of Ireland. In any case, a high proportion of English planters held Puritan beliefs, similar to those held by Presbyterians. Now Wentworth, assisted by Henry Leslie, a Scot appointed Bishop of Down by King Charles in 1635, demanded acceptance of the *Book of Common Prayer* and the rule of bishops.

Leslie made his first visit to Down in July 1635 to demand from his clergy subscription to the doctrines and liturgy of the Church of Ireland. Five ministers in the diocese refused, so they were summoned to meet him in church in Belfast on 10 August. There, in his sermon, Leslie vilified those ministers who had succumbed to Presbyterianism:

> *He that will take upon him the office of a minister, not being called by the Church, is an intruder and a thief that cometh not in by the doore, but climbeth up another way ... They think by the puff of their preaching to blowe downe the goodly orders of our church, as the walls of Jericho were beaten downe with sheepes hornes. Good God! is this not the sinne of Uzziah, who intruded himself into the office of the priesthood? ... They have cryed downe the most wholesome orders of the Church as Popish superstitions ...*

After a tense debate, the ministers were deprived of their office and financial support. Forced to leave Ireland, they decided to join other Presbyterians determined to go to New England to preserve their religious liberty. In the autumn of 1636, the *Eagle Wing*, a ship of 150 tons built at Groomsport, was ready to sail for the New World. Setting out from Belfast Lough with 140 passengers on 9 September, the *Eagle Wing* was driven across the North Channel to Loch Ryan by contrary winds. After repairing a leak, the emigrants sailed out into the Atlantic and got almost as far as the Newfoundland Banks. One passenger, the excommunicated minister of Killinchy, John Livingston, wrote an account of what happened next:

> But if ever the Lord spake by his winds and other dispensations, it was made evident to us, that it was not his will that we should go to New England. For we met with a mighty heavy rain out of the north-west, which did break our rudder, which we got mended ... Seas came in over the round-house ... and wet them all that were between the decks ... We sprung a leak that gave us seven hundred strokes in two pumps in the half-hour glass. Yet we lay at hull a long time to beat out the storm, till ... it was impossible to hold out any longer.

After prayer, they decided to return, reaching Belfast Lough on 3 November.

Meanwhile, the Scots were preparing to resist the king's demand for conformity. Tens of thousands signed the National Covenant, a pact between them and God to refuse the *Book of Common Prayer* and the rule of bishops. Aware that many Presbyterians in Ulster had signed the Covenant, Wentworth drafted a command that all Scots over the age of sixteen must take an 'oath of abjuration of their abominable covenant'.

This 'Black Oath' had to be taken kneeling and if it was refused, Bishop Leslie had the power to fine, imprison and excommunicate. Members of one family were fined £13,000 and imprisoned at their own expense in Dublin. But the anger of the Presbyterians was as nothing compared with the mounting fury of the native Irish, ready in Ulster to rise in rebellion.

The 1641 Massacres

. . .

AT THE BEGINNING OF October 1641, a plot was finalised among the indebted Gaelic lords: Conor Maguire would seize Dublin Castle by an elaborate ruse and at the same time Sir Phelim O'Neill would lead a revolt in Ulster. But the authorities got to hear of the plan on 22 October. Dublin Castle was put in a high state of defence and soon afterwards Lord Maguire and other conspirators were seized and imprisoned in the fortress they had planned to capture. The Dublin plot had been foiled, but that same night the rebellion in Ulster began.

The native Irish of Ulster, led by Sir Phelim O'Neill, rose in furious rebellion on the night of Friday 22 October 1641. Charlemont, Mountjoy, Castlecaulfield and Dungannon fell to the insurgents within hours of each other. Sir Conn Magennis led a successful assault on Newry at nightfall on Saturday. Lurgan, in flames, capitulated on Sunday, and Lisburn came under siege.

Lisburn held out. Three times the insurgents were driven back. A herd of 400 head of cattle driven against the gates failed to batter them down. Belfast, Antrim, Carrickfergus, Larne and Ballygally were thus given time to resist. Meanwhile, in all the rest of Ulster, only the island town of Enniskillen and the walled city of Derry were able to hold out.

On Sunday 24 October, Sir Phelim issued a proclamation from Dungannon, declaring that the rising

> is no ways intended against our Sovereign Lord the King, nor the hurt of any of his subjects, either of the English or Scottish nation, but only for the defence and liberty of our selves and the Irish natives of this kingdom.

THE
Ouer-throw of an
Irish rebell, in a late battaile:
Or
The death of Sir *Carey Adoughertie*, who murdred
Sir George Paulet *in Ireland*; *and for his re-*
bellion hath his head now standing ouer
Newgate in Dublin.

Imprinted at London for I. Wright, and are to be sold at
his shop neere Christ Church gate. 1608.

From a London news pamphlet, 1608: 'The Overthrow of an Irish Rebel'

The Irish victories were so rapid in the first few days that the leaders did not know what to do with those who had surrendered. For example, after they had robbed and stripped the settlers in Cavan, the O'Reillys simply released them, 'turned naked, without respect of age or sex, upon the wild, barren mountains, in the cold air, exposed to all the severity of the winter; from whence in such posture and state they wandered towards Dublin'.

Rebel commanders at first attempted to distinguish between the English (regarded as the enemy) and the Scots settlers. Sir Phelim issued this instruction: 'I protest that no Scotsman should be touched', and in Cavan Philip O'Reilly ordered his men 'not to meddle with any of the Scottish nation, except they give cause'. Soon, however, the leaders lost control of their men and all the colonists – Scots as well as English – were in peril. Hungered by harvest failures, and listening to wild prophecies and rumours of a Puritan plot to massacre them, the Irish threw themselves with merciless ferocity on the settlers.

All authority collapsed in a climate of fear and want; the native Irish, inflamed by rumour, religious passion and a lust for revenge, fell ferociously on the planter families of Ulster. The most notorious massacre was at Portadown in the middle of November. William Clarke told how Manus Roe O'Cahan drove him

> with such other English as they could find to the number of threescore persons which belonged to the said Parish of Loughgall and put them all in the Church there ... imprisoned for the space of nine days with at the least 100 men, women and children during which time manie of them were sore tortured by strangling and halfe hanging ... after which time of imprisonment hee with an 100 men, women and children or thereabouts were driven like hogs about six miles to Porte of Doune to a river called the Band and there they forced them to goe upon the Bridge ... and then stripped the said people naked and with their pikes and swords and other weapons thruste them down headlong in to the said river and immediately they perished and those of them that assayed to swim to the shore the rebels stood to shoot at.

Elizabeth Price confirmed that the prisoners were driven

> *off the bridge into the water and then and there instantly and most*
> *barbarously drowned the most of them. And those that could not*
> *swim and came to the shore they knocked on the head, and so after*
> *drowned them, or else shot them to death in the water.*

Like William Clarke, Mrs Price was kept alive because she was thought to be hiding money; in an effort to find it, her tormenters 'had the soles of her feet fried and burnt at the fire, and [she] was often scourged or whipped'.

After the massacre at Portadown, other Protestant settlers were herded into a house at Sewie nearby and burnt to death. Ann Smith and Margaret Clarke escaped through a hole in the wall; they were knocked on the head and left for dead but survived to give evidence of the atrocity.

Ellen Matchett described a similar incident where settlers were burnt to death in a house where they had taken refuge. She was 'miraculously preserved by a mastiff dog that set upon these slaughtering and bloody rebels'. She survived with others in hiding, emerging 'sometimes to get the brains of a cow, dead of disease, boiled with nettles, which they accounted good fare'.

Anne Blennerhasset saw colonists hanged from tenterhooks in Fermanagh. By the southern shore of Lower Lough Erne, the Maguires slaughtered the entire garrison of Tully Castle after promising the quarter. The most horrific massacre took place near Augher in south Tyrone: here nearly 400 Scots who surrendered were put to the sword.

The bloodshed was not all one-sided. Sir William Cole and his men made a sally from Enniskillen and, having rounded up 200 Irish, butchered them all.

Just how many colonists were killed in the massacres of 1641 will never be known. Perhaps a thousand were slaughtered in Co. Armagh alone and modern estimates range between 10 per cent and 25 per cent of the settler population. One Scot, travelling through Ulster in November, observed:

> *The most woeful desolation that ever was in any country in the sudden is to be seen here. Such is the sudden fear and amazement that has seized all sorts of people that they are ready to run into the sea.*

A flood of refugees soon reached Scotland. Over 500 landed on the Isle of Bute and there were similar reports from Ayr, Irvine, Portpatrick and Stranraer. On 1 February 1642, the Scottish Privy Council ordered a collection throughout the country for 'by famine they will miserablie perish if they are not tymouslie supplied'. Once news of the rebellion reached Scotland, many of those with estates in Ulster, or relatives or friends with estates there, began to gather bodies of volunteers to be sent to Ireland.

The tension between Scottish Covenanters and London caused agonising delays. Finally, on 3 April, after landing at Carrickfergus, Major-General Robert Monro set out southwards with a Scots army in pursuit of the Irish. A hardened veteran of the Thirty Years War in Germany, he simply slaughtered his captives, first at Kilwarlin Wood, then at Loughbrickland, and finally at Newry.

A world turned upside down

. . .

THE 'OLD ENGLISH' WERE descendants of Norman colonists, and of the people they brought over the Irish Sea with them. They lived mostly in Dublin, the area surrounding it once known as 'the Pale', in other ports, in inland towns and on the fertile plains. Though nearly all of them were able to speak Irish fluently, they were proud to call themselves English – specifically 'Old English' to distinguish themselves from the 'New' English who had arrived in the sixteenth century. The Old English were loyal to the Crown, and many of them had fought in the Lord Deputy's armies. But they were also Catholics and were loyal to the Pope.

The Old English had high hopes that James I would grant them toleration. He did not. Nor did his successor, Charles I. On 22–23 October 1641, the Ulster Irish had risen in revolt. In the weeks that followed, thousands of British colonists had been driven out; thousands more had been massacred; and the whole of the north, apart from Derry, Lisburn, Belfast and Carrickfergus, had fallen to the rebels.

The victorious insurgents took Dundalk and began to lay siege to Drogheda. The Catholic Old English gentlemen responded to the Dublin government's call to arms, but as they marched north to confront a 'detestable conspiracy by some evil-affected Irish papists', they – as papists themselves – recalled that they had been subject to religious persecution and the threat of confiscation of their property. Charles I had pushed them too far. At Tara and Knockcrofty in Co. Meath, they changed sides to join the rebellion begun by the native Irish.

Battle of Naseby during the English Civil War, 1645

Long-promised Irish exiles sailed from the European mainland to join their compatriots in arms. Many were experienced veterans of the Spanish army. The most distinguished was Owen Roe O'Neill, nephew of the great Earl of Tyrone. In July 1642, he landed at Doe Castle in north Donegal, there to begin training a professional army to confront the heretics. Meanwhile, the Old English established an alternative government made up of representatives elected across the island, the Confederation of Kilkenny. When the English Civil War broke out on 22 August 1642, the Confederation hesitated fatally and lost the best chance to take control of all of Ireland.

The curse of Cromwell

. . .

FEW PERIODS OF IRISH history are as confusing as the 1640s. These were years of massacres, innumerable sieges, dozens of battles and hundreds of skirmishes; this was a time of religious hatred, burnt crops and smoking ruins, when the defeated and the innocent were cut down without mercy. In addition, generals and their men changed sides, sometimes with bewildering frequency, partly in response to the changing fortunes of Royalists and Parliamentarians across the Irish Sea.

In April 1642, Major-General Robert Monro, a hardened veteran of the religious wars in Germany, led an army of 10,000 men across the North Channel to help fellow Scots driven back by the native Irish. He shot and hanged, scouring the countryside about, making sure any Irish captured, one officer reported, were 'cutte downe, with sume wyves and chyldrene for I promis, such gallants gotis but small mercie if they come in your comone sogeris handis'.

Owen Roe O'Neill spent four years training his Ulster army in modern fighting methods. He was ready when Monro moved out of Antrim to march south against the Confederation in June 1646. With fresh Scottish reinforcements, Monro advanced with 6,000 men and six field pieces drawn by oxen. On the River Blackwater, at Benburb, O'Neill attacked from the rear. As his men were pounded by Monro's cannon, Owen Roe harangued his men:

> *Let your manhood be seen by your push of pike! Your word is Sancta Maria, and so in the name of the Father, Son, and Holy Ghost advance! – and give not fire till you are within pike-length!*

With no guns but an equal number of men, the Irish steadily pressed the Scots back to the river, slaughtering them. Monro escaped only after he had cast away his coat, hat and wig. Between one-third and one-half of the Scots were killed, the Irish sustaining only trifling losses.

The Battle of Benburb was the greatest and most annihilating victory in arms the Irish ever won over the British. Yet this great victory was thrown away. Though all the north was now at his mercy, Owen Roe turned south to help hardliners oust the moderates at Kilkenny. Fatally divided, the Confederates would be in no condition to face the victors in the English Civil War – the Roundheads and their leader, Oliver Cromwell.

Portrait of Oliver Cromwell, English general and statesman

On 30 January 1649 Charles I was executed. Now Parliament sent Cromwell over to crush opposition in Ireland. His opponents were routed at Rathfarnham in their attempt to deny the commander-in-chief a safe landing in Dublin. From the outset Cromwell made it clear that he intended to avenge the 1641 massacres of Protestants in Ulster:

> *You, unprovoked, put the English to the most unheard of and most barbarous massacre without respect of sex or age, that ever the sun beheld, and at a time when Ireland was in perfect peace.*

More than two blood-soaked years were to follow, remembered as 'the curse of Cromwell'.

'To Hell or Connacht'

. . .

CROMWELL OPENED HIS IRISH campaign in 1649 by besieging the walled port of Drogheda. For an entire week, he positioned his cannon with infinite care. Then, on three sides, the guns battered the walls for two days until the breaches were judged large enough for an assault. As resistance collapsed, Cromwell reported, 'our men getting up to them were ordered by me to put all to the sword; and, indeed, in the heat of the action, I forbade them to spare any that were in arms in the town'. His estimate was that some 2,000 were slaughtered in this way. Over a hundred taking refuge in the tower of St Peter's were burned to death. All priests and friars found in the town were killed – or, as Cromwell put it, their 'heads were knocked promiscuously together'.

For Cromwell, the slaughter was God's revenge for the Ulster massacre of 1641:

> *I am persuaded that this is a righteous judgement of God upon these barbarous wretches, who have imbrued their hands in so much innocent blood, and that it will tend to prevent the effusion of blood for the future.*

While Ironsides marched north to recover Ulster, Cromwell forged his way southwards. With the loss of only about twenty men, he took the port of Wexford: the total number of soldiers and townspeople put to death there was not far short of 2,000. The Lord Lieutenant relentlessly pressed on. The Tipperary town of Clonmel put up stiff resistance: Cromwell lost some 2,000 men during the assault in May 1650. A few days later he returned to England, leaving his son-in-law, Henry Ireton, in charge.

Siege of Drogheda, massacre of civilians, 1649

Many thousands more died violently before the fighting stopped in February 1653, when the western islands of Inishbofin, Inishturk and Clare Island surrendered. The destruction of war was evident everywhere. Dr William Petty, the army's physician-general, estimated that 504,000 native Irish and 112,000 colonists and English troops had perished between 1641 and 1652. Bubonic plague began to take its toll. Colonel Richard Lawrence wrote:

> *The plague and famine swept away whole countries that a man might travel twenty or thirty miles and not see a living creature, either man, beast, or bird, they being either all dead or had quit those desolate places.*

Feeding on corpses of cattle, horses and – no doubt – people, packs of wolves grew fat and numerous. In December 1652, a public wolf hunt was organised in Castleknock on the very outskirts of Dublin.

By 1654 more than 200 men had been executed by Cromwell's special commission. Catholic priests had been given twenty days to get out of Ireland. Many who dared to stay were hunted down and put to death. The rebel commander Sir Phelim O'Neill was captured, convicted in Dublin and hanged, drawn and quartered. The poet Seán O'Connell described Cromwell's conquest of Ireland as 'the war that finished Ireland'. This was close to the truth. Much of the island had been laid waste. The government even reported that orphan children were being 'fed upon by ravening wolves'.

Cromwell had once declared that the Catholics of Ireland could go 'to Hell or Connacht'. In his 1652 Act of Settlement, he spelled out what he meant by this. Only those who could prove 'constant good affection' to the cause of Parliament could keep their estates. Very few in Ireland could prove this: hence almost all Catholic landowners were to lose their estates entirely and get smaller ones west of the River Shannon – in the province of Connacht.

Miserable groups of Catholics, carrying passports and certificates issued by revenue officers, gathered at Loughrea in Co. Galway. Here, commissioners considered their claims to land in Connacht. Catholics almost disappeared as a property-owning class east of the Shannon. Indeed, out of 380 Catholics who had owned land in Co. Wexford before the war, 297 were left with nothing at all by 1657. Many Irishmen who had lost everything took to the hills and bogs to live as bandits – or, as they were called at the time, tories.

Cromwell and the
Scots in Ulster

. . .

DURING THE VIOLENT CONVULSIONS of the 1640s, only military help from Scotland had saved the Plantation of Ulster from extinction. Now, in 1649, the Scots colony was threatened by the might of Cromwell. Led by Lord Montgomery of the Ards, Scots settlers in Ulster, following the example of their homeland, had declared for Charles II. While campaigning in Munster, Cromwell sent Colonel Robert Venables northwards to deal with them. Early in December, Venables cut the settlers' army to pieces near Lisburn, killing 1,000 men, many hacked down in a relentless cavalry pursuit. Colonel Tam Dalyell then surrendered Carrickfergus.

Belfast had not resisted Venables, and yet we are informed that 800 Scots who had brought their wives and children to plant themselves there were turned out of the town.

Would the Scots be turned out of all their lands in Ulster? Cromwell's prescription that all those who could not prove 'constant good affection' to the Parliamentarian cause would be punished applied to royalist Protestants as well as Catholics. Very few in Ireland could provide such proof. In 1653, the year when peace at last returned to Ireland, the government issued a proclamation ordering 260 Scots from Antrim and Down, including Lord Montgomery, to be transplanted to Tipperary.

After Cromwell's death, King Charles II arrived in Dover on 25 May 1660

In the end, however, Cromwell realised that he needed the support of Protestants, whatever their past allegiances had been. The Tipperary transplantation plan was dropped. Protestants who could not prove constant good affection were allowed to keep their estates, provided they paid fines. The Marquis of Antrim, Randal MacDonnell, as a Catholic, was Ulster's most high-profile victim of the new policy. The government confiscated his estates amounting to some 300,000 acres. Other Catholic estates, such as those of rebel leaders, including Sir Phelim O'Neill and several members of the Magennis family in Iveagh, were also confiscated.

During the 1650s Scots who had fled across the North Channel during the rebellion steadily returned to Ulster to bring their lands back into full production. Though they had to keep a wary eye on Anabaptists in power in Dublin, Presbyterian ministers were allowed to return and get their incomes restored. Lady Clotworthy persuaded Colonel Venables to allow her minister, Mr Ferguson, to return to Antrim and, as the Reverend Patrick Adair recalled:

> *After this, the rest of the brethren returned from Scotland with passes from the English government there ... For Cromwell did labour to ingratiate all sorts of persons and parties ... Upon this favourable reception by those in power for the time, the brethren thought it their duty of meeting together presbyterially, as they had formerly done ... They met at Templepatrick, Cairncastle, Comber, Bangor, &c., for a while, till at last they settled their meetings as before. This was in the year 1654, when this poor Church had a new sunshine of liberty.*

Between 1653 and 1660 the number of Presbyterian ministers in Ulster grew from around half a dozen to seventy. When Charles II was restored to his throne in 1660, the Ulster Scots rejoiced. Not wanting to go on his travels again – as he said himself – the king was in no position to upset Cromwell's land settlement. A few favourites were restored to their estates, the most prominent being the Marquis of Antrim. Soon, however, Presbyterians found that the Church of Ireland returned to favour and renewed its insistence on conformity. In 1661, sixty-one Presbyterian ministers were turned out of the churches of Ulster by the bishops. Ministers were not restored to their livings, but in 1672 they were given a regular stipend, known as the *regium donum*, or 'royal gift'. Presbyterians, however, like Catholics, were excluded from public office (such as being members of town corporations) and this became official in the 1673 Test Act – the test being proof of the receipt of communion in a Church of Ireland church.

The Irish economy made a remarkable recovery during the long reign of Charles II. The British settler population steadily recovered its numbers. Once again the leading immigrants were Scots. By 1669 Scots made up an estimated 60 per cent of the British inhabitants of Ulster, and 20 per cent of the population as a whole. And with every crisis in Scotland, more took ship for Ireland. King Charles had the Solemn League and Covenant declared illegal in Scotland, and the attempt to reimpose Anglican Church rule there led to an uprising of Covenanters. Crushed at Bothwell Brig in 1679, many surviving Covenanters fled to Ulster to swell the Scots population there.

When Charles II died in 1685, however, the Scots in Ulster faced a fresh crisis.

Three kings and thirteen apprentice boys

. . .

WHEN CHARLES II DIED in 1685, his Catholic brother became King James II. Protestants on both sides of the Irish Sea dreaded what would come next.

They did not have to wait long. In 1687 a Catholic, Richard Talbot, was appointed Lord Deputy, the king's governor in Ireland. The sixteenth child of an impoverished Kildare landowner, he had been one of the few royalist officers to escape Cromwell's massacre in Drogheda. Now created the Earl of Tyrconnell, he was a man dedicated to the Catholic cause.

Tyrconnell busied himself clearing Protestants out of the Irish army and the country's administration. Following the birth of a male heir to the throne in June 1688, thereby ensuring the Catholic succession, the Protestant gentlemen of England became convinced that King James would have to go. William of Orange, ruler of the Dutch Republic, accepted their invitation and landed with an imposing army at Torbay in the south west of England on 5 November 1688.

While King James was in London making frantic efforts to stop his support from melting away, Protestants in Ulster were rallying for their own defence against Tyrconnell's Catholic troops. On 3 December 1688, an anonymous letter was found lying in a street in Comber, Co. Down, addressed to Lord Mount Alexander. It began:

> *Good my lord, I have written to you to know that all our Irishmen through Ireland is sworn that on the ninth day of this month they are to fall on to kill and murder man, wife and child ...*

Almost certainly a forgery, the 'Comber Letter' nevertheless galvanised the Protestant population of Ulster. Indeed, one of the aldermen of Derry was reading out the letter to citizens when a messenger arrived warning that Lord Antrim and his troop of soldiers were approaching. The Earl of Antrim had been ordered by Tyrconnell to place a garrison in the walled city. Fortunately for the Protestants of Derry, Lord Antrim was elderly and a little crazy, and it took weeks before he was ready to move. He insisted, for example, that all his Redshank soldiers should be over six foot tall. Nevertheless, the appearance finally of 1,200 Catholic soldiers on 7 December caused instant alarm inside the walls.

The Protestant Bishop of Derry advised citizens to admit Lord Antrim's troops. But when the Redshanks entered the Waterside and began to cross the Foyle, thirteen apprentice boys seized the keys from the main guard, raised the drawbridge at Ferryquay gate and closed the gates. This swift action by the apprentice boys, an army captain recalled, 'acted like magic and roused a unanimous spirit of defence; and now with one voice we determined to maintain the city at all hazards, and each age and sex conjoined in the important cause'.

On 23 December 1688, James fled to France, and, on 13 February 1689, William and his wife Mary, a Protestant daughter of James by his first marriage, were declared joint sovereigns of England, Scotland and Ireland. Louis XIV now persuaded James to go to Ireland to recover his kingdom; the French king's plan was to keep William busy in Ireland while he overwhelmed the Dutch Republic.

On 12 March 1689, a French fleet of twenty-two ships steered into the Bandon estuary and James stepped ashore at Kinsale. From there to Cork and north to Dublin the Irish turned out to give him a rapturous welcome, as one of his officers recalled:

> All along the road the country came to meet his majesty with staunch loyalty, profound respect, and tender love as if he had been an angel from heaven. All degrees of people and of both sexes were of the number, young and old; orations of welcome were made to him at the entrance to each town, and rural maids danced before him as he travelled.

Men took off their coats and laid them in the mud before his horses' hooves. In Carlow, he 'was slobbered with the kisses of the rude countrywomen, so that he was forced to have them kept away from him'.

Engraving of King William III and his wife Queen Mary who shared the English monarchy in the late seventeenth century (circa 1690)

James entered Dublin in triumph on Palm Sunday. Two harpers played on a richly decorated stage; below it friars, holding a large cross, were singing; bells rang; guns fired in salute; and there were 'about forty oyster-women, poultry- and herb-women in white, dancing'. The Lord Mayor and Corporation presented James with the keys of the city while pipers played 'The King Enjoys His Own Again'. The king dismounted and approached Dublin Castle on foot. All fell silent as James received benediction from the Archbishop of Armagh. Overhead the white standard of the Stuarts was unfurled with the motto

> *Now or Never*
> *Now and Forever*

Then a great cheer erupted from the dense crowd. These people were pinning all their hopes on this deposed king.

Meanwhile, Louis XIV had sent out another formidable fleet. Over 2,000 seasoned French troops came ashore, bringing with them engineers and an impressive quantity of munitions and artillery. Very soon King James had control of the whole island – or rather, *almost* the whole island, because there were two or three places in the north which refused to accept his authority. One of these was Derry.

'No surrender!'

. . .

AFTER THE THIRTEEN PROTESTANT apprentice boys had closed the gates of Derry against the forces of the Catholic King James II, the mayor expelled the remaining Catholics from the city and issued this proclamation:

> *We have resolved to stand upon our guard and to defend our walls, and not to admit of any papists whatsoever to quarter amongst us.*

Meanwhile, the 'Jacobites' – those who remained loyal to King James – were sweeping northwards. From all over the north, Protestants poured into Derry, then under the command of Lieutenant-Colonel Robert Lundy. As well as a garrison of over 7,000 men, perhaps another 30,000 colonists sought sanctuary in the city. So, in a very real sense, the fate of the entire Protestant settlement in Ulster depended on Derry's ability to hold out.

In April, men from the Derry garrison were overwhelmed by James's French and Irish troops. Thomas Ash recorded in his diary that the Williamites had been beaten 'although we were five to one against them, which caused suspicion that Colonel Lundy was traitor to our cause'.

When Lundy, the governor of Derry, refused the support of two regiments sent out from Liverpool, that suspicion became a certainty. The citizens revolted, overthrew Lundy, and appointed as joint governors in his place Major Henry Baker and the Rev. George Walker, the Church of Ireland rector of Donaghmore. They were to provide inspired leadership, and they both humanely allowed Lundy, disguised as a common soldier, to slip away over the walls. Walker described the prospects of a successful resistance:

> We had but few horse to sally out with and no forage; no
> engineers to instruct us in our works; no Fireworks, not so much
> as a hand-grenado to annoy the enemy; nor a gun well mounted
> in the town.

Well-mounted or not, some of the guns in the city were impressive.
The largest was 'Roaring Meg', given to the city in 1642 by the
Fishmongers' Company. And there was no shortage of powder and
handguns.

THE APPRENTICE BOYS OF DERRY SHUTTING THE GATES.

Siege of Derry, 1689

King James travelled from Dublin to join his besieging army. On
18 April he advanced towards the walls and offered terms. He was
greeted with cries of 'No surrender!' This was followed by a sustained
barrage of shot and ball from the city walls. Just out of range, James
sat motionless on his horse for several hours in the pouring rain.
Then the king was persuaded to return to Dublin, where the French
ambassador observed that 'His Majesty appears to me to be very
mortified over his latest proceeding.'

The defenders had entrenched themselves on a hillock to the west of the city, where a windmill stood. The Jacobite general Richard Hamilton resolved to drive them back:

> *General Hamilton, observing that the rebels made a walking place of this entrenched ground for the preservation of their health, and that they gave great annoyance with their cannon from the said mill and with their long fowling-pieces ... Whereupon he commanded, on the sixth of May, an attack to be made upon the entrenchment.*

The assault was a complete failure. As an alternative strategy, Hamilton drew the net tighter, cutting the city off from much of its water supply. Just downstream, the French constructed a boom, made of fir beams fastened with chains, to stretch across the Foyle. Derry was now completely cut off.

At the end of May 1689, a train of heavy guns sent by King James arrived to intensify the bombardment of the city which had not ceased since the beginning of the siege.

Captain George recalled:

> *One bomb slew over seventeen persons. I was in the next room one night at my supper (which was but mean) and seven men were thrown out of the third room next to that we were in, all killed and some of them in pieces.*

The walls were not breached, however, and a French general, the Marquis de Pointis, ruefully concluded that 'The state of affairs is such that the attacking must no longer be thought of and it will be well if without raising the siege we shall have to wait on hunger.'

After months of siege, the defenders were starving. Walker's memoir provides a price list for July:

> *Horse-flesh 1/8d a pound; a quarter of a dog 5/6d (fattened by eating the bodies of the slain Irish); a dog's head 2/6d; a cat 4/6d; a rat 1/0d; a mouse 6d; a small flook taken in the river, not to be bought for money ...*

George Holmes observed:

> *I believe there died 15,000 men, women and children, many of which died for want of meat. But we had a great fever amongst us and all the children died, almost whole families not one left alive.*

Major-General Percy Kirke had sailed into Lough Foyle on 11 June with thirty vessels in the hope of assisting the besieged city. But for six weeks he waited, unwilling to risk the Jacobite guns at Culmore, downstream from Derry. Finally, moved by pleas for help and a stern order from his superiors, Kirke made a move on Sunday 28 July. While one warship engaged Culmore, a longboat and three small vessels sailed up the Foyle.

The wind dropped completely, but the flowing tide pushed the leading vessel, the *Mountjoy*, against the boom, snapping its chains. The ship's captain died as he ordered his men to respond to the Jacobite guns, and the *Mountjoy* stuck fast in the mud, but was freed in the recoil to drift up to the city.

Thomas Ash, who survived the 105 days of siege, recorded in his diary:

> *Oh! To hear the loud acclamations of the garrison soldiers round the Walls when the ships came to the quay ... The Lord, who has preserved this City from the Enemy, I hope will always keep it to the Protestants.*

For the Protestants, this epic defence gave inspiration for more than three centuries to come.

Enniskillen and
the Boyne

. . .

DURING THE SIEGE OF Derry, Jacobites – the forces of James II – had been tied down for months in a vain attempt to starve the island town of Enniskillen into submission. Then, on the day that the *Mountjoy* was breaking the boom at Derry, Lieutenant-General Justin MacCarthy arrived with a formidable Jacobite army. The men of Enniskillen – soon to be known as Inniskillingers – drove these troops back in confusion and on 31 July 1689, with the battle cry 'No Popery', closed in on MacCarthy at Newtownbutler. With his much larger army, MacCarthy should have won, but his men were not ready for the furious onslaught. Of 500 men who in fleeing tried to swim across the lough, only one survived. The rest were hunted down and slain. The victors ruthlessly put over 2,000 Jacobites to the sword.

For William of Orange, the steadfast refusal of Derry to surrender and the victory at Newtownbutler provided a vital breathing space – he could depend on a safe base in Ireland from which to drive out King James.

The Duke of Schomberg's Williamite army met no opposition as it came ashore at Ballyholme in north Down on 13 August 1689. After taking Carrickfergus by storm, this elderly French Huguenot veteran moved too slowly. When he finally camped north of Dundalk, he refused action. With their tents pitched by a marsh, Schomberg's soldiers were ravaged by fever. As the army chaplain George Story tells us, around 1,700 died at Dundalk and another 1,000 in vessels taking the sick back to Belfast, where 3,762 died.

There were several that had their limbs so mortified in the camp, afterwards, that some had their Toes, and some their whole Feet that fell off as the Surgeons were dressing them; so that upon the whole matter, we lost nigh one half of the Men that we took over with us.

With a heavy heart, William realised he had no choice but to go to Ireland himself. Early in June 1690, he assembled an army of continental size at Hounslow Heath in London. On the road to Chester a train of no fewer than 3,000 oxcarts carrying supplies stretched for more than eighteen miles. Then Sir Cloudsley Shovell's squadron of warships escorted William's fleet of about 300 vessels across the Irish Sea into Belfast Lough on 14 June. Never before had Belfast greeted so many men of distinction: Godard van Reede, Baron de Ginkel of Utrecht; Hans Willem Bentinck, the king's close adviser; the Duke of Würtemberg-Neustadt, the German commander of the Danish force; Count Henry Nassau; Prince Georg of Darmstadt, brother of Christian V of Denmark; and many others. This pale, asthmatic monarch had brought with him by far the largest invading force Ireland had yet seen.

The Jacobites withdrew from Dundalk to take up battle positions on the tidal south bank of the River Boyne, just west of Drogheda. William marched south and by Monday 30 June, he had deployed his troops on the north side of the river. The international composition of his army underlined the fact that it represented the Grand Alliance against France. The core of his army was made up of Dutch, Danish, French Huguenot and German veterans of continental campaigns. His English troops were mostly raw recruits, reinforced by Ulster Protestant skirmishers, described by Story as being 'half-naked with sabre and pistols hanging from their belts ... like a Horde of Tartars'.

Numbering 36,000, the Williamites were at least 10,000 stronger than the Jacobites and far superior in firepower. That Monday night the king held a council of war. A detachment would ride inland to the fords at Slane, to make it look as if this was where the main attack would be. Meanwhile, when the tide was right, he would direct a frontal assault across the river.

Sending troops upstream in a feint successfully drew the French away. This advantage having been gained, the ground shook as William's artillery pounded the Jacobite positions and the Dutch Blue Guards waded up to their armpits across the river at Oldbridge, holding their weapons over their heads. The Irish Jacobite cavalry fought back fiercely, but in the end, the Williamites triumphed by superior firepower and weight of numbers. The Duke of Schomberg and the Rev. George Walker, the hero of the Siege of Derry, were killed in the fighting.

The landing of the Duke of Schomberg at Carrickfergus, August 1689

The Battle of the Boyne was not a rout; the Irish and French retired in good order to fight for more than another year. Yet the battle was decisive. It was a severe blow to Louis XIV's pretensions to European domination, and it was celebrated by the singing of a *Te Deum* in thanks to God in Catholic Vienna. James II could no longer think of Ireland as a springboard for recovering his throne. For Ulster Protestants, the battle ensured the survival of the plantation and a victory to be celebrated from year to year.

Galloping Hogan, Sarsfield and the walls of Limerick

. . .

FOLLOWING HIS DEFEAT AT the Boyne on 1 July 1690, King James II dashed straight for Dublin. Here he made an ungracious speech to his Privy Council. The Irish soldiers, he said 'basely fled the field and left the spoil to the enemies, nor could they be prevailed upon to rally ... so that henceforth I never more determined to head an Irish army and do now resolve to shift for myself and so, gentlemen, must you'.

And shift himself he did. The next day he left for Waterford to sail for France, never to return. No wonder the Irish Jacobite commander Patrick Sarsfield observed: 'Change but kings and we will fight you over again.'

The Jacobite army adopted Sarsfield's plan to withdraw westwards and hold a line running along the River Shannon. Meanwhile, William III arrived at Dublin, making his camp just north of the city at Finglas, and on Sunday 6 July the 'Deliverer' entered the city in triumph, listened to a sermon in St Patrick's Cathedral, and watched the Dublin Protestants run about 'shouting and embracing one another and blessing God for his wonderful deliverance as if they had been alive from the dead'.

King William was anxious to move on in pursuit of the Jacobites. He had reason to be worried because he had just received bad news: on the day before his victory at the Boyne, the French fleet had inflicted a disastrous defeat on the Williamite navy at Beachy Head. And he had information that Louis XIV was sending to Ireland twenty-four additional vessels with men and munitions.

During William's slow progress southwards by Waterford and Carrick-on-Suir, the Jacobites worked frantically to improve the defences of Limerick. On 7 August, William halted about eight miles southwest of the city to await the arrival of his train of heavy guns and carts drawn by no fewer than 400 horses. But at midnight on 9 August, Patrick Sarsfield stole out of Limerick with 500 men. Guided by 'Galloping' Michael Hogan through the Tipperary mountains, on the following night they surreptitiously drew near to the siege train of 153 wagons which had made camp in a meadow. The password, curiously, was 'Sarsfield' – this 'Galloping' Hogan discovered from an old woman selling apples. So, challenged in the dark by a sentry, Sarsfield cried out: 'Sarsfield is the word, and Sarsfield is the man!'

Carters and horses were ruthlessly cut down, but the life of one gunner was spared in return for demonstrating how the cannon could be put out of action. Then 800 cannonballs, 12,000 pounds of gunpowder, 1,600 barrels of match and 500 hand grenades, along with tin pontoon boats, were heaped in a circle and a long powder trail laid. Hogan lit the fuse. The earth shook with the explosion, the loudest man-made sound yet heard in Ireland, and people far away in Co. Clare were wakened from their beds. After a brief silence there followed the crumbling sound of the ruined Ballyneety Castle close by crashing down from the shock waves. The holes left in the ground by the explosion can still be seen today.

King William had to wait for heavy guns from Waterford before he could begin to besiege Limerick. Using sacks of wool as protection against bullets and shrapnel, the Dutch got the cannon close to the walls of Limerick and made a breach. On the afternoon of 27 August, the Williamites assaulted the breach. John Stevens, an English Jacobite, was one of the first defenders and recorded how the city held fast: 'The fight was for some time renewed and continued with sword in hand and the butt end of the musket … The action continued hot and dubious for at least three hours … till the enemy wholly drew off. A great slaughter was made of them … there could not be much less than 3,000 killed.'

It was clear there would be no quick end to this war. The Williamites withdrew from their attempt to seize the city of Limerick in August 1690. King William returned to direct affairs from London.

The Jacobites, holding the River Shannon and all the land to the west of it, and delighted by their recent success, refused offers of a compromise peace.

William appointed Godard van Reede, Baron de Ginkel, as his commander in Ireland. It was a wise choice. Campaigning was a miserable affair during the persistent rains of winter. On 27 December Ginkel wrote: 'The enemy are burning all before us, and the Rapparees are so great a number that we can find neither forage nor cover, which

hinders much our march.' Named for their main weapon, a short pike known in Irish as a rapaire, the rapparees were Irish skirmishers. They did much to frustrate Ginkel's attempts to bring the war in Ireland to a conclusion. As well as reinforcements and fresh supplies sent by Louis XIV, the Jacobites acquired a new commander, Charles Chalmont, the Marquis de Saint-Ruth. St-Ruth had no fewer than 16,000 foot soldiers, 3,000 cavalry and 2,000 dragoons to stop Ginkel – with a smaller force – from taking Athlone, a town at a vital crossing of the Shannon.

Lithograph of the siege of Limerick, dated 1848

173

Athlone, Aughrim, Limerick and a treaty

...

ATHLONE GUARDED THE PRINCIPAL crossing over the River Shannon. The Marquis de Saint-Ruth, in command of the Jacobite army, was determined to prevent Baron de Ginkel, the Williamite general, from taking it.

Ginkel launched the heaviest bombardment ever in Irish history on the night of 21 June 1691. For ten days, without let-up, the town and Jacobite fortifications were pounded and reduced to rubble. John Stevens was in the thick of the fighting in defence of the bridge over the Shannon:

> *What with the balls and bombs flying so thick that spot was a mere Hell on Earth, and so many cannon and mortars incessantly playing on it there seemed to be no likelihood of any man coming off alive.*

But how was the Shannon, the largest river in these islands, to be crossed? Ginkel decided to test a ford below Athlone. On 7 June he sent three Danes under sentence of death for mutiny to try the crossing in return for their lives. Yes, they reported – after wading across and back – the river was fordable. On 30 June 1691, the assault began. A church bell gave the signal for the grenadiers to enter the water, which came up to their chests. Each man had been given a golden guinea to whet his courage.

The Jacobites, caught from behind, were completely taken by surprise. In less than half an hour Athlone fell to King William's army. St-Ruth pulled back sixteen miles to the south west, near the village of Aughrim. There he prepared a set-piece battle on the limestone Galway plain. His plan was to lure the Williamites into a treacherous bog in front of his line.

At first, these tactics seemed to work. A thick mist enveloped Ginkel's army as it moved out of Ballinasloe on Sunday 12 July. Ginkel's Huguenots were drawn into the bog, cut off and slaughtered, while the Danes strove in vain to relieve them. The Irish pikemen stood firm even when, it was reported, 'the blood flowed into their shewse', and Ulster Jacobites, led by Gordon O'Neill, spiked a battery of Williamite guns. In anticipation of a speedy victory, St-Ruth cried out: '*Le jour est à nous*, the day is ours, *mes enfants!*'

At that moment a cannonball, fired at extreme range, took off his head. This chance incident created total confusion in the Jacobite ranks. Guided by members of the Trench family, French Protestants who had settled in Co. Galway, Ginkel sent his cavalry by a causeway over the bog. As these horsemen made a devastating assault over this narrow stretch of dry ground, the Jacobite cavalry – the flower of the Old English gentry of Ireland – turned tail and abandoned their foot soldiers to their fate.

The assault on Athlone, 20 June 1691

The Battle of Aughrim was the bloodiest battle ever fought on Irish soil. The French commander, the Marquis de Saint-Ruth, three major generals, seven brigadiers, twenty-two colonels, seventeen lieutenant-colonels and over 7,000 men of other ranks were killed. When news of this victory for King William's army spread north, the Protestants of Ulster set bonfires blazing, as they would do year after year thereafter.

The French and the Irish Jacobites decided to make a last stand in Limerick city. Patrick Sarsfield took over command from the Duke of Tyrconnell, King James's dying Lord Deputy. An intense contest ensued. This second siege of Limerick was conducted on a scale never again equalled in Irish history.

The Rev. George Story, an English chaplain in Ginkel's army, described what happened in his journal:

> *September the 8th, our new Batteries were all ready. Those fell to work all at a time, and put the Irish into such a fright, that a great many of them wish'd themselves in another place, having never heard such a Noise before, or I hope never shall in that Kingdom.*

This furious bombardment continued without let-up for the next fortnight. Then Ginkel decided to storm the gaping breach in the walls, as George Story records:

> *September the 22nd ... For our Granadeers were so very forward ... and pursued them so close, that a French Major who commanded at Thoumound Gate, fearing our mens entering the Town with their own, he ordered the Draw-bridge to be pluck'd up, and left the whole Party to the Mercy of our Souldiers. They were laid in Heaps upon the Bridg higher than the Ledges of it; so that they were either all killed or taken ... The number of the dead is said to be six hundred, amongst whom we may reckone over hundred fifty four that were drowned in being forced over the Fall of the Draw-bridg.*

On the following day, Ginkel wrote to William's representatives in Dublin to assure them that it was impossible for him to take the city of Limerick by assault. That same day, however, the French and the Irish held a council of war and agreed to ask Ginkel for a capitulation and a ceasefire. The ensuing discussions were conducted with great courtesy – helped, no doubt, by a boatload of Bordeaux wine brought over for the Williamite officers by Patrick Sarsfield. By 3 October 1691, terms had been agreed and both sides signed what became known as the Treaty of Limerick.

The articles of the treaty appeared lenient. But it was one thing for a Dutch general to sign a generous treaty to end a war. It was quite another for the Protestant gentlemen in the Westminster and Dublin parliaments to agree to those terms. With very good reason, the Treaty of Limerick was to become known as the 'Broken Treaty', and it embittered relations between the Irish and the English for more than two centuries.

'Seven ill years'

...

The eruption of Hekla in Iceland

IN 1693 HEKLA IN Iceland erupted with terrible force, spewing huge quantities of volcanic dust into the stratosphere. At the same time, on the other side of the world, the volcanoes of Serua and Amboina erupted in the Dutch East Indies, adding to the atmospheric haze filtering out the sun. Ruined harvests resulted in a terrible famine in Scandinavia: Finland lost a third of its population. In Scotland, the harvest failed in 1693 and every following year to the end of the century. The Scots called these the 'seven ill years'. Some parts suffered more than even during the Black Death in the fourteenth century. The starving tried to survive by eating nettles and grass and then, fever-ridden, poured into the towns, dying there in thousands. Andrew Fletcher of Saltoun reckoned that one in five died from hunger, and others reported that a third of the people starved to death. It seems likely that the seven ill years killed at least a tenth of Scotland's population as a whole. Patrick Walker, an itinerant pedlar, wrote:

> I have seen, when meal was all sold in the markets, women clapping their hands, and tearing the clothes off their heads, crying, 'How shall we go home and see our children die in hunger?'

A Lowlander in the Highlands reported:

> Some die by the wayside, some drop down in the streets, the poor sucking babs are starving for want of milk, which the empty breasts of their mothers cannot furnish them, everyone may see death in the face of the poor that abound everywhere.

Ireland escaped the worst effects of this climatic downturn. Many survivors of the Scottish famine headed for the Narrow Sea to begin a new life in Ulster.

The Penal Laws

...

Queen Anne (1665–1714), Queen of England, Scotland and
Ireland and subsequently Queen of Great Britain and Ireland

ALL THINGS CONSIDERED, THE treaty signed with Baron de Ginkel, King William III's general, was a fair one. Those Jacobite officers and men who had surrendered would be pardoned and keep their property provided they took an oath of allegiance. Catholics all over Ireland were to have freedom of worship. Those who preferred to join the armies of Louis XIV could leave for France. Around 12,000 did so: these exiles soon became known as the 'Wild Geese', but unlike the myriads of white-fronted, barnacle and brent geese which fly in from the north every autumn, very few of them ever returned to Ireland.

In London, King William signed the treaty. But a contemporary broadsheet put forward the view that Ginkel had been outwitted by the Jacobite negotiators – 'We fight like heroes but like fools we treat'. Soon it became clear that members of both the Westminster and Dublin parliaments would refuse to accept the main terms of the Treaty of Limerick. The outcome of this 'Broken Treaty' was a succession of acts passed by both parliaments which collectively would become known as the Penal Laws.

> *Whereas, it is Notoriously known, that the late Rebellions in this Kingdom have been Contrived, Promoted and Carried on by Popish Archbishops, Bishops, Jesuits, and other Ecclesiastical persons of the Romish Clergy ...*

So began a bill put forward in the Irish parliament, and passed into law in 1697, to exile monks, friars, Jesuits and the Catholic hierarchy. Other penal laws against Catholics followed rapidly, one after another. William viewed the strident demand for further laws against Catholics with some distaste. But in the spring of 1702, the king's horse tripped on a molehill. William was thrown to the ground and died shortly afterwards from complications arising from his injuries. Anne, the Protestant daughter of James II, was now queen.

Encouraged by Queen Anne, both parliaments set about drafting fresh laws to restrict the rights of Catholics. The 1704 Act to Prevent the Further Growth of Popery was the crowning piece of this legislation. These laws – known as the Penal Code – were enacted over a long period, thirty-nine years in fact. The final penal law, depriving Catholics of the vote, did not enter the statute book until 1728. The principal laws can be summarised as follows:

No Catholic could buy land.

No Catholic could have a lease for longer than thirty-one years.

When a Catholic died, his estate would not be inherited by the eldest son but would be divided equally among all sons. If one son became a Protestant, he could inherit the entire estate.

No Catholic could become a barrister, a solicitor, a judge or a member of a grand jury.

Catholics could not sit in parliament or vote in elections.

A Catholic could not be a civil servant, a sheriff, or a member of a town council.

Catholics could neither send their children abroad to be educated nor establish schools at home.

Catholics could not be guardians of orphans.

Catholics could not carry arms, join the army, or own a horse worth more than £5.

Catholics were excluded from living in many important provincial towns.

Catholics could worship freely, but their churches could not have steeples or display crosses. Priests had to register with the government and take an oath of loyalty. Archbishops, bishops, Jesuits, monks and friars had to leave the country.

Catholic pilgrimages, especially the one to Lough Derg in Co. Donegal, were forbidden.

It soon transpired that many of the Penal Laws were impossible to enforce. But the laws concerned with political rights, jobs and landed property were rigidly imposed, with long-term consequences. The code was directed principally at Catholics of education and property. The aim was the disarming and 'dismounting' of Catholic gentlemen so that they could never again organise and conduct a rebellion. Humble Catholic farmers and labourers, humiliated though they might be, were not so severely affected, for the Penal Laws were not really concerned with the Catholic lower orders.

Mutilating the Treaty of Limerick beyond recognition, the Irish parliament took possession of the estates of Catholics who had backed King James in any way, including exiles and those killed in the war. Close to a million acres of land were confiscated. In 1688, Catholics held 22 per cent of the land of Ireland. By the time Queen Anne died, only 14 per cent was left to them. By 1780 the proportion of land owned by Catholics – three-quarters of the population – had dropped to an all-time low of 5 per cent. How can this be explained?

For a start, the Penal Laws prevented Catholics from buying land. And if one son became a Protestant, he could inherit the entire estate. Only 5,500 Catholics converted to the Established Church – that is, the Church of Ireland – between 1703 and 1789. However, these converts were drawn almost exclusively from the Catholic gentry eager to avoid the subdivision of their estates and to find careers for younger sons in the legal profession. Virtually no Catholic estate of any significance was left in the entire province of Ulster when Alexander MacDonnell, the fifth Earl of Antrim, 'turned' upon reaching the age of 21 in 1734.

Scots 'are coming over here daily'

. . .

THE LAST DECADE OF the seventeenth century and the first years of the next saw a new surge of Presbyterian Scots coming into Ulster. Even before the Jacobites had been defeated, it was observed that 'vast numbers of them followed the Army as Victuallers ... and purchased most of the vast preys which were taken by the Army in the Campaign and drove incredible numbers of cattel into Ulster'. The Church of Ireland Archbishop of Tuam, Edward Synge, estimated that 50,000 Scots families came to Ulster between 1689 and 1715. This was certainly an exaggeration; but the true figure was high, probably around 40,000 persons.

The Catholic Bishop of Clogher, Hugh MacMahon, wrote in 1714:

> *Although all Ireland is suffering, this province is worse off than the others, because of the fact that from the neighbouring country of Scotland, Calvinists are coming over here daily in large groups of families, occupying the towns and villages, seizing the farms in the richer parts of the country and expelling the natives.*

There was some truth in this observation. It is quite wrong to conclude that in the Plantation of Ulster, the native Irish were left only with the poor land. But by the end of the seventeenth century the colonists, English as well as Scots, were concentrating in the more fertile lands such as the Clogher, Lagan, Bush and Foyle river valleys. Earlier, estate owners, short of tenants, had been willing to let farms to the Catholic Irish. Now that prospective British tenants were more abundant, they preferred to lease the good land to their co-religionists. The Catholic Irish in many parts of the north were not expelled, but they often had little choice but to rent farms on land previously described as 'waste' – bogland and hillsides which in the past had been used only for summer grazing.

The clergy of the Established Church, the Church of Ireland, were particularly alarmed by this flood of Scots immigrants. In several parts of Ulster, Presbyterians formed overwhelming majorities – Jonathan Swift was unhappy at Kilroot not just because he was thwarted in love but also because he had almost no Anglicans living in his parish. Ulster Presbyterians threatened the privileges of the Established Church and made inroads into Anglican congregations too often neglected by worldly or absentee clergy. Presbyterianism was particularly well-organised and disciplined. Congregations grouped into presbyteries which supervised their affairs through regular visitations. There were five presbyteries in 1689 and seven by 1691. From 1691 ministers and selected elders began to meet annually as the Synod of Ulster. Discipline was strict: ministers and elders could punish offences such as adultery, fornication, drunkenness, slander, failure to pay debts and Sabbath-breaking. Dr Edward Walkington, Church of Ireland Bishop of Down and Connor, indignantly complained that 'They openly hold their sessions and provincial synods for regulating of all matters of ecclesiastical concern'.

Priest saying mass in cabin in a village, nineteenth century

William King, Archbishop of Dublin, insisted that Ulster Presbyterians were very different from other Protestants in Ireland: 'They are a people embodied under their lay elders, presbyteries and synods ... and will be just so far the King's subjects as their lay elders and presbyteries will allow them.'

At this time, all the states of Europe were confessional states, each with only one official religion. Louis XIV went so far as to expel Protestants, the Huguenots, from France in 1685. Many, including those with surnames such as Morrow and Molyneux, were to find refuge in Ulster. The Islamic Turkish Empire, which then ruled the Balkans, put the rest of Europe to shame with its tolerant approach to Christian and Jewish minorities. In central and western Europe, realms were either Catholic or Protestant. Indeed, in nearly all Protestant states only one variety of Protestantism was established. The Church of Scotland was Presbyterian. The Church of England was Anglican with the monarch as head of the Church. And London insisted that the Established Church in Ireland must be Anglican. Here Catholics formed a large majority and they suffered greatly from their refusal to conform.

'Jet-black
prelatic calumny'

. . .

THE 1704 ACT TO Prevent the Further Growth of Popery was by far the most comprehensive of a series of statutes depriving Catholics of their rights. After its passage, a senior judge observed: 'The law does not suppose any such person to exist as an Irish Roman Catholic.'

The 1704 Act also included penal legislation directed at Presbyterians. Because they were concentrated in Ulster, the authorities in Dublin feared their power. In any case, since Anne had come to the throne in 1702, the High Tories were in office in London, determined to enforce conformity to the Anglican Church.

The 1704 'Popery Act' restored the sacramental test: it stated that any person holding public office must produce a certificate that he had received the sacrament of the Lord's Supper 'according to the usage of the Church of Ireland ... immediately after divine service and sermon'. Since Catholics were already disqualified by previous penal laws, this sacramental test was really directed at the Presbyterians, who now could no longer be members of municipal corporations or hold commissions in the army or militia.

Ulster Presbyterians were now in something of a quandary. They were outraged by the test but, at the same time, they heartily approved of the Popery Act. Nevertheless, from his cell in Newgate, Daniel Defoe, the author of *Robinson Crusoe*, launched a fierce attack on the test. In his pamphlet *The Parallel; or Persecution the Shortest Way to prevent the Growth of Popery in Ireland*, Defoe declared that since the Williamite War, Ulster Presbyterians *instead of being remembered to their honour have been ranked amongst the worst enemies of the Church, and chained to a Bill to prevent the further growth of Popery ... Will any man in the world tell us that to divide Protestants is a way to prevent the further growth of Popery, when this united force is little enough to keep it down? This is like sinking the ship to drown the rats, or cutting off the foot to cure the corns.*

Sure in the knowledge that Presbyterians would always rally to the Protestant cause in times of danger, the Church of Ireland continued to harass dissenters, those Protestants who were not Anglicans. Dr William Tisdall, vicar of Belfast, shared the view of Dean Jonathan Swift that Presbyterians were more to be feared than the Catholics themselves. Swift may have helped Tisdall to compose a pamphlet attacking the Presbyterians, ironically titled *A Sample of True-Blew Presbyterian Loyalty in all Changes and Turns of Government*. The citizens of Belfast, overwhelmingly Presbyterian, reacted by obstructing the vicar's collection of 'house-money' to support his clergy. They also brought back their Presbyterian minister, John McBride, who had been forced to flee to Scotland in 1708 when Tisdall accused him of being a Jacobite. Tisdall was quite unable to suppress pamphlets he condemned as scurrilous, including McBride's denunciation of the vicar, entitled *A Sample of Jet-black Prelatic Calumny*.

On 10 December 1712, ten Presbyterian ministers and two probationers drawn from all over Ulster gathered at Belturbet in Co. Cavan to set up a new congregation. Hearing of the meeting, the Dean of Kilmore, Dr Jeremiah Marsh, rallied the local Anglicans 'to stop these pernicious designs ... to pervert the people'. The ministers were arrested and a county grand jury was empanelled to bring in the unanimous verdict that the Presbyterians were guilty of disturbing the peace. A couple of months later Robert Wodrow, an agent of the Scottish Presbyterians visiting Ulster congregations, reported: 'I find our brethren there are in very ill circumstances. High church is rampant and flaming.'

Jonathan Swift, 1667–1745, was a satirist, essayist, political pamphleteer, poet and cleric

But events in Scotland suddenly brought an end to this persecution. On 16 January 1707 the peers and commoners of the Estates, the Scottish parliament, had voted in favour of a union between Scotland and England, although this union was deeply unpopular with large sections of the Scottish people. When Queen Anne died without an heir in 1714, George, Elector of Hanover, was invited to become king. Louis XIV immediately recognised the Catholic son of James II as King James III. In 1715, led by the Earl of Mar, Highlanders rose in furious revolt in support of James. Ten thousand Jacobites swept south, but on 13 November they were halted at Sheriffmuir by troops under the command of the Duke of Argyll. It was all over by the time James, later known as the Old Pretender, disembarked at Peterhead from a French vessel on 22 December. He sailed away a few weeks later.

Ulster Presbyterians unhesitatingly stood by their Protestant king, George I. For their loyalty, they were rewarded with an Act of Toleration in 1719. Catholics, branded as Jacobites, continued to be oppressed by the Penal Laws.

'Like a contagious distemper'

. . .

THROUGHOUT THE SEVENTEENTH CENTURY, and particularly during the 1690s, tens of thousands of Scots had crossed the Narrow Sea to Ulster. Then, during the first years of the eighteenth century, this migration stopped rather suddenly. After a string of bad harvests in Scotland, yields of corn were so good that there was a surplus for the burgeoning gin trade in London. At the same time, in Ulster, the restless Scots and their descendants began to contemplate starting a new life across the Atlantic Ocean.

The British colonisation of North America had begun at around the same time as the Plantation of Ulster in the early seventeenth century. By the beginning of the eighteenth century – despite abrasive competition with the French and wars with native peoples – the American colonies were thriving. The first emigrants from Ireland were drawn from the Laggan district in north-east Donegal and it was clear that the exodus had begun in earnest by 1718. In that year, eleven Presbyterian ministers and nearly 300 members of their congregations petitioned the governor of Massachusetts and New Hampshire, Samuel Shute, for a grant of land there. At least one ship brought a hundred passengers from Londonderry to New York, and the *Boston News Letter* reported the arrival of eleven ships from Belfast and Derry in the summer and autumn of 1719. Between 1717 and 1719 as many as 7,000 emigrants left Ulster for America.

The authorities in Dublin were alarmed at this draining away of a Protestant population which had been so painstakingly settled in Ulster during the seventeenth century. William King, Archbishop of Dublin and a commissioner for the Irish government, wrote in 1718:

'No papists stir ... The papists being already five or six to one, and being a breeding people, you may imagine in what condition we are like to be in.'

Ten years later, Hugh Boulter, Archbishop of Armagh, deputising for the viceroy, informed the Duke of Newcastle:

> *The humour has spread like a contagious distemper, and the people will hardly hear any body that tries to cure them of their madness. The worst is that it affects only Protestants, and reigns chiefly in the North, which is the seat of our linen manufacture.*

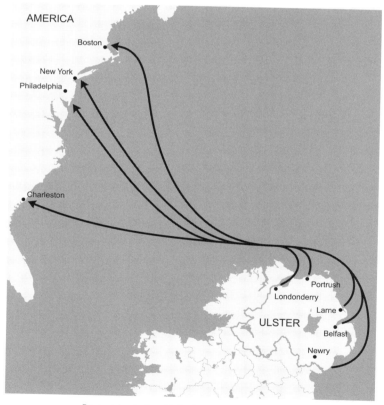

Routes taken by Scottish Presbyterians to North America

Indeed, most Catholics had at this stage neither the resources nor the inclination to go to the American colonies, which were, in any case, still overwhelmingly Protestant. The great majority leaving Ulster were Presbyterians, known in America as the 'Scotch-Irish'. In 1729 an *Address of Protestant Dissenting Ministers to the King* argued that the sacramental test – excluding those who were not members of the Church of Ireland from public office – was found by Ulster Presbyterians to be

> *so very grievous that they have in great numbers transported themselves to the American Plantations for the sake of that liberty and ease which they are denied in their native country.*

Almost certainly this was not the main cause, though Presbyterian ministers had a key part to play in organising the first sailings across the Atlantic. Ezekiel Stewart of Portstewart observed in 1729:

> *The Presbiteirin ministers have taken their shear of pains to seduce their poor Ignorant heerers, by Bellowing from their pulpits against their Landlords and the Clargey, calling them Rackers of Rents and Scruers of Tythes ... There are two of these Preachers caryed this affair to such a length that they went themselves to New England and caryed numbers with them.*

In these more settled conditions, when memories of wars in Ireland were fast fading, demand for land rose sharply. As leases expired, rents were jacked up – not so much by the great proprietors (such as the London Companies and the Earl of Abercorn) but by 'middlemen', those who rented large tracts from them. It was these middlemen, those who 'underset' (or sublet) these farms, who doubled and tripled rents over as few as fifteen years.

Bliadhain an Áir:
'Year of the Slaughter'

. . .

EARLY EIGHTEENTH-CENTURY IRISH society was founded on dispossession and exclusion. Those who gained from the ruin of the Catholic gentry were Protestant landowners and their relatives. The term 'Protestant Ascendancy' was only coined in the 1790s, but it very neatly describes the charmed circle of aristocrats, squires, clergy and prosperous lawyers, along with their relatives, who formed Ireland's privileged elite in the eighteenth century.

The Obelilk near Castletown 140 feet high

Conolly's Folly in Maynooth, Co. Kildare, was built at a cost of £400 to provide employment for the poor of Celbridge when the famine of 1740–1 was at its worst

The Battle of Aughrim and the capitulation of Limerick in 1691 decided the political future of Ireland for the next two centuries and more. For much of the preceding hundred years, the island's soil had been drenched in blood. Now Ireland, indisputably back under the rule of its larger neighbour, was to experience a century of peace, the longest in its history. That peace was to give Ireland a prosperity it had not known before. But it was by no means immune to disaster.

During January 1740, Arctic weather descended on Ireland, so intense that vast numbers of fish were found dead around the shores of Strangford Lough and Lough Neagh. Lasting seven weeks, this 'Great Frost' froze the sea around both English and Irish ports, stopping the carrying of coal across the Irish Sea. A whole sheep was roasted on top of nineteen inches of ice on the River Shannon at Portumna, 'at the eating of which they had great mirth, and drank many loyal toasts'. For the ordinary people of Ireland, this Siberian weather was a disaster. The temperature plummeted so greatly that potato stores in straw-covered clamps in the ground were turned to inedible pulp. Richard Purcell wrote from north Cork:

> The eating potatoes are all destroyed, which many think will be followed by famine among the poor, and if the small ones, which are not bigger than large peas and which be deepest in the ground, are so destroyed as not to serve for seed, there must be sore famine in 1741 ... I think this frost the most dreadful calamity that ever befell this poor kingdom.

Huge numbers of cattle and sheep had been killed by the extreme cold. Then, for those animals which survived, there was little or no grazing – the usual rains did not follow when a thaw set in during February. In April, a correspondent from north Wexford wrote to the Dublin newspaper *Pue's Occurrences*:

> Without rain what is to come of us? The corn that is sowed is perishing, the corn we have in our haggards is so prodigious dear the poor cannot purchase it ... As for flesh meat they cannot

smell to it, they have lost all their sheep long ago, and now their last stake, their little cows are daily and hourly dropping for want of grass.

The drought was so severe that streams that usually turned the waterwheels to power corn mills and woollen tuck mills dried up. In the tinder-dry conditions, fires raged in many towns: 150 houses burned down in Carrick-on-Shannon, fifty-three in Wexford town, and twenty in the village of Moate, Co. Westmeath.

Violent gales blew in September, followed by blizzards in October and two terrible storms in November. On 9 December, the heavens opened with such force that floods were reported across the island – a correspondent in Navan witnessed 'the greatest flood in the River Boyne that was ever known in the memory of man'.

On the following day, temperatures dropped and the Arctic weather returned. The only outcome now could be famine – a famine so terrible that 1741 would be remembered as *Bliadhain an Áir*, 'Year of the Slaughter'.

Their bodies weakened by hunger, people fell prey to disease, including smallpox and dysentery, known then as the 'bloody flux'. John Usher, a land agent at Lismore, Co. Waterford, wrote to his employer in London that 'a bloody flux and a violent fever rages so all over the country that scarce a day passes that we do not bury fifteen or sixteen even in this small place'. 'For my own part', he concluded, 'were it not for the business of this place I would fly for my life.' From west Cork, Sir Richard Cox wrote: 'By all I can learn, the dreadfullest civil war, or most raging plague never destroyed so many as this season.' The Rev. Philip Skelton, curate of Monaghan parish, reported that

the dead have been eaten in the fields by dogs for want of people to bury them. Whole thousands in a barony have perished, some of hunger and others of disorders occasioned by unnatural, unwholesome and putrid diet.

Archbishop Hugh Boulter got this anonymous letter from Cashel: 'I have seen the aged father eating grass like a beast ... the helpless orphan exposed on the dunghill, and none to take him in for fear of infection ... the hungry infant sucking at the breast of the already expired parent ...'

Out of a population of 2,400,000, between 310,000 and 480,000 died as a direct result of famine and fever in 1741. A greater proportion of the population died in this *one* year than during the *six* years of the Great Famine in the 1840s, when the population was more than three times larger than it was in 1741.

The extreme weather affected all of western and northern Europe but no country, except for Norway, suffered as much as Ireland. Those in authority in Dublin had failed to put into effect the most elementary measures needed to safeguard the destitute from starvation. For example, though the dearth in Prussia was acute, and the state was at war, timely and efficient action by its government prevented a catastrophe. In England, the Poor Law obliged each parish to provide relief to the old, the sick, the destitute and the 'casual poor'. In Scotland, the system of poor relief was not compulsory, but it seemed to work as well as the obligatory system in England.

In Ireland, parliament had failed to legislate for any kind of safety net. Those responsible for governing Ireland, at both a national and a local level, lacked the funding, the staff and the machinery to provide relief – and, in some cases, the will to act humanely in time of crisis.

Flaxseed and prosperity

. . .

AT THE BEGINNING OF the seventeenth century, Ulster was reckoned to be the poorest of Ireland's four provinces. By 1700, it was unquestionably the richest. How can this be explained? First, in order to attract British tenants to their estates in Ulster, landlords (unlike those in Scotland) were obliged to let out farms on long leases usually lasting thirty-one years (but sometimes as many as fifty). Settlers were given time to drain, lime and ditch their land, bringing their farms into full production without the fear of eviction. During most of the seventeenth century, colonists depended on cattle, just like the native Irish, as the main source of farm income. Nevertheless, government officials noticed that Scots in Ulster were more diligent than the English there in ploughing up the sward to grow corn.

Scotland, like England, was a birthplace of what later was to be known as the Agricultural Revolution. New methods of rotating crops and fertilising them, to eliminate fallow ground, and better ploughs, which delved deeper into the mineral-rich subsoil, were gradually introduced to Ulster across the Narrow Sea. But by far the clearest explanation for Ulster's new prosperity was the growth of the linen industry.

Huguenots, French Protestants, have usually been given credit for bringing the linen industry to Ulster. Actually, from very early times the native Irish had grown their own flax and made their own linen. This type of linen was still being made for local sale in the eighteenth century; however, its width was too narrow for the export market. It was really the Scots, and families from the north of England settling in Ulster, who established the manufacture of linen suitable for sale abroad. In 1700, 50 per cent of all Scotland's exports to England by value were made up of linen. Scots making a new home in Ulster in the seventeenth century brought their skills with them, and the majority of them set parts of their farms aside for the growing of flax. Some of the leading Ulster planters, such as the Clotworthys of south Antrim, encouraged their tenants to grow and spin flax to tide them over in hard times. Not only could flax be easily sold for ready cash in the market, but it could also be kept at home and processed, spun and woven into linen for sale to drapers. These merchants then took the linen webs to the Linen Hall in Dublin and from there exported them to London.

In 1699, Westminster passed a Woollen Act forbidding the export of Irish woollen goods in order to protect the interests of English producers. This drastic legislation, which killed off a thriving trade, caused an outrage which united Protestants and Catholics alike. London, however, did not want to ruin the Irish economy and, in compensation, acted to encourage linen exports. Restrictions on the importation of linen to the American colonies directly from Ireland were removed in 1705.

During the early decades of the eighteenth century, the domestic weaving of linen became the main economic activity of eastern Ulster: Antrim, Armagh, Down, Monaghan and the eastern parts of Londonderry, Tyrone and Cavan. Weavers could not allow their hands to become rough by heavy farm work – in case they would catch in the fine warp and weft – and so food had to be imported from other parts of Ireland to areas concentrating on producing linen cloth. Often, weavers were satisfied with holdings just large enough for a cottage which could house a loom and spinning wheels, and with enough land to grow flax and enough grass for a cow to supply the family with fresh milk.

By the end of the 1720s, linen, nearly all of it produced in Ulster, accounted for a quarter of the total value of exports from Ireland. The success of this industry in turn greatly stimulated the emigration of Ulster Scots to the American colonies. The emergence of a flourishing trade in flaxseed explains this development. Just as its blue flowers were fading, the flax was pulled, ripped up roots and all, so that no part of the stem was lost and the fibres in the stem were as long as possible. This had to be done before the plant went to seed. It was, therefore, more economical for a family of weavers to buy the seed from elsewhere. Early in the century, seed was nearly all from the Baltic, shipped to Ulster by Dutch merchants. Then, in 1731, Westminster permitted the shipment of flaxseed directly to Ireland from the Colonies. In 1733 it stimulated the trade with a bounty or subsidy and America became the exclusive supplier of flaxseed to Ulster.

Ship owners landing seed at Derry, Belfast, Coleraine and Newry did not want to return across the Atlantic in half-empty vessels. The most lucrative cargo proved to be people anxious for a fresh start in the New World.

Woman spinning flax

EPISODE 58

The second city
of the Empire

. . .

The Custom House, Dublin

DURING THE EIGHTEENTH CENTURY, Britain became a
world power. Possessing a powerful navy, it conquered territory from
its rivals France, Spain, Portugal and Holland, extended its control in
the Indian subcontinent, developed colonies in North America, and
began its settlement of Australia. Strict laws prevented Ireland from
trading directly with the Colonies, but English vessels brought into

Irish ports tea from the Far East, sugar from the West Indies, tobacco from Virginia, fine muslin from India and other exotic luxuries. To pay for these overseas goods, and also for English coal, Ireland exported linen, corn, butter, salt pork and other farm produce.

No city in Ireland benefitted more from the expansion of the British Empire than Dublin. Captain William Bligh – yes, the same captain of *Mutiny on the Bounty* fame – supervised the impressive deepening of the Liffey estuary to allow vessels to come up at all tides to the new stone-lined quays. The population, which had been 58,000 in 1683, was close to 129,000 by 1772, and 182,000 (including the garrison) by 1798, making Dublin the second-largest city in the British Empire.

During this time, the viceroy held court at Dublin Castle. In the 1750s, the handsome Bedford Tower was erected there, and the castle was extended and given an elegant square built of red brick and cream stone. Edward Lovett Pearce, descended from the seventeenth-century rebel leader Rory O'More, designed a magnificent new parliament house in College Green with a line of stone columns in the new classical style. Across the island, expanding trade, a rising population and – above all – the long period of peace increased the income of the Protestant landowners. Much of the money they collected from their tenants they spent in Dublin. Here they needed to be present to attend the sessions of parliament and the law courts. And, of course, they wanted to show off by entertaining lavishly and find suitable husbands for their daughters.

As well as erecting great mansions on their estates, these gentlemen built magnificent townhouses in Dublin constructed of cut stone. The first to be put up in the new Georgian style was Tyrone House, built for Marcus Beresford, Earl of Tyrone, in 1740. Then followed many others, including Powerscourt House in William Street, built for Richard Wingfield, Viscount Powerscourt; Leinster House in Kildare Street, completed for James Fitzgerald, first Duke of Leinster, in 1745, and now the home of Dáil Éireann; Northland House, built for the Knox family of Dungannon in 1770, and now the Royal Irish Academy; and Charlemont House, designed by and built for James Caulfield, first Earl of Charlemont of Co. Armagh, and later the Municipal Gallery of Modern Art.

Other Protestant gentlemen became urban developers. They included Luke Gardiner, the first Viscount Mountjoy, who planned and laid out Gardiner Street and Mountjoy Square; the sixth Lord Fitzwilliam of Meryon, who developed Merrion Square and Fitzwilliam Street (the longest Georgian street in the world); and Dr Bartholomew Mosse, who developed Rutland Square, now Parnell Square. On the same site, Dr Mosse erected the Rotunda Lying-in Hospital – the first maternity hospital in either Britain or Ireland. The Assembly Rooms attached to the Rotunda rapidly became Dublin's social hub, where concerts and other events were put on to raise funds for the hospital.

Most of these Protestant gentlemen and their families had become newly rich in only one or two generations. Visitors from England often found them to be noisy, wild, brash, extravagant and hard-living – in particular, hard-drinking. Lord Chesterfield, when he was Lord Lieutenant, was horrified by the 'beastly vice' of excessive drinking of French wine which destroyed 'the constitutions, the faculties, and too often the fortunes of those of superior rank'. Heavy drinking naturally took place on festive occasions when endless toasts were given, the most popular being to 'the glorious, pious and immortal memory of the good and great King William, who delivered us from popery, slavery, arbitrary power, brass money, and wooden shoes'. This caused that perceptive observer of Irish society, Sir Jonah Barrington, to remark:

> Could His Majesty King William learn in the other world that he had been the cause of more broken heads and drunken men, since his departure, than all his predecessors, he must be the proudest ghost, and most conceited skeleton that ever entered the gardens of Elysium.

According to John Bush, an Englishman who visited Dublin in 1794, a 'middling drinker' would drink four bottles of claret – that is, red wine from Bordeaux – without showing any effects. No man was considered a serious drinker in Dublin who could not, he wrote, 'take off his gallon cooly' – that is, the equivalent of six modern bottles drunk at a single sitting.

Dublin, indeed, was a city of excess and extremes.

'The Irish gentry are an expensive people'

. . .

THE POPULATION OF IRELAND rose from around two million in 1700 to about two and a quarter million by 1740 and reached over five million by 1800. In consequence, the demand for land increased sharply, and this allowed landowners to raise their rents. Now the nobility and gentry could afford to knock down or abandon uncomfortable castles and fortified houses that had been erected in more turbulent times and replace those outmoded dwellings with new luxurious mansions.

Without exception, all looked east across the Irish Sea for inspiration. The classical style became the vogue when Sir Gustavus Hume, High Sherriff of Co. Fermanagh, commissioned the German architect Richard Cassels to build his country seat on the western peninsula of Lower Lough Erne in 1728. At about the same time William Conolly, Speaker of the Irish House of Commons and the richest man in Ireland, erected what is still regarded as the most magnificent Georgian great house in Ireland, Castletown, fifteen miles west of Dublin. Almost as splendid was Carton nearby, designed by Cassels for Robert Fitzgerald, nineteenth Earl of Kildare.

It cost Armar Lowry-Corry, first Earl of Belmore, some £390,000 to build Castle Coole in Co. Fermanagh. He chartered a brig to bring Portland stone from the Isle of Wight to a specially constructed quay at Ballyshannon; from there the blocks were carted ten miles to Lough Erne to be taken by barge to Enniskillen, and more bullock carts were used for the last two miles to complete the delivery. Visiting in 1796, the French *émigré* the Chevalier de Latocnaye found the interior 'full of rare marbles, and the walls of several rooms are covered with rare stucco work produced at great cost, and by workers brought from Italy ... Temples should be left to the gods.' When the earl died in 1802, his estate had debts of £370,000. Lord Belmore's extravagance was exceeded by that of Frederick Hervey, simultaneously Earl of Bristol and Bishop of Derry. After visiting the earl-bishop's huge palace at Downhill on the rugged Londonderry coast, de Latocnaye wrote:

> *Oh, what a lovely thing it is to be an Anglican bishop or minister! These are the spoiled children of fortune, rich as bankers, enjoying good wine, good cheer, and pretty women, and all for their benediction. God bless them!*

During a tour of Ireland in 1732 the English historian John Loveday remarked: 'The Irish gentry are an expensive people, they live in the most open hospitable manner continually feasting with one another.'

Certainly, there are numerous accounts of gargantuan meals and extended drinking bouts. John Boyle, fifth Earl of Orrery, wrote in 1736:

> *Drunkenness is the touchstone by which they try every man ... A right jolly glorious-memory Hibernian never rolls into bed without having taken a sober gallon of claret to his own share ... It is a Yahoo that toasts the glorious and immortal memory of King William in a bumper without any other joy in the Revolution than that it gives him a pretence to drink so many more daily quarts of wine. The person who refuses a goblet to his prevailing toast is deemed a Jacobite, a papist and a knave.*

Beauchamp Bagenal of Dunleckney House in Co. Carlow was so fond of duelling that he kept a brace of pistols loaded upon his dinner table. When the meal was over, the claret being produced in a cask, he would tap the cask with a bullet from one of his pistols, while he kept the other for any of his guests who failed to do justice to his wine. John Eyre, a baron living in Co. Galway, served his meals at Eyrecourt with so little ceremony that guests were expected to cut off hunks from the whole roasted ox he had hung up by its heels.

William Conolly, speaker of the Irish House of Commons

Feasts at Shane's Castle by Lough Neagh in Co. Antrim were altogether more refined. Sarah Siddons, the celebrated English actress, visited her friend Lady O'Neill there in 1783:

> It is scarce possible to conceive the splendour of this almost Royal Establishment, except by recollecting the circumstances of an Arabian Night's entertainment. Six or eight carriages with a numerous throng of Lords and Ladies and gentlemen on Horseback began the day by making excursions about this terrestrial paradise, returning home but just in time to dress for dinner. The table was served with a profusion and elegance to which I have never seen anything comparable ... A fine band of musicians played during the repast. They were stationed on the Corridor, which led from the dining room into a fine Conservatory, where we plucked our dessert from numerous trees of the most exquisite fruits, and where the waves of the superb Lake wash'd its feet while its delicious murmurs were accompanied with strains of celestial harmony from the Corridor.

It would be impossible to imagine a greater contrast between such scenes of opulence and refinement and the squalor and destitution in which the peasantry lived.

'In America they
may get good land'

. . .

SO THAT THE BIBLE could be privately consulted every day for guidance, the Presbyterian Church laid great emphasis on teaching its members to read. Incoming Scots did much, therefore, to make Ulster the most literate corner of Ireland. Presbyterians there could also read handbills advertising the opportunities awaiting them across the Atlantic. In 1729 the Justices of Assize for the North West Circuit of Ulster remarked on the lure of the New World for Protestants aggrieved at rent increases. They noted the success of agents sent around the province by ships' masters who

> *assure them that in America they may get good land to them and their posterity for little or no rent, without either paying tithes or taxes, and amuse them with such accounts of those countries as they know will be most agreeable to them.*

British settlers in North America had found that flax grew readily there and raised crops every year, letting the plants mature well into the autumn. Then, in a process known as 'rippling', they drew the sheaves of flax through large fixed combs to detach the seeds. At this stage, their flax was no longer good for making fine linen, but the seed commanded a ready price. Hogsheads of flaxseed were bought by travelling dealers, known as 'scowbankers', and taken downriver to New York, Philadelphia, Boston and other ports.

The American colonies also supplied Ulster with flaxseeds. In 1743 the Philadelphia merchant Samuel Powel wrote that 'the call for flaxseed to Ireland continues & increases ... It puts our people to sowing a great deal'. By 1751 Philadelphia alone was shipping out more than 69,000 bushels of seed a year, all of it destined for Ireland. In turn, settlers in America were eager to buy Irish linen with the money they had raised in selling flaxseed. By 1760 Ulster was exporting 17 million yards of linen a year, most of it bound for the Colonies.

Costly fine linen did not take up nearly as much room as seed on the return journey. Ship owners, therefore, competed with each other to fill the vacant space with passengers. The flaxseed trade and the emigrant trade were thus two sides of the same coin in this transatlantic commerce. Those who could afford it paid a fare of around £4 a person for the passage.

Since labour was scarce in America, merchants there put money up to pay for passengers who, in return, signed indentures before the mayor of the port of embarkation to work for no pay for around four years. The services of these 'indentured servants' were then sold, usually to farmers, for about £12 each, Pennsylvania currency.

Scrutching flax – processing cotton in preparation for spinning

Other passengers, who ran out of money on the passage over, were known as 'redemptioners'. They also had to sign agreements and were allowed ashore to seek out friends and relations to find the cash owed. Redemptioners caused a good deal of trouble, as frequent insertions in the press indicated:

> *This is to desire Thomas Smiley, George Caldwell, Henry Robinson, and James Henderson, who came Passengers from Ireland with Capt. James Aspinall, in the Snow Frodsham, in the year 1735, that they would immediately pay the respective Sums for which they stand engaged, to James Mackey of Philadelphia, or they may expect to be arrested.*

Most of the emigrants, setting out from Derry, Belfast, Larne, Newry, Coleraine and Portrush, disembarked at Delaware, Philadelphia, New York or Boston. Arthur Dobbs, from Castle Dobbs near Carrickfergus, had become governor of North Carolina and he made energetic attempts to attract the Scotch-Irish to settle in his colony. In 1761, the South Carolina assembly voted to pay £4 sterling for the passage of each poor Protestant brought to the colony. In the Low Country there, enslaved Africans were in a majority and plantation owners feared slave insurrections if Europeans were too few in number. Also, they felt, rightly, that the Scotch-Irish would be particularly skilled at colonising the 'backcountry', or hinterland. Charleston merchants John Torrans and John Poag engaged John Greg from Belfast to rustle up Ulster emigrants. Greg's ship *Falls* of Belfast, and the *Prince of Wales*, owned by Mussenden, Bateson and Company of Belfast, soon filled with passengers. They also hired the *Success*, a brigantine of 85 tons built in Philadelphia and part-owned by William Caldwell from Derry.

Soon these Scotch-Irish would be busy opening up the backcountry and coming into armed conflict with native Americans, just as their forbears had done with the native Irish in the previous century.

Volunteers, Grattan and the madness of King George

. . .

BRITAIN WAS ENGAGED IN major wars almost continuously from the start of the Seven Years War against France in 1756 until Waterloo in 1815. Of these various wars, none was more consequential than the American War of Independence. It so depleted British military resources that the prohibition against having Roman Catholics in the army was lifted, out of necessity. Among those enlisted in the British colours was the great Irish-language poet Eoghan Rua Ó Súilleabháin, who joined the navy and wrote a praise poem for his commander, 'Rodney's Glory'. He wrote it originally in English – he was versatile – and it was later rendered into Irish, in which language it is best known.

Irish Volunteers, 1784

The requirement for troops left Ireland emptied of regular soldiers and incapable of offering any defence against a French invasion. To fill this military vacuum, there sprang into life, as if spontaneously, a volunteer movement of Protestant civilians. Within a year, Volunteer corps had been founded in every county and the total aggregated to 50,000 men. Its members were generally from the more affluent classes, as they had to pay for their own uniforms and armaments. They trained and drilled in order to protect Ireland against a French invasion, expected imminently.

But there was no French invasion. Instead, the Volunteers turned their attention to local Irish grievances against the London government, using their newly acquired muscle as persuasion. In November 1779, the Volunteer leaders organised a huge and disciplined demonstration in Dublin's College Green, right in front of the Parliament House. London's Irish position was terribly weak: the war in America, where the French did turn up, and to decisive effect, was going badly. Lord North's government was in a poor position to resist the demands of its Irish elite.

Principal among these was the demand for free trade, meaning the removal of all restrictions on Irish exports. Under a series of English acts going back to the 1690s, exports of lucrative commodities such as cattle and wool were prohibited, the better to protect English commerce in such areas. Moreover, Ireland could not trade freely with colonies such as those in the Caribbean. London realised that the Volunteers commanded a majority in the Irish parliament and were prepared to pass 'short money' bills, guaranteeing supply for only six months.

London capitulated and the Anglo-Irish elite gained their free trade demands. This triumph merely emboldened the Volunteers. In February 1782, they held a convention in Dungannon, Co. Tyrone, to demand legislative independence. This meant repealing English acts which effectively made legislation passed in Dublin subject to review or repeal by Westminster. The motions passed at Dungannon were blunt:

Resolved unanimously, that a claim of any body of men, other than the Kings, Lords and Commons of Ireland, to make laws to bind this kingdom, is unconstitutional, illegal, and a Grievance.

And again, in a public address issued to the Irish population, in effect to the whole body of the Volunteers:

We thank you for your noble and spirited ... efforts, in defence of the great constitutional and commercial rights of your country ... The almost unanimous voice of the people is with you; and in a free country, the voice of the People must prevail. We know our duty to our Sovereign, and are loyal.

The echoes of the American colonial complaint, also springing from the discontents of a community weary of being treated as second-class Englishmen, were unmistakable. But the People, so defined, comprised only roughly 10 per cent of the Irish population: the Anglican elite. They got their legislative independence under the guidance of their most eloquent tribune, Henry Grattan, for whom the short-lived parliament that emerged was named.

But they refused to reform that parliament to permit greater participation by Roman Catholics and Presbyterians. The political nation was identified wholly with the Anglican elite, a traditional *ancien régime* perspective at a time of revolutionary turmoil: America was about to be lost and the French Revolution, proposing bottom-up popular (not top-down royal) sovereignty, was only a few years away. The failure to reform – and the fact that the Irish administrative machine, the civil service, remained under London control – doomed Grattan's Parliament.

A key moment came in 1788–9 with the regency crisis. King George III fell ill and was incapacitated. The Prince of Wales (later George IV) was proposed as regent *pro tem*, but some in the Irish parliament wished to install him as King of Ireland in his own right, to assert Dublin's independence from Westminster. John (Black Jack) Fitzgibbon, the most clear-headed of the Irish administration conservatives, saw through this with brutal clarity:

I remind the gentlemen of Ireland that the only security by which they hold their property ... is the connexion of the Irish crown with, and its dependence upon, the crown of England ... When we speak of the people of Ireland, it is a melancholy truth that we do not speak of the great body of the people ... Sir, the ancient nobility of this kingdom have been hardly treated. The act by which most of us hold our estates was an Act of violence – an Act subverting the first principles of the Common Law in England and Ireland ... Every acre of land which pays quit rent to the Crown is held by title derived under the Act of Settlement ... If the addresses of both Houses can invest the Prince of Wales with Royal power in this country, the same address could convey the same power to Louis XVI or His Holiness the Pope ...

The king recovered. The moment passed. But Fitzgibbon had seen through the pretensions of Grattan's Parliament – and by extension those of the colonial Anglican elite – with relentless and unanswerable logic.

The United Irishmen

. . .

THE FRENCH REVOLUTION CHANGED everything. Its democratic and nationalist principles found echoes far and wide, not least in Belfast. In July 1791, the second anniversary of the revolution was celebrated in Belfast, and the Society of United Irishmen was founded there in October of that year. All the founders were educated Protestants, as was Theobald Wolfe Tone, a gifted pamphleteer whom they invited up from Dublin and who gave them their mission statement:

> We have no national government – we are ruled by Englishmen, and the servants of Englishmen ... Such an extrinsic power ... can be resisted with effect solely by unanimity, decision, and spirit in the people, – qualities which may be exerted most legally ... by that great measure essential to the prosperity and freedom of Ireland – an equal representation of the people in parliament ...

The democratic impulse had a particular appeal to Presbyterians, echoing the Church's governance structures. But Tone, the southerner, found northern Protestants quite ignorant of their Catholic fellow countrymen.

The revolution, for all its ripple effects, remained a domestic French matter until April 1792, when France declared war on Austria and Prussia. The French broke this first anti-revolutionary coalition in September with the famous cannonade at Valmy that routed the Prussians. Thereafter, however, the revolution curdled into violence, culminating in the execution of the king in January 1793 and the Terror that followed until the guillotining of Robespierre the following July ended it. But by then, Great Britain was at war with France – and was to remain so, on more than off, for the next twenty-three years until Waterloo. This had direct implications for the United Irishmen.

In effect, the movement went from political persuasion to revolutionary conspiracy. For this, it needed numbers. They were provided by the Defenders, Catholic secret societies based in south Ulster, whose sectarianism was a world removed from the secular idealism of Wolfe Tone and the others. Their Protestant equivalents were the Orange Order, a consolidation of pre-existing secret societies.

The war with France not only drove the United Irishmen underground, but it also accelerated the London government's desire to further settle the Catholic question in Ireland, lest it become a festering grievance and an invitation to French meddling. The early years of the war went very badly for the British and equally well for the French, who now had by far the best army in Europe. To appease Ireland, British Prime Minister William Pitt the Younger appointed Earl Fitzwilliam as viceroy with a reform mandate, in particular the removal of remaining legal disabilities on Catholics, of which the right to sit in parliament – later called Catholic Emancipation – was the most pressing.

Fitzwilliam failed. His reform ambition broke on the rock of Irish Protestant resistance, a mindset that had been pithily articulated by a statement from the Dublin Corporation:

> A *Protestant King of Ireland; a Protestant parliament; a Protestant hierarchy; Protestant electors and Government; the Benches of Justice, the Army and the Revenue, through all their branches and details, Protestant; and the system supported by a connexion with the Protestant realm of England.*

These views found an echo in the Dublin Castle administration, which was able to command a majority in the Irish House of Commons. Just as influential were the objections of the king, George III, who regarded any further concessions to Catholics as a violation of his coronation oath. Fitzwilliam was recalled in less than a year. There was to be no reform.

In the meantime, Wolfe Tone had become tangled up in a pro-French conspiracy in Dublin and escaped the gallows by the skin of his teeth. He went to America, from where he made his way to France. There, he became acquainted with James Monroe, the American ambassador, who introduced him to Lazare Carnot, the most influential figure in the French government. The result was a powerful French expedition to Ireland which reached Bantry Bay in west Cork in December 1796. Many of the ships, including the flagship carrying the leader, Hoche, had been lost or scattered at sea but still 15,000 crack troops arrived in the bay just before Christmas:

> O the French are on the sea, says the Shan van Vocht;
> O the French are in the bay, they'll be here without delay,
> And the Orange will decay, says the Shan van Vocht.

The capture of Wolfe Tone

But they never got ashore. Unseasonal contrary winds denied them and eventually they cut their cables and returned to France. It had been a very close shave for the British, for Ireland was almost defenceless. Tone, who had been commissioned as a French officer, was on board one of the ships and wrote in his journal that they had been so close that he could have tossed a biscuit ashore: 'Well, England has not had such an escape since the Spanish Armada and that expedition, like ours, was defeated by the weather.'

Could the planned rising go ahead without the French?

General Lake and the Orange Order

. . .

THE IRISH ADMINISTRATION CERTAINLY thought that it would. The government passed an Insurrection Act and imposed martial law in disturbed districts. There followed a ferocious dragonnade focused initially on Ulster. Yeomanry corps, an entirely Protestant militia, were mobilised in every county in the province. Catholics, and especially Defenders or those suspected of being Defenders, bore the brunt of the government action. But it was also directed at members of the United Irishmen, which meant that many Presbyterians – sympathetic to the democratic principles of the French Revolution – were also targeted.

The new army commander in Ireland, General Gerard Lake, made no secret of his policy, which was one of outright state terror. In the first ten days of the operation, which began in Belfast and soon spread to the countryside, over 5,000 firearms and an immense number of pikes were seized. The yeomanry were given a free hand, burning houses and flogging suspects. The Presbyterian minister at Broughshane, Co. Antrim, was an eye-witness:

> *I saw Samuel Bones of Lower Broughshane receive 500 lashes – 250 on the back and 250 on the buttocks. I saw Samuel Crawford of Ballymena receive 500 lashes. The only words he spoke during the time were 'Gentlemen, be pleased to shoot me'; I heard him utter them. I saw Hood Haslett of Ballymena receive 500 lashes ...*

Almost fifty United Irish prisoners were executed, including Presbyterian ministers. The most celebrated victim was William

Orr, hanged after a farcical trial where the jury found conflicts of evidence and vainly recommended clemency.

> *Here our murdered brother lies –*
> *Wake him not with women's cries.*
> *Mourn the way that manhood ought;*
> *Sit in silent trance of thought.*

So wrote William Drennan, one of the leading Presbyterian intellectuals and himself a United man. The memory of William Orr is still revered in Ulster, even by people long since politically unionist. Lake's ferocious campaign spread south into Leinster, eventually reaching Co. Wexford in the south east, where the depredations and cruelty of his troops were a material factor in sparking the reaction that resulted in the rising in that county in May–June 1798.

Lake's brutality drew hatred from its victims and criticism from many on his own side. A new commander-in-chief, Sir Ralph Abercrombie (who did not last long), found the army in a hopeless condition:

> *The Irish army is in a state of licentiousness which must render it formidable to everyone but the enemy – this is proved by the very disgraceful frequency of courts-martial.*

Members of the Dublin administration were likewise disapproving, one of them describing Lake's dragonnade as 'a public and indiscriminate censure – almost an invitation to a foreign enemy'.

This judgement would be vindicated before long. One of Lake's conspicuous sins of omission in Ulster was his studied avoidance of another armed group, the recently formed Orange Order. This was a lower-class Protestant solidarity group, a consolidation of a number of ad hoc groups that had been engaged in localised violence against Catholics in Co. Armagh since the 1780s. These had been answered in kind by the Catholics, now consolidated as the Defenders; horrible atrocities were perpetrated by both sides.

Gerard Lake, first Viscount Lake, 1744–1808. Commander British forces in Irish Rebellion 1798

It came to a head in September 1795. Near Loughgall, in mid Co. Armagh, an affray took place between Defenders and the Peep o' Day Boys, the most prominent Protestant group. These latter, being both reinforced by a similar group from across the county border in Down, and being better armed, won. About thirty Defenders died.

The victorious Protestants retired to the nearby house of James Sloan in Loughgall and there they founded the Orange Order. It is still with us, one of the most enduring legacies of the 1790s and as far removed from the heady idealism of the French Revolution as one could imagine.

The same could be said of the Defenders. Co. Armagh was the most densely populated county in Ireland, with consequent competition for labour which was often the proximate trigger for disturbances. The county was balanced demographically between Anglicans and Presbyterians, mainly in the north and centre, and Catholics in the south in the area known as the Fews. The Enlightenment, upon which every kind of non-sectarian idealism must depend, had not penetrated here. Instead, ancestral hatreds going back to the plantations and the 1641 uprising were still fresh in the collective memory.

Just one example of Orange intimidation can stand for the atmosphere on both sides. A woman and her brother in Keady in south Armagh received the following warning from the local Orangemen:

> Be all the Secruts of hell your house Shall Be Burned to the Ground. Both his Soul & your Shall be Blwed To the Blue flames of hell. Now Teak this for Warnig, For if you Bee in this Contry Wednesday Night I will Blow your Soul to the Low hills of hell And Burn the House you are in.

Rebellion: Wexford and Antrim, 1798

. . .

IN MARCH 1798, THE Dublin leadership of the United Irishmen was betrayed by a spy and arrested by Major Sirr, the chief of police. The documents discovered were deeply incriminating and showed that plans for a rebellion were well advanced. The most socially distinguished member of the leadership, Lord Edward Fitzgerald, escaped the trawl for the moment but was captured in May. He was wounded and soon died.

The state terror thus released now reached a heightened pitch in the counties south and west of Dublin. In the village of Ballitore, Co. Kildare, Mary Leadbetter, a Quaker, recorded in her diary:

> *They set fire to some cabins near the village – took P. Murphy ... apparently an inoffensive man, tied him to a car opposite to his own door, and these ... officers so degraded themselves so far as to scourge him with their own hands.*

The triangle, to which suspects were pinioned and flogged until they confessed, and the dreaded pitch cap now made their appearance. But while these depredations cowed many people, they drove as many again into arms. On the night of 23 May, the rising broke out. It was largely confined to Co. Wexford but was no less intense for that; what had been planned as a national rising had been foiled by the capturing of the United leadership earlier.

> *Rouse, Hibernians, from your slumbers!*
> *See the moment just arrived,*
> *Imperious tyrants for to humble,*
> *Our French brethren are at hand.*

They were not, and after some early engagements in Co. Kildare, the Wexford men soon found themselves alone. They gave a good account of themselves. On 27 May, a detachment of the North Cork Militia – ironically, Irish-speaking Catholics for the most part – met with an irregular band of rebels at Oulart Hill, near Enniscorthy in the centre of the county. Equally ironically, the rebels – under the command of a priest, Fr John Murphy of Boolavogue – were English-speaking. It was almost unknown for irregulars to defeat regular troops in the open field, but they did – helped by a foolish decision to attack the rebels uphill.

The result was a bloody skirmish in which 105 of the 109 militiamen who attacked were killed. The government promptly abandoned central Co. Wexford, including the key market town of Enniscorthy. The rebels invested in Wexford town; the Meath Militia was sent to relieve it but was beaten back. United Irish prisoners were released from Wexford jail. From the county town, the rebels marched west to New Ross, a town on the upper tidal reaches of the River Barrow, and there was fought the decisive battle.

It was now 5 June. The town was defended for the government by troops under the command of Major-General Henry Johnston, augmented by a substantial force of the Dublin Militia under Colonel Luke Gardiner. The United men overwhelmed the Three Bullet Gate, a key entry to the town on the south-east side. Gardiner died here, and there followed a vicious all-day battle in the narrow streets. After seven hours, it seemed that the United Irishmen had carried the day. But they were exhausted; Johnston rallied his men and counter-attacked. The rebels were routed, and the army was unrestrained in its victory. Major Vesey, now commanding the Dublin Militia, admitted: 'The carnage was shocking, as no quarter was given, the soldiers were too exasperated and could not be stopped.'

About a hundred wounded rebels were burned to death in a temporary hospital. At about the same time, a similar number of loyalist prisoners were burned to death in a barn at Scullabogue, a short distance to the east.

Pitchcapping: a form of torture used by the British military on Irish rebels during the 1798 rebellion

The very next day, a rather different rising erupted in counties Down and Antrim. This was mainly the work of Presbyterian United Irishmen; it was significant that these were the two counties with the fewest Catholics and so relatively immune from the sectarian poison which infected Armagh and was just now manifesting itself in Wexford. Here the idealism of the United movement was not compromised by ancestral passions.

The first serious action was an attack on Antrim town, which was repulsed by regular troops. But the decisive battle was in Co. Down, at Ballynahinch on 12 June. It resulted in an outright victory for the government. The east Ulster rebellion was over in a week.

Resistance in Wexford hardly lasted longer. On 21 June, on Vinegar Hill just above Enniscorthy, Lake's regulars destroyed the rebel forces in what was the final battle of the Wexford rising. The loss at New Ross had been the turning point. There followed predictable and brutal reprisals. The defeated rebels had committed atrocities in Wexford town and were now repaid in their own coin, with interest:

> *When I was mounted on the gallows high*
> *My aged father he was standing by;*
> *My aged father he did me deny,*
> *And the name he gave me was the Croppy Boy.*

The United Irishmen wore their hair cropped, in the fashion of the French Revolution.

Like the great revolution itself, the idealism of the Wexford men had curdled. The government was no better – but then it never was. About thirty thousand people had died, the bloodiest few weeks in Irish history.

The Act of Union

. . .

THE EUROPEAN WAR WAS the context in which everything must now be seen. While Ireland was not the obvious strategic threat to England that a glance at a map might suggest, no London government could risk it falling into the hands of a continental enemy, which in the late 1790s meant France. After all, the French had been as close as a whisker in Bantry Bay in 1796 and there were clearly a significant number of rebellious and discontented Irish who would offer them every assistance should they attempt to come again.

So Pitt resolved on a solution that was the very opposite of Wolfe Tone's dream: full union with Great Britain in a unitary state. For Pitt, the last straw was the inability of the Irish ascendancy to maintain law and order at a time when Britain herself was in genuine peril. Thus far, the war had gone badly for Britain – which suffered military defeats and a naval mutiny that threatened existential danger – and for its continental allies, principally Austria and Prussia. France stood garlanded with victories, with the genius of the young Bonaparte freshly announced.

Central to Pitt's scheme was the final emancipation of the Irish Catholics. Most of the anti-Catholic Penal Laws had already been repealed. Now it only remained to remove the two significant surviving ones. Catholics were still excluded from some senior public positions, such as the senior judiciary, and from sitting in parliament as MPs. The small Catholic elite – educated and moneyed – had to be embraced in the proposed new arrangement, so that they might feel that they had a stake in the new state.

This plan met with firm opposition from two sources. First, large numbers of the Irish ascendancy, probably a majority at the outset, were bitterly opposed. As usual, the clear-headed reactionary 'Black Jack' Fitzgibbon, Earl of Clare, declared that the only circumstances in which he would contemplate supporting a union were if these penal restrictions on Catholics were left in place. He could count, and he had no intention of enabling a 'popish democracy'. Even more significant was the adamantine opposition of King George III, who regarded any further concessions as a betrayal of his coronation oath. To mollify the king, Pitt very reluctantly dropped the emancipation proposals.

Then there was the question of the Irish parliament. Since Grattan's legislative independence in 1782, Westminster – where Pitt was assured of a majority on the issue – could no longer make laws binding on Ireland. So the Irish parliament had to be persuaded to commit hara-kiri. The under-secretary at Dublin Castle, Edward Cooke, summed up what was required. The union proposal needed to be 'written-up, spoken-up, intrigued-up, drunk-up, sung-up and bribed-up'.

William Pitt the Younger, 1759–1806, was a prominent British Tory statesman and the prime minister of the United Kingdom

This last was crucial, for the exclusively ascendancy parliament had been the great joy and pride of Irish Anglicans, and they had little spontaneous desire to see it disappear. Few were as clear-headed as Black Jack Fitzgibbon, who could see the bigger picture, both for the ascendancy and for Great Britain in times of war. So the viceroy, Cornwallis, the chief secretary, Castlereagh, and Cooke set about their business: bribery in cash, offices and peerages. An early parliamentary vote was won by the government, but only by one vote – not enough for such a momentous measure – so the Castle had to redouble its efforts.

It was hard pounding. Cornwallis declared:

> *My occupation is now of the most unpleasant nature, negotiating and jobbing with most corrupt people under Heaven ... I despise and hate myself every hour for engaging in such dirty work.*

Every man who controlled a pocket borough in the Irish parliament – inconsequential little places, villages at best and some not even that – was compensated at the enormous sum of £15,000 per borough; 'places' and 'pensions' were promised along with annual payments, all guaranteed by the Crown. Barons became earls. Illegally, secret service funds were used to finance the bribery.

It was impressive even by the standards of an unsqueamish age. And it worked. On 26 May 1800, the government carried the Union in the Dublin parliament by sixty votes, with the legislation to come into effect on 1 January following. One hundred Irish MPs were now to go to the House of Commons at Westminster and thirty-two peers to the Lords. The Church of Ireland became part of a united Anglican Church, no longer a mere sister of the Church of England.

The more radical Protestants, such as the Orange Order, opposed the Union to the end, seeing it as an eventual back door for Catholic Emancipation. Most Catholics welcomed it for the same reason. The most conspicuous exception was a young barrister from Co. Kerry then making his name. This was Daniel O'Connell.

Daniel O'Connell and the road to Emancipation

...

THE YEAR 1803 BROUGHT an aftershock of 1798. An inept rebellion in Dublin led by young Robert Emmet, son of the surgeon to the viceroy, was over almost as soon as it began. Everything went wrong; the rising ended within a day and brought little lustre to the cause. By the evening of 23 July 1803, the attempt at insurrection was palpably failing – many of the few remaining rebels were drunk – and it resulted in little more than the murder of a liberal judge, Lord Kilwarden. His companion, Rev. Richard Wolfe – ironically, a member of the same family for which Wolfe Tone had been named – was also hacked to death.

Emmet was arrested, tried and executed. But his speech from the dock, before his inevitable conviction, went down in history and secured his place in the nationalist pantheon.

The Irish Catholics, still hoping for the delivery of the emancipation originally promised by the union proposal, were quiet for most of the decade following 1798 and 1803. But the proposal had proved fatal to Pitt, who had resigned over the issue, as it was to prove to Greville's Whig government in 1807. The king's opposition was the rock on which it broke every time. Its day was not yet.

Instead, the Catholics were consumed by the veto crisis. Britain wanted a veto on Irish Catholic episcopal appointments and many, perhaps most, of the conservative leadership were prepared to comply. It was not unprecedented or unique: the King of Prussia exercised such a veto over the appointment of Polish bishops. But for the younger, bourgeois radicals in the Catholic movement, it was utterly unacceptable. This was the issue that first brought Daniel

O'Connell to public notice. It was a bitter division but O'Connell got his way, as he was to do in so many things over the following thirty years. He had announced himself as anti-Union in 1800 and now, a decade later, as the leader of a group asserting the independence of the Catholic Church from the state of which they were a part. These twin issues were the *leitmotif* of his career.

Simultaneously, much of Ireland was racked by agrarian violence. In Ulster, the Defenders of the 1790s had mutated into the Ribbonmen of the early nineteenth century, who were essentially the same thing: a rural Catholic defence vigilante force. Facing them locally was the Orange Order, generally better armed and equipped. In Munster, agrarian disturbances had been a feature since the 1760s, when the Whiteboys – so called because they wore sheets as a disguise – had protested violently against such practices as the enclosure of common land, the replacement of tillage by pasture and tithes payable for the upkeep of the clergy of the Church of Ireland. They were most active in north central Munster, and forty years later their successor organisation, the Caravats, were strongest in the same areas.

Daniel O'Connell

Their principal opponents were the Shanavests, usually more well-to-do farmers, so these agrarian troubles were as much a class war as a protest against prevailing conditions. But they were certainly that – and sectarian to boot. This was not helped by contemporary attempts at proselytising, usually prompted by well-meaning but ignorant English evangelicals. This produced a millenarian reaction, as in the widespread belief that 1825 would spell doom for Irish Protestants. A spy informed the government that

> They spoke of a prophecy to be fulfilled in the year 1825, for the overthrow of the tyranny of Orangemen and government, and that there will be but one religion.

Catholic clergy and educated gentlemen were embarrassed by this sort of thing, but Daniel O'Connell, while hardly endorsing it, harnessed it to his political ambition. Emancipation had been refused twice by the king and again in 1821, when a bill was carried in the Commons but failed in the Lords. Internally the anti-vetoists under O'Connell's leadership had asserted a kind of ecclesiastical independence. He now proceeded to project this sensibility into an otherwise demoralised movement. Irish Protestants were now reconciled to the Union, for not only had it not brought Emancipation, but it also continued the old system of separate government and administration in Ireland, which meant a near-monopoly of plum jobs for Protestants. In 1823, Richard Lalor Sheil – one of O'Connell's principal lieutenants – despaired of twenty years of futile campaigning for Emancipation:

> I do not exaggerate when I say that the Catholic question was nearly forgotten. No angry resolutions issued from public bodies ... The unnatural ascendancy of a handful of men over an immense and powerful population ... were gradually dropping out of the national memory ... It was a degrading and unwholesome tranquillity. We sat down like galley-slaves in a calm.

Even as Sheil uttered these words, the situation was about to be transformed. In that same year, Daniel O'Connell founded the Catholic Association, to agitate Westminster for full Emancipation. It was the beginning of modern Ireland.

Mass movement politics and Catholic Emancipation

. . .

THE CATHOLIC ASSOCIATION HAD a slow start. Full members paid a guinea (twenty-one shillings or just over a pound) a year, out of reach of the poor. But O'Connell then proposed a category of associate membership at a penny a month. The association was transformed. People flocked to it, now having a stake – however modest – in a national enterprise. The Catholic clergy rowed in and provided the parish structure as a means of local organisation; the 'Catholic Rent' could be collected, at a farthing (a quarter of a penny) a week, at church gates after Sunday mass. The huge sum of £20,000 was raised in the first year.

O'Connell had conjured into existence the first mass populist political movement in the modern world. It threw Westminster into confusion, faced with an unprecedented half-million people mobilised for a political cause. Legal actions against O'Connell and the association either failed or were circumvented.

In 1826, a general election was called. In Co. Waterford, the powerful Beresford family ruled the roost – or had. In this election, the voters, all tenants of the Beresfords, risked their tenancies and, in a show of solidarity, elected a young liberal pro-Emancipation landlord, Henry Villiers-Stuart, in place of Lord Thomas Beresford. Even Beresford's faithful huntsman voted for Stuart, explaining to Beresford: 'Long life to yer honour, I'd go to the world's end with yer honour, but sure, please your lordship, I cannot go agin my country and religion.'

Formation of the Catholic Association

It was a transfer of loyalty on a massive scale, from ascendancy landowners to the Catholic Church and its political associates. The huntsman's association of 'country and religion' – faith and fatherland – had been a hidden sensibility among Catholics; now it emerged into daylight and proved enduring.

There followed a farcical attempt by one of O'Connell's more enthusiastic but tactless lieutenants to carry the agitation for the Catholic cause into Ulster, but it broke in the face of mobilised Protestant resistance on the southern margins of the province, an ominous portent for all future nationalist ambition. Then came the Clare by-election.

The Duke of Wellington was now prime minister and he appointed William Vesey-Fitzgerald, MP for Clare, to his cabinet. In accordance with custom, Vesey-Fitzgerald had to stand for re-election, expecting to be returned unopposed. Instead, O'Connell himself stood against him. As a Catholic, he could not take his seat if elected, but he stood anyway in a contest soon drenched in uncompromising sectarian rhetoric. O'Connell himself set the tone:

> as a Catholic, I cannot, and of course never will, take the oaths prescribed to members of parliament ... The oath at present required by law is, 'That the sacrifice of the mass, and the invocation of the Blessed Virgin Mary, and other saints, as now practised in the Church of Rome, are impious and idolatrous'. Of course, I will never stain my soul with such an oath; I leave that to my honourable opponent, Mr Vesey-Fitzgerald. He has often taken that horrible oath ... I would rather be torn limb from limb than take it.

Vesey-Fitzgerald was, ironically, pro-Emancipation but it availed him naught. He was a Protestant, and that was enough. O'Connell won by 2,057 to 982. His victory was promptly declared void. He stood again and was returned unopposed. Vesey-Fitzgerald wrote to Peel, the home secretary and Wellington's right-hand man:

> We were watching the movements of tens of thousands of disciplined fanatics, abstaining from every excess and indulgence, and concentrating every passion and feeling on one single object ... Is it consistent with common prudence and common sense to repeat such scenes and to incur such risks of contagion?

Peel, a political realist, agreed. He needed to convince Wellington, a reliable reactionary, and to overbear King George IV, who was as fussed about his coronation oath as his father had been. Peel succeeded, but only after severe political turbulence in London. An Emancipation Bill was prepared and became law in April 1829. There was a heavy price, however: the small tenants whose holdings were valued at forty shillings (£2) were disenfranchised. They had been the backbone of O'Connell's electorate and risked their tenancies to vote for him in defiance of their landlords. Now they had nothing to show for it. The voting qualification for county elections in Ireland was raised to a whopping £10.

O'Connell was a supreme political calculator, and he calculated that this was a price worth paying. He has been much criticised for it in retrospect by people who never had to face the sort of pressures he did. But his arrival at Westminster, where he proved to be a star, and the almost simultaneous change to a Whig administration, helped to transform the governance of Ireland.

The Tithe War

...

Tithe War in Ireland: a visit from the Tithe Proctor

A STARTLING FACT ABOUT the years 1801–50 in Ireland is that for only five of them did normal law apply. For the other forty-five, Ireland was governed by special powers. This meant that, however reluctantly, the British state took a more active role in Ireland in excess of anything it would attempt in Great Britain itself. This reflected London's disillusionment with the Protestant ascendancy and what was perceived to be its inability to govern Ireland efficiently. In effect, Irish governance was moving from a devolved model to more direct rule.

As chief secretary from 1812 to 1818, Robert Peel began this process. He formed a Peace Preservation Force in 1814, a proto-police force – the first anywhere in the United Kingdom, anticipating Peel's formation of the Metropolitan Police in London in 1829. Despite protests that such a force was un-British, it went ahead.

Peel also tackled a nasty famine in 1816–17 head on, setting up a central relief committee to disburse funds extracted from a very reluctant Treasury. When Peel left Ireland, the active British state stalled until the arrival of the Whigs in government in 1830.

The new chief secretary, Edward Stanley, established a system of primary education known as national schools. They were proposed on a non-sectarian basis, but this drew the fire of all the churches, so as a result the system quickly became denominational.

O'Connell made a formal alliance with the Whig government in 1835, in place of the informal understanding he had maintained since 1830. In the same year, Thomas Drummond, a Scot, was appointed Irish under-secretary, in effect the head of the Irish civil service. He was familiar with Ireland and had formed the view that the tyranny of the ascendancy was at the root of much Irish unrest. His prescription was not coercion or special powers but a fair, disinterested administration that would win public confidence. He encouraged Catholics to assume positions in public life, appointed them to important legal posts, and oversaw the evolution in 1836 of Peel's Peace Preservation Force into the (Royal) Irish Constabulary, which soon proved a success and reduced crime in the countryside.

Before this and despite Catholic Emancipation, the Irish administration had been overwhelmingly Protestant. In 1833, there was not a single Catholic judge or paid magistrate. Positions of influence were almost all in Protestant hands, something that made any residual Protestant opposition to the Union evaporate. In a few years, Drummond threw this pattern into reverse, encouraging Catholic participation on an unprecedented scale. In 1838 he rebuked the Tipperary magistrates who were pleading for coercive measures to quell rural disorder by reminding them that

> *Property ... has its duties as well as its rights ... To the neglect of these duties in times past is mainly to be attributed the diseased state of society ... and it is not in the enactment and enforcement of statutes of extraordinary severity but chiefly in the better and more faithful performance of those duties ... that a permanent remedy for such disorder is to be sought.*

No grievance was more acute than the legal obligation to pay tithes for the upkeep of the clergy of the Church of Ireland. This was resented given the minority status of that church and the imposition of the tax – one-tenth of income, generally payable in kind – on persons not in communion with it. It had been a running sore as far back as the Whiteboy disturbances in north central Munster in the 1760s. Moreover, from 1735 to 1823, pasturage had been excluded from the scheme, which meant in practice that wealthy Anglican landowners were exempt, while their poorer Catholic tenants were liable.

The situation came to a violent head in the 1830s in what was known as the Tithe War. Post-Emancipation, Catholic confidence swelled. Attempts to enforce payment – or, worse, to distrain goods for non-payment – met with violence. The Tithe War started in Co. Kilkenny in 1830 when the cattle of a parish priest were so distrained. It ballooned into a successive series of protests, with many deaths, burglaries, burnings, maimings of cattle and attacks on houses. In a few cases, Protestant clergy were murdered. In 1833, the withdrawal of police and yeomanry from tithe enforcement took some of the heat out of the situation, but the agitation continued until 1838.

O'Connell had kept his distance from all this while not denouncing it and was careful to keep his own response within the law. He helped the Whig government to frame legislation that finally ended the Tithe War. The Tithe Rent Charge (Ireland) Act reduced the quantum and made it a rent charge, collectable by the landlords. But the entire episode was a reminder that Ireland remained a potential powder keg, accounting for the persistence of all that special legislation.

Repeal of the Union

· · ·

THE WHIGS WERE VOTED out of office in 1841 and Peel
returned as prime minister. That meant the end of the O'Connell–
Whig alliance for the moment; it could achieve nothing more by
way of Irish reforms in opposition. As it was, O'Connell judged the
reforms to date to be the minimum that could be extracted and was
particularly unhappy about the Poor Law Act of 1838. This was the
work of an Englishman, ignorant of Ireland, who simply ignored the
recommendations of a knowledgeable Irish commission of enquiry –
one that included both the Roman Catholic and Anglican archbishops
of Dublin – and more or less extended the English system to Ireland,
where conditions were so different. O'Connell now turned to the
second great cause of his political career: repeal of the Union.

> *The Repeal and the Repeal alone is and must be the grand basis
> of all future operations, hit or miss, win or lose. The people will
> take nothing short of that ... I say there can be no other basis of
> association save the Repeal, the glorious Repeal.*

But who were the people who would take nothing short of repeal?
In Leinster, Munster and Connacht – overwhelmingly Catholic
provinces – it was a fair claim to make and O'Connell was lionised
as the Liberator. But Ulster was different and held a pan-Protestant
majority, principally comprising Presbyterians and Anglicans. As had
been proved in 1828, any attempt to carry the O'Connell movement
into the northern province was likely to meet with resistance.

O'Connell himself had never once been to Ulster in his sixty-
six years, despite having been the dominant figure in Irish life for a
quarter of a century. Now, in 1841, he went – and a very dusty reception

he got. The initial plan for a procession north was abandoned, the government having stationed troops there just in case. Instead, he made his way by carriage, passing through the heartland of Protestant Ulster en route to Belfast, his destination. Instead of being lionised, huge crowds assembled in Dromore, Hillsborough and Lisburn, where they burned him in effigy. He snuck into Belfast and did not dare leave the sanctuary of his hotel for a few days. He then stepped out on the hotel balcony to harangue the crowd but could not make himself heard above the yells and howls of the hostile mob.

When he did go out, there were disturbances: stone-throwing, broken windows – including at O'Connell's hotel – and the local repeal newspaper, the *Vindicator*, came under attack. O'Connell's principal adversary was Dr Henry Cooke, a conservative Presbyterian clergyman, and a man as intelligent and formidable in debate as O'Connell himself. Addressing a meeting, he summed up his case:

> *Look at the town of Belfast. When I was myself a youth I remember it almost a village. But what a glorious sight does it now present – the masted grove within our harbour – our mighty warehouses teeming with the wealth of every climate – (cheers) – our giant manufactories lifting themselves on every side ... All this we owe to the Union ... Mr O'Connell, look at Belfast, and be a repealer – if you can.*

Whatever about the Union, the Industrial Revolution had arrived in east Ulster. That's what underlay Cooke's unanswerable material boast. As we'll see (in episodes 74 and 75), the revolution took root there but left the other three provinces almost untouched.

It was there, back to safe ground, that O'Connell now returned. He organised a series of monster meetings – enormous public rallies, generally at sites of historic association, to impress the government by sheer force of numbers. Even *The Times*, inveterately hostile to O'Connell – and all subsequent Irish nationalism – estimated that the crowd at Tara, Co. Meath, was over a million. Over forty similar meetings – still huge, although not quite on the scale of Tara – were held across Ireland (outside Ulster) in 1843. The last one of the year was scheduled for 8 October at Clontarf, just north of Dublin and the site of a famous Gaelic victory over the Vikings in 1014 – or so it was represented: in fact, there had been Vikings on both sides and Dublin continued to be a Viking city until the arrival of the Normans.

All the monster meetings to date had been peaceful, orderly, and the product of a disciplined, well-led movement. Such peaceful mass meetings were unheard of elsewhere in contemporary Europe. Still, the government held its nerve. It denounced the meeting on the eve of the event, declaring it illegal. O'Connell, who had always operated within the law, if only just at times, called the meeting off, something for which generations of more radical nationalists later condemned him. Instead, he was convicted on a trumped-up charge of 'seditious conspiracy'; thus the Liberator found himself comfortably imprisoned in Richmond Penitentiary in London – where the bemused governor made over his own house to the great man – until his sentence was overturned by the House of Lords. But that was effectively the end of the repeal campaign.

Instead, Ireland stood on the brink of the greatest catastrophe in her modern history.

Daniel O'Connell campaigning for the repeal of the
Act of Union at a meeting in Trim, Co. Meath, in 1843

On the eve of
the Great Famine

...

IN A SINGLE LIFETIME, the seventy years prior to 1845, Ireland experienced an unprecedented population explosion. The population doubled by a *net* four million people – even allowing for the emigration of about one and a half million – to over eight million in the first completely reliable census, that of 1841. This was facilitated by the astonishingly high yields of the staple potato, which anchored a dreary but very healthy diet. This huge increase in numbers, concentrated at the bottom of a subsistence economy, put enormous pressure on land and gave landlords no incentive to reduce rents in what was a seller's market.

All English and continental travellers to pre-Famine Ireland – and there were many of them – agreed on the astonishing levels of poverty they found there. Thus Gustave de Beaumont, the French social observer:

> *I have seen the Indian in his forests, and the negro in his chains, and thought, as I contemplated their pitiable condition, that I saw the very extreme of human wretchedness; but I did not then know the condition of unfortunate Ireland ... In all countries, more or less, paupers may be discovered; but an entire nation of paupers is what never was seen until it was shown in Ireland ...*

The first phase of the Industrial Revolution in England and the employment opportunities it offered were what drove pre-Famine emigration. But early industry was also beginning to supply cheap, mass-produced textiles with which domestic spinning and handlooms could not compete, thus robbing the Irish poor of an important supplementary source of income. The same applied to simple agricultural tools like scythes and ploughshares, which could be delivered to market more cheaply from industrial England than the local blacksmith could match. Ever greater numbers now led a hardscrabble existence on ever-smaller plots of land dependent entirely on the potato monoculture. This pattern was worst in the west, where the land was the poorest.

The 1841 census reported some stark findings. Two houses out of every five in Ireland were one-roomed, windowless mud cabins whose conditions in wet weather – of which there was no shortage in Ireland – can readily be imagined. Ninety-three per cent of Irish farms were of less than thirty acres when sixty acres were considered a small farm in Scotland. Three-quarters of the rural poor were landless labourers and cottiers. It all rested on the reliability of the potato, and in 1845 the potato failed – catastrophically.

Irish cabin, eighteenth century

In that year, Daniel O'Connell turned seventy and was visibly fatigued. He never recovered his authority after Clontarf. Moreover, the 1840s were a restless decade throughout Europe. The period was known in German as the *Vormärz* or pre-March, a reference to the year of revolutions that first broke out in March 1848 and rattled the structures that had been put in place at the Congress of Vienna after the Napoleonic Wars. This restlessness was felt in Ireland, too. The Young Ireland movement – initially a subset of the repeal movement, but ever more alienated from O'Connell as the decade progressed – was an echo of Mazzini's Young Italy and also influenced by the Romantic cultural nationalism of German philosophers such as Herder.

The movement proposed such a cultural nationalism, and a robust one at that. Thomas Davis, a Protestant, was its leading figure. He was the principal mover behind a new journal, *The Nation*, which was a roaring success from its first issue in 1842. Davis was a minor poet of some talent:

> *When boyhood's fire was in my blood*
> *I read of ancient freemen,*
> *For Greece and Rome who bravely stood,*
> *Three hundred men and three men.*
> *And then I prayed I yet might see*
> *Our fetters rent in twain,*
> *And Ireland, long a province, be*
> *A Nation Once Again*

Young Ireland's Romantic, non-sectarian and ever more militant nationalism had an obvious appeal to Protestants, well aware of O'Connell's association of faith and fatherland and his pragmatic, transactional approach to politics. It found a cause in its support for the Queen's Colleges, non-sectarian universities proposed by the British government. This alienated the Young Irelanders ever more from the ageing Liberator, who opposed the colleges precisely because they were non-sectarian.

It did something else as well. In its non-sectarian, implicitly republican disposition it recalled the idealism of the United

Irishmen, which had been occluded by the sectarian outrages of 1798 and then ploughed under entirely for a generation by O'Connell's compelling genius.

> *Who fears to speak of Ninety-Eight?*
> *Who blushes at the name?*
> *When cowards mock the patriots' fate,*
> *Who hangs his head in shame?*
> *He's all a knave, or half a slave*
> *Who slights his country thus;*
> *But a true man, like you, man,*
> *Will fill your glass with us.*

Thus wrote John Kells Ingram, a young Protestant scholar, in *The Nation* in 1843. The political pulse was quickening, even as demographic disaster beckoned.

'The food of the whole nation has perished'

. . .

NOBODY KNEW WHAT *PHYTOPHTHORA infestans* was. It was a microscopic fungus brought in from America that proved fatal to the cultivation of the potato, the staple food of the Irish poor. It first announced itself in September 1845 across north-west Europe but only in Ireland, which was overwhelmingly dependent on this single food source, did it prove so lethal.

The fungus was unknown to contemporary science. But its effects were soon all too clear. One anonymous witness summed them up succinctly:

> *Suddenly ... the withering breath of a simoon* [*a desert wind*] *seemed to sweep over the land, blasting all in its path. I myself saw whole tracts of potato growth changed, in one night, from smiling luxuriance to a shrivelled and blackened waste.*

The potato stalks turned black and reduced the tubers in the soil to a stinking pulp. The crop was inedible and famine was quickly and accurately forecast. Most of the island, except for the west and parts of Ulster, was affected that first year. But the blight reappeared the following year, 1846, and this time the entire island fell victim. This was a demographic catastrophe. There was mass starvation.

The Tory government of Robert Peel had taken direct action in November 1845, establishing a central relief commission, and purchased £100,000 worth of maize from America, later remembered bitterly by Irish nationalists as 'Trevelyan's corn', named for Charles Trevelyan, the head of the Treasury.

Against the grumbles of doctrinaire free traders, this intervention resulted in the first cargoes of maize – so-called Indian meal – arriving in February 1846, to be sold at cost. It helped but did not – could not – cure. Then Peel committed political suicide by repealing the Corn Laws – which had kept the price of corn high as a silent subsidy to British producers – and was succeeded by a Whig government under Lord John Russell, free trade absolutists to a man. They had an ally in Trevelyan.

The commissary-general for Ireland, Sir Randolph Routh, proposed banning the export of Irish corn but was overruled by Trevelyan:

> *Do not encourage the idea of prohibiting exports, perfect free trade is the right course … We beg of you not to countenance in any way the idea of prohibiting exportation … There cannot be a doubt that it would inflict a permanent injury on the country.*

Trevelyan advised Russell's government to curtail the distribution of subsidised food and to extend a programme of public works. The poor must work for their food. As to the home market, that was to be left to the beneficence of private enterprise.

In early 1846, Fr Theobald Mathew, later celebrated as a temperance campaigner, wrote to Trevelyan of a journey from Dublin to Cork:

> *I beheld with sorrow one wide waste of putrefying vegetation. In many places the wretched people were seated on the fences of their decaying gardens, wringing their hands and wailing bitterly the destruction … The food of a whole nation has perished.*

New public works were proposed, carefully ensuring that they did not interfere with any private-sector commerce. These new works were to be funded entirely by the rates – Irish property was to pay for Irish poverty, something quite beyond the capacity of Irish property, much of it already mortgaged or otherwise encumbered. Peel's corn depots were closed down. Too late, Trevelyan tried to buy corn abroad, but there was none to be had in any market after the poor European harvest.

Scene at the gate of a workhouse, circa 1846

In October 1846, the repeal journal the *Vindicator* made a simple appeal:

> *'Give us food, or we perish' is now the loudest cry that is heard in this unfortunate country ... It is heard in every corner of the island ... It is a strange cry to be heard within the limits of the powerful and wealthy British empire.*

But no: the prescription was that the starving must buy food with money earned from employment in public works. That was what classical free-trade economics demanded. And that is what was done. The result was mass starvation. A comparison with Belgium is helpful. It was the country apart from Ireland most affected by the blight; 95 per cent of the crop in Flanders was destroyed in 1845. The Belgian government's response was to remove all tariffs on food imports, ban exports temporarily, buy food for import wherever it could be had and subsidise local authorities. This was enlightened self-interest; the authorities feared food riots. Belgium suffered but did not starve.

Ireland starved. Such relief works as had been approved took time to get off the ground, hampered by the lack of basic equipment such as handcarts and wheelbarrows, a shortage of engineers to direct operations, and deteriorating weather in the autumn of 1846. The longest and most severe winter in living memory had begun. The island of Ireland was prostrate.

Black '47

. . .

THE YEAR 1847 WAS remembered in the Irish language as *Bliain an Áir*, the year of the slaughter. In English, it was simply remembered as 'Black '47'. The village of Skibbereen in west Cork came to stand as a symbol of all the remote places in Ireland, most of them on or near the west coast, that were worst affected by the Great Famine in this, its most terrible year. As early as January 1847, the *Cork Examiner* sent its reporter to Skibbereen. He reported as follows:

> *In huts I have visited, I have seen children reduced to skeletons, in some instances; in others bloated beyond expression by hideous dropsy, and creeping around the damp wet floors of their miserable cabins, unable to stand erect ...*
>
> *It is too late to rescue the hundreds of diseased and stricken wretches from destruction – their fate is sealed without a hope – their earthly sufferings will speedily terminate.*

This report echoed that of a local magistrate, Nicholas Cummins, who had also visited Skibbereen and had written to the Duke of Wellington in these terms a month earlier:

> *My Lord Duke,*
>
> *Being aware that I should have to witness scenes of frightful hunger, I provided myself with as much bread as five men could carry, and on reaching the spot I was surprised to find the wretched hamlet apparently deserted.*

I entered some of the hovels to ascertain the cause. In the first, six famished and ghastly skeletons, to all appearances dead, were huddled in a corner on some filthy straw ... I approached with horror, and found by a low moaning they were alive ... Suffice to say, that in a few minutes I was surrounded by at least 200 of such phantoms ... The same morning the police opened a house on the adjoining lands ... and two frozen corpses were found, half devoured by rats ...

Quaker soup kitchen in Cork city. Quakers were instrumental in establishing soup kitchens across the country, particularly in some of the worst affected districts

And so it went on throughout that dreadful year, and not just in Skibbereen. Private charitable initiatives tried to compensate for the inertia of the London government. An association formed 'for the relief of extreme distress in the remote parts of Ireland and Scotland' at Rothschild's Bank raised £470,000. The Society of Friends, better known as the Quakers, simply set out with commendable directness to feed the starving people. The *Illustrated*

London News, whose reports were to be hugely influential in spreading the word of the calamity internationally, described their 'soup house' in Cork:

> *at a loss, or rather cost, of from £120 to £150 per month to supporters of the design. The present calls are from 150 to 180 gallons daily requiring 120 pounds of good beef, 27 pounds of rice, 27 pounds of oatmeal, 27 pounds of split peas, and 14 pounds of spices, with a quantity of vegetables. Tickets, at one penny each, are unsparingly distributed.*

This, and other private initiatives, many of them American, set the standard. Of the latter, that of Elihu Burritt from Boston deserves mention. He visited Skibbereen in February 1847, escorted through the village by the parish priest. His accounts of the place echoed the horrors of other witnesses. His relief appeals raised $100,000 to buy provisions, and a US warship delivered this bounty to Cork harbour in short order. At last, all of this prompted a change in government policy.

In what was an admission of failure, Russell's administration began the free distribution of soup. This required the establishment of a formidable new bureaucracy to manage the programme; by July 1847, three million people were being fed daily. No single measure saved more lives. Still, the deaths continued, hunger now compounded by fevers – typhus and relapsing fever, in particular, taking their toll on a dreadfully weakened population. Hospitals and workhouses were overflowing; emigrant ships were packed.

In the midst of all this, O'Connell died and his rivals in Young Ireland tripped off a brief summer rebellion in Co. Tipperary in 1848 that amounted to little more than a farcical affray. Ireland was in no physical condition for rebellion. After 1848, the worst of the Famine abated, although it lingered for a few more years.

The census of 1851 summarised the calamity. Ten years earlier, the Irish population had been 8.2 million; now it was 6.5 million. In a single decade, 20 per cent of the population was lost to death and emigration.

It is hard to dissent from the summary of Cormac Ó Gráda the economic historian:

> in the end, the Irish were desperately unlucky ... Nothing quite as horrific as Phytophthora infestans had appeared before, in Ireland or anywhere else. Moreover, had the fungus arrived either some decades earlier or later, the damage would not have been so horrific ... A delay of four decades, and phytophthora would have faced both ... bluestone counter-remedy and a countryside more thinly peopled.

The Famine was never forgotten, nor was the grudging response of London.

Fenians and disestablishment

. . .

James Stephens, founder
of the Irish Republican
Brotherhood

IN THE WAKE OF the Famine, Irish politics atrophied. O'Connell was dead and Young Ireland had proved a damp squib. But nationalism had not died; to the contrary, it was transformed by the calamities of the 1840s. In 1858, James Stephens, who had been 'out' in 1848, founded the Irish Republican Brotherhood (IRB) in Dublin. The following year, in New York, John O'Mahony, another old '48-er, founded the Fenians, a sister organisation by whose name the entire movement became known. It was an out-and-out republican, revolutionary movement, with little time for parliamentary methods.

The Fenians in Ireland found an organiser of real ability in Stephens. He had fled to Paris after the 1848 fiasco but returned in 1856. An engineer by profession, he had imbibed Parisian revolutionary influence while there. Back home, he tramped the entire country recruiting for his new movement.

He walked about three thousand miles in all, finding many who were sympathetic to his revolutionary message. It was a tough time to spread this word, but he sowed a seed that germinated in time. Stephens was vain, bombastic and quarrelsome, but his sincerity was palpable, and O'Mahony's sister organisation in New York brought exiled and embittered Irish-Americans into the revolutionary equation for the first time. They never left.

Stephens urged immediate action:

> The attempt ... should be tried in the very near future if we wanted at all to keep our flag flying; for I was as sure as of my own existence that if another decade was allowed to pass without an endeavour of some kind or another to shake off an unjust yoke, the Irish people would sink into a lethargy from which it would be impossible for any patriot ... to arouse them.

The flag in question was the tricolour of green, white and orange, brought back from Paris in the revolutionary year of 1848 by Thomas Francis Meagher, a radical Young Irelander. But it was the death of another old '48-er, Terence Bellew McManus, in 1861 that first showed the Fenian flag and established a tension – never fully resolved thereafter – between Fenianism and the Catholic Church, and specifically its powerful leader Paul Cullen, Archbishop of Dublin and soon to be the first Irish cardinal.

The Fenians shipped McManus's body home from San Francisco and arranged for a 'show funeral', inaugurating another strong Fenian tradition, although facing implacable hostility from Cullen, who forbade the use of official church facilities. This did not deter a public turnout of between 20,000 and 30,000 for McManus's final committal in Glasnevin cemetery. It was a triumph for Stephens, the principal organiser.

The secret organisation had grown at a hectic pace, especially among urban lower-middle-class young men previously excluded from the public square. It was especially strong in west Cork, where Jeremiah O'Donovan Rossa had incorporated his Phoenix Society of Skibbereen into the national movement. Hope of American assistance was frustrated by the outbreak of the US civil war; by the time it was over in 1865, the Fenians in Ireland had been well and truly infiltrated by spies. The Dublin Castle authorities took pre-emptive action against them in September of that year. Stephens' newspaper was shut and he and most of its leaders were arrested, although Stephens managed to escape from custody.

Moreover, the American movement split. Civil war veterans launched a fruitless raid on Canada, being the nearest available British territory. Stephens, whose conduct had become ever more erratic, was deposed; an Irish-American expeditionary force sailed the Atlantic and tripped off a rebellion in 1867 that was scarcely more successful than the doomed fiasco of '48. Once again, the British authorities were well prepared, with spies and informers everywhere. The Catholic hierarchy made its disapproval crystal clear. But there were aftershocks, and they were consequential.

A raid on Fenians in Manchester resulted in an attempt to spring prisoners from a prison van. A policeman died and three Fenians were hanged as a result: the Manchester Martyrs. A further attempt to rescue a leading Fenian from Clerkenwell jail in London went all wrong and resulted in an explosion that saw the deaths of seventeen people in nearby houses and severe injuries to fifty more. This seemed like the acme of failure, but it drew the British government's attention to Irish affairs as nothing else could do – inaugurating another persistent tradition – and resulted in some immediate reforms.

Of these, the most significant was the disestablishment of the Church of Ireland, thus breaching a core article of the Act of Union. It had been joined indissolubly to the Church of England under article 5 of the Union, but notwithstanding was now cut adrift by Gladstone, the new prime minister. The Irish Question had come to the very centre of British political life, where it was to remain until 1922 and – in the case of what became Northern Ireland – until the present day.

The Industrial Revolution in east Ulster

. . .

ULSTER WAS DIFFERENT. IT had been different to the rest of the island in the critical matter of religion since the seventeenth-century plantation. Now, in the nineteenth century, there was added the further difference of the Industrial Revolution, which took hold there – especially in Ulster east of the Bann – but left the rest of Ireland almost untouched.

From the eighteenth century, Ulster had developed an economy that did not simply meet subsistence requirements but produced modest domestic surpluses through piecework, especially in linen manufacture. For a while, cotton outpaced linen, but Ulster could never compete with Lancashire, and once a means was discovered to process flax by power-spinning machines, linen resumed its primacy.

In the first quarter of the nineteenth century, there was a commercial revolution in east Ulster centred on the Lagan valley. Canals were built; the railway was established early; banks and other reliable financial houses provided the sinews of commerce; industrial mills appeared in profusion. All this created an urban economy that drew people in from the countryside to work, although they brought with them old sectarian hatreds and rivalries as well.

In 1828, Mulholland's York Street cotton mill went on fire and was rebuilt – but as a linen mill. An enormous premises by the standards of the times, it became the focus of the pre-eminence of Belfast as a centre of the international linen trade. By 1850, there were sixty-two such mills in Belfast alone. No wonder that Dr Henry Cooke, a conservative Presbyterian divine and the most formidable Irish opponent that Daniel O'Connell ever faced, was able to boast as he did on the occasion of O'Connell's one and only visit to Ulster in 1841.

A late nineteenth-century view of Royal Avenue in the city centre of Belfast

His speech made plain the junction between industrial advance and adherence to the Union with Great Britain. In effect, east Ulster had become an extension of the economy of north-west England, west Scotland and south Wales.

On Tuesday 10 July 1849, the Victoria Channel in Belfast harbour was opened, allowing large vessels to come up the Lagan at any state of the tide. This mattered because the Belfast region had few of the natural resources, iron and coal for instance, necessary for industrial development and required imports of raw materials. This even included linen, long established in Ulster but needed now in such quantities that imports were imperative. By 1852, Belfast had outstripped Dublin to become the first port in Ireland both by value and by tonnage; it had established its own banking system, effectively independent of the capital; and in the White Linen Hall in the centre of Belfast had seen the key location for the trading of that vital commodity move from Dublin to Ulster. The *Belfast News-Letter* reported the opening of the Victoria Channel as follows:

> *Along the whole line of the opposite quay, loud huzzas from a dense multitude of spectators rent the air ... A scarlet flag, inscribed with the words 'The New Channel Opened', was then unfurled from the mizzen mast head ... The booming of cannon announced the completion of the auspicious event, and 'Rule Britannia' resounded from the deck.*

While all this was happening in east Ulster, the rest of Ireland remained in the grip of the Famine and its aftermath. The contrast was startling: Ulster was becoming ever more different, almost surreally so, to the rest of Ireland. It had always had marked regional differences, even away back in Gaelic days, and these were then accentuated by the plantation, but the establishment of heavy industry was utterly transformative. It was also marked by the shift in Presbyterian sensibility in a generation, from the brave naivety of the republican rebels of 1798 to the uncompromising unionism of Henry Cooke in 1841.

It was not all modernity, for the rural influx to the industrial towns not only hugely increased Catholic numbers – producing in Derry, of all sacred Protestant spaces, a Catholic majority by the end of the century – but also the sectarianism that had for long scarred the countryside. There were Catholic–Protestant riots in Belfast at regular intervals from the 1850s, something only recently abated. But the underlying tensions remain.

However, the nineteenth century and its Industrial Revolution were the high-water mark of Protestant – and especially Presbyterian – Ulster. The contrast with the rest of the island was now so stark and startling as to defy much contemporary understanding. Nationalism – overwhelmingly southern and Catholic – had a blind spot about Ulster and was in denial about its vast difference from the impoverished and agrarian three provinces of the south. This persistent denial over generations inclined to wish Ulster unionism away as a chimera, but it was no such thing. It was unbearable for nationalists to consider the island as anything but a natural unit; therefore a regional minority must bend and accommodate itself to the majority position. Bending and accommodating were habits that Protestant Ulster found extremely difficult and was disinclined to acquire.

The Ulster apogee

. . .

BY 1901, BELFAST HAD passed out Dublin and was now the largest city by population in Ireland. At its centre stood the brand-new city hall, on the site of the old White Linen Hall, a bloated Victorian exercise in civic pride – and beautiful withal. Nearby, at the corner of Donegall Square and Donegall Place, stood the lovely *Jugendstil* building housing the Royal Irish Linen Warehouse, otherwise named for its founding partners, Robinson & Cleaver.

It opened in 1888 and from the start, it was the pre-eminent city centre store for the newly rich Ulster bourgeoisie. Irish linen was indeed its main stock in trade and it exported linen products all over the world. Some estimates reckoned that one-third of all parcels sent overseas from Belfast originated in this one shop.

It was not just linen. The Belfast region – again, principally centred on the Lagan valley – produced other textiles, tobacco products, engineering and many of the goods and commodities that we associate with heavy industry's high noon in the decades before World War I. But at its very heart was shipbuilding.

When the Victoria Channel was opened in 1849, the spoil disturbed by the dredging was used to create an artificial island, named Queen's Island. Here, Robert Hickson, a Liverpool engineer who managed a large ironworks upstream at Cromac, decided to build ships with the iron he was finding it difficult to sell at a profit. To assist him, he engaged Edward Harland, a twenty-three-year-old engineer from Newcastle-upon-Tyne.

Harland launched his first ship in October 1855, and his craft soon caused a sensation in the shipping world because of their revolutionary design, with their 'increased length without any increase in the beam'. In 1858, Harland bought out Hickson with funds supplied by Gustav

Schwabe, a partner in a Liverpool shipyard. Schwabe's nephew, Gustav Wolff, joined Harland and eventually became his partner. Their nimble ships drew orders from as far afield as the American Confederate states during the civil war, anxious as they were to run Union blockades. Within ten years, Harland & Wolff was at the cutting edge of shipbuilding engineering and established a lasting connection with the White Star Line of Liverpool, for whom it eventually was to build the most famous ship ever to sail and sink, the *Titanic*.

Cover page of the *Illustrated London News* depicting the launching of the SS *Oceanic* in Belfast, January 1899

From its foundation in the 1850s until World War I and after, Harland & Wolff was one of the world's great shipyards and was the linchpin of Belfast's industrial heyday. In the early 1890s, it was the largest shipyard in the United Kingdom. Other, smaller yards such as that of Workman Clark developed in its shadow.

Belfast was now an imperial city. In 1895, H.O. Lanyon, president of the Belfast Chamber of Commerce, was able to speak as follows, based on the city's production figures for the preceding year:

> *I find the length of yarn produced in the year amounts to about 64m miles, making a thread that would encircle the world 25,000 times. If it could be used as a telephone wire, it would give us six lines to the sun, and about 380 besides to the moon. The exports of linen measured about 156m yards, which would make a girdle for the earth at the Equator three yards wide, or cover an area of 32,000 acres, or it would reach from end to end of the Co. Down, one mile wide.*

Mackie's was the largest company in the world manufacturing linen machinery; the York Street Flax and Weaving Company was likewise the biggest of its kind in the world. Belfast was a powerhouse of skilled labour. By the end of the nineteenth century, it also had the largest tobacco factory *in the world*, tea machinery and fan-making works, a handkerchief factory, a coloured Christmas card printing firm, a dry dock and a spiral gasometer. Cantrell & Cochrane was the largest manufacturer of soft drinks in the world.

Nowhere else in Ireland had enjoyed such economic success which was, even by international standards, astonishing. Three-quarters of Belfast's population was Protestant and identified the city's success firmly with the Union with Britain. They were utterly opposed to home rule. But three-quarters of the population of Ireland as a whole was Catholic and ever more set upon a devolved parliament in Dublin. Something had to give.

The Land Question

. . .

ENGLISH PROPERTY LAW VESTED all rights in the owners of the land. Tenants had no rights in law, although they might have local customary rights established by tradition and precedent. These latter were, however, not widespread in Ireland and almost non-existent outside Ulster. There, the so-called Ulster Custom compensated tenants for improvements made to their holdings. In 1870, Gladstone passed the first of a long series of Irish land acts to give statutory authority to this customary right throughout Ireland.

Although problematic in the short term, the act established the important principle that parliament and the law should offer legal protections to tenants rather than simply upholding the rights of landed property. Over the next thirty years, various other acts extended this principle – often in the face of heated opposition from landed interests with a perfectly understandable reluctance to compromise the core principle of secure property rights for proprietors.

Charles Stewart Parnell,
Home Rule League

It was one of a series of important reforms enacted by Gladstone's first government (1868–74), none more important for Ireland than the Secret Ballot Act of 1872, which ended the practice of open roll-call voting – superintended, naturally, by landlords and their agents to ensure tenants' compliance with the landlords' wishes. This reform was to have its effect before long.

In the 1874 general election, which saw Gladstone out and Disraeli in, the Liberal vote in Ireland collapsed and transferred to a new entity under the rubric of 'home rule'. This was effectively the revival of O'Connell's old repeal campaign. The home rulers were a diverse group led by a decent but ineffectual barrister, Isaac Butt. Straight away, however, the editorial reaction of the leading Protestant newspaper in Ulster, the *Belfast News-Letter*, to this departure was telling: 'Home rule is simple Rome rule, and if home rule were accomplished tomorrow, before that day week Rome rule would be evident.'

With Disraeli in Downing Street, home rule looked like a hopeless cause anyway. But a by-election in Co. Meath in 1875 returned a tall, spare young man – a landlord from Co. Wicklow – in the home rule interest. Charles Stewart Parnell proved to be a political genius.

But first, before any advance could be made on the home rule front, the Land Question took centre stage. A series of disastrous harvests in the second half of the 1870s was the proximate cause of trouble. The deeper, longer-term problem was one beyond the reach or control of anyone in Ireland: the opening up of European markets to agricultural produce generated in the vast prairies of the United States and Argentina and the development of fast, refrigerated ships to deliver it to market.

Conditions in the west of Ireland, in particular, were dire. Incessant rainfall made saving and drying turf for fuel near impossible; even worse, the potato blight returned, with the Famine still well within living memory. The *Freeman's Journal* reported on conditions in Co. Mayo in August 1879:

> *The prospect of an abundant harvest is at an end; the chance even of a tolerable one hangs dangerously in the balance … The two props of the Mayo farmer's homestead have collapsed miserably upon his head. The potatoes are bad, the turf is worse.*

Many families owed two or three years' rent. However, as the eviction notices arrived the tenant farmers resisted. Galvanised by the editor of the *Connaught Telegraph*, James Daly, at least 10,000 gathered at Irishtown, on the edge of Westport, Co. Mayo, on 20 April 1879. Out of this emerged the Land League, dedicated to resisting all attempts at eviction. Many establishment home rulers were alarmed by this development, but Parnell seized it as the means to pick the lock of the landlord system. He told the crowd:

> *You must show the landlords that you intend to keep a firm grip of your homesteads and lands. You must not allow yourselves to be dispossessed as you were dispossessed in 1847.*

What followed was the land war, organised by the Land League. Crucially, it now had the support of the political home rulers with Parnell at their head, having displaced Butt. Just as crucially, it also drew the support of the Fenians, the Americans in particular, who set aside their aversion to day-to-day politics to join with Parnell's home rulers and the Land League in a historic junction of interests known as the New Departure.

The cry now was for fundamental reforms of the Irish land tenure system, to extend tenants' rights, to secure rent reductions, and to refuse to pay what were judged to be exorbitant rents. Parnell raised funds on a spectacularly successful American trip and established himself at the head of this agrarian coalition. Michael Davitt, a Mayoman, had first floated the idea of a campaign to boycott anyone who took up the holding of an evicted tenant. Parnell promptly endorsed it.

> *When a man takes a farm from which another has been evicted, you must show him on the roadside when you meet him, you must show him at the shop counter, you must show him in the fair and at the market place and even in the house of worship, by leaving him severely alone, by putting him in a sort of moral Coventry, by isolating him from the rest of his kind as if he were a leper of old …*

Charles Stewart Parnell

. . .

THE MOST FAMOUS PRACTICAL example of Parnell's prescription in action was over the winter of 1880–81: the isolation of Captain Charles Boycott, a landowner in Co. Mayo and an agent for Lord Erne. He issued eviction notices to desperate tenants in arrears and was promptly subjected to intimidation by supporters of land reform. He tried importing loyalist gangs from Ulster to lift his potatoes and thresh his corn. Eventually, it was done, but at a cost that was ten times the value of the crop. The loyalists were also boycotted – the usage became universal – without any violence, the protesters displaying the discipline urged on them by the *Connaught Telegraph*:

> *Be calm, be cool and, at the same time, resolute and determined ... Treat those mailed and buckshot warriors with silence and contempt ... Show the world over by your calm, but resolute demeanour, that you are worthy of your name and traditions.*

By now Parnell had established himself as the undisputed leader of a revived Irish nationalism. He was the acknowledged head of the land campaign, which saw success when Gladstone's second government passed a further tenant relief act in 1881. Parnell protested that it did not go far enough and was clapped in Kilmainham jail for a while.

The 1880 general election that had returned Gladstone to power had also returned sixty-one home rulers under Parnell's now unchallenged leadership, many of whom would be his officer corps as he built the party into a unified, formidable parliamentary machine over the next five years. So now Parnell stood at the head of both the land agitation and Irish parliamentary representation movements.

It was the beginning of his glorious decade, the crucible for all later nationalist achievements. But first, there was tragedy.

On 6 May 1882, a group called the Invincibles – a maverick Fenian offshoot – murdered the under-secretary (the head of the Irish civil service in Dublin Castle) and the chief secretary (the cabinet minister for Ireland) in the Phoenix Park in Dublin. It was a quite shocking event, and Parnell so felt that control was slipping from his grasp that he actually offered his resignation to Gladstone. The prime minister declined. Parnell had been released from Kilmainham only four days earlier, having made an informal alliance with Gladstone and the Liberal Party which was to endure.

Irish Land League poster from 1881 demanding non-payment of rents to secure release of some nationalists, including Parnell

Parnell gradually wound down the land campaign, without ever fully abating disturbances in the countryside. The emphasis was now on the political issue, home rule; in other words, devolved domestic government for Ireland. This was inadvertently advanced by Gladstone's government when it passed the Third Reform Act (1884) which greatly extended the parliamentary franchise to include all male heads of households. It tripled the Irish electorate so that about one in two male adults now had the vote – an extension of democracy that was to produce a dramatic result in the general election of the following year.

The 1885 general election was the first held under this new, wider franchise. It produced a sweeping victory for Parnell's home rulers in the three southern provinces, claiming eighty-six seats for a party now firmly under Parnell's iron control. But in Ulster, as ever, things were different. Its parliamentary seats were divided almost equally between home rulers and anti-home rule unionists. This result marked out Ulster exceptionalism in a particularly stark way. Nonetheless, Parnell's eighty-six MPs now held the balance of power at Westminster. Which way would they throw their influence?

Gladstone effectively decided for them. He declared his open support for home rule – a truly revolutionary démarche for the leading British politician of the era – and thus secured Parnell's support. The price was to be the introduction of a Home Rule Bill in parliament. The decision sent shock waves through unionist Belfast and there were severe sectarian riots. More pertinently, the unionist cause now attracted the first of many English Tory grandees in its support: Lord Randolph Churchill, louche, erratic but, like his son Winston to come, a stunningly good orator. He told a rapt audience in the Ulster Hall:

> On you it primarily rests whether Ireland shall remain an integral portion of this great empire sharing its glory ... or whether, on the other hand, Ireland shall become the focus and centre of foreign intrigue and deadly conspiracy.

Or, as Lord Randolph had summarised it upon his arrival at Larne: 'Ulster will fight, and Ulster will be right.'

But for the moment, this seemed a marginal, provincial nuisance. This was the hour of Parnell's triumph. He had taken Irish nationalism from its tentative, almost prostrate condition ten years before and raised its principal demand to the central position in British public life. He was truly now 'the uncrowned king of Ireland', in the contemporary phrase. Even if the bill failed this time – as it did – it would surely succeed in time. The Irish Question had arrived with a vengeance.

The birth of
Ulster unionism

. . .

SUDDENLY, THE ARRIVAL OF home rule in parliament – or the imminent prospect of it – galvanised Protestant Ulster. As for nationalists, they could not imagine the island as anything other than a geographical unit. To be fair, it was something that everyone took for granted. The results of the 1885 general election suggested some sort of radical division – a pattern that would be replicated in all subsequent elections – but projecting that into an actual physical partition was beyond the imagination of just about everyone in the 1880s.

Parnell set out the nationalist case in the House of Commons:

> *We cannot give up a single Irishman. We want the energy, the talents and the work of every Irishman to ensure that this great experiment shall be a successful one. The best system of government for a country I believe to be the one which requires that government should be the result of all the forces within that country.*

But what was 'that country'? The 1881 census had shown that there were 866,000 Protestants in Ulster and almost all, Liberal or Conservative, passionately opposed home rule. They were all right for the moment: the Home Rule Bill failed in the Commons, and ninety-three Liberals voted with the Tories to defeat it, opening a split in the Liberal Party that would never quite heal.

The day after the parliamentary defeat there were riots in Belfast, bad even by the now well-established traditions of rioting in the city. There were sectarian attacks in the docks; a celebratory unionist crowd, 2,000 strong, looking to loot a liquor store on the Shankill Road, drove back the RIC who attempted to stop them. Seven died before the Highland Light Infantry intervened at 10 p.m., finding several children unconscious from the drinking of looted alcohol. The Rev. Hugh Hanna spoke for many from his pulpit in St Enoch's Presbyterian Church:

> It was right that the loyalty of the land should celebrate as it did what God has given us ... But that celebration has cost us dear. It incurred the wrath of a government that has been traitorous to its trusts ... The armed servants of that government are sent to suppress rejoicing loyalty by the sanguinary slaughter of a people resolved to resist a wicked policy.

This latter remark picked up on the fact that many of the police were southern Catholic officers brought in as reinforcements. So began a hot summer of fighting between loyalists and police, and between sectarian mobs. One Belfast journalist, Frank Frankfort Moore, witnessed an attack by Protestants on a Catholic procession. He had seen riots in Cape Town, London and rural Ireland, but never anything like this:

> None of the principals in these actions knew anything of strategy compared with those who engineered the sacking of York Street upon that dark night in August 1886 ... Scarcely a light was to be seen; still I had no difficulty in making out the movements of the dense crowds surging in every direction, and shot after shot I heard above the shouts that suggested something very like Pandemonium. Once or twice I was carried along in the rush of people before a police charge ... I felt that I had learned something of the impotence of every arms except artillery in the case of street fighting.

By September, when the weather turned and the rain came, there were officially thirty-one dead; the true figure was probably nearer fifty. Nor were disturbances confined to Belfast, although they were most intense there: Derry, Portadown and Ballymena all experienced them that summer.

If local unionist politicians and civic leaders were horrified by the thought of home rule – although it had failed at the first parliamentary attempt – these riots and sectarian attacks were populist expressions of a similar sentiment, at least on the Protestant side. They were mirrored by the disappointment of the parliamentary failure on the Catholic side. But both sides knew that the home rule genie was out of the bottle and could not easily be stuffed back in. On both sides, there was the expectation – inducing nationalist hope and unionist dread – that the question would be put again. And how would it all end?

This binary understanding was to dominate Irish affairs for the next thirty-five years and continues to haunt the island to the present day. Unionist resistance to nationalist ambition was now out in the open, in the public square, having hitherto been confined to the peculiar local sectarian tensions of the northern province. Southern Protestants were unionists as well, for the greater part, but they were a scattered regional minority, islands in a nationalist ocean. In Ulster, however, and especially east of the Bann, Protestantism and unionism – they were pretty well synonymous – were concentrated in a determined local majority.

Illustration of rioting in Belfast in 1886

Parnell ascendant

. . .

PARNELL'S HISTORICAL REPUTATION IS strangely muted. This is understandable: before him was the gigantic achievement of O'Connell followed by the cataclysm of the Famine; after him came the drama of the Easter Rising and the Irish Revolution. In all that, it is easy to occlude the utterly transformative effect that Parnell had on Irish history – and on British history too.

The best way to measure Parnell's impact is to consider the state of Irish nationalist politics in the thirty years before his rise. Post-Famine, Ireland outside Ulster was prostrate and exhausted. The Fenian efforts were pretty ineffectual at the time. In the 1870s, especially in the years of Disraeli's Tory government (1874–80), Irish nationalist ambitions did not register at all at Westminster. Ten years later, after Parnell, they were front and centre. In many respects, the Irish Question as put was the Parnell Question. He made the weather.

Gladstone's conversion to home rule and the introduction of the First Home Rule Bill in the Commons in 1886 were the key moments in all this. Prior to that, no British government took Irish nationalism seriously. Ireland was a security problem, a source of civil unrest, but not a political or constitutional problem for London. After 1886, it was – and there could be no going back.

These were the years of Parnell's ascendancy. In 1885, for reasons that would in a few years' time become plain, Parnell foisted the quite unsuitable Captain William O'Shea on Galway as home rule candidate against furious local opposition and serious discontent in the parliamentary party. Each member was pledge-bound to support party policy and, although O'Shea declined to be so pledged, Parnell still pressed on. The reason was Parnell's passionate affair with

O'Shea's wife, Katharine, with whom he had three children, two of whom survived; a seat in the Commons was the price of O'Shea's silent complaisance. In addressing this delicate issue, the *Freeman's Journal* identified Parnell's place in Irish life:

> The issue is not between Captain O'Shea and Mr Lynch [*the local favourite*] but whether at the very moment of the crisis, when the question of home rule hangs in the balance, when Mr Parnell almost holds it in the hollow of his hand, Galway will strike a blow at his prestige and his authority ... The power of Mr Parnell has consisted, and must consist, in English statesmen recognising that he is the personal embodiment of the Irish nation, delegated by them to speak and act on their behalf.

That was a fair statement of the case. Parnell got his way despite the doubts of his more talented and independent-minded lieutenants in the parliamentary party, men such as John Dillon and the waspish Timothy Healy. And then came the Home Rule Bill and the Liberal alliance and the years when Parnell was adored in Ireland and admired – and rather feared – in England. One American journalist in *The Nation* wrote thus of Parnell in 1887:

> The deference which is paid to him by his followers has no close parallel anywhere within my knowledge ... Most nearly he rules them as an emotionless archbishop might rule the priests of a province. He is the embodiment of authority, a being to be obeyed, to be salaamed to, to be addressed with ceremonious deference; yet, who must in turn keep up all the dignities of his high post, must have no favourites, must be urbane and polite and considerate, and must be at once approachable and solitary. It is really the Catholic training and instincts of the Irish members, I fancy, which has developed this curious hierarchical relation, and it is not made the less interesting by the fact that their primate is a Protestant.

Then, in 1889, came Parnell's crowning victory. A story in *The Times*, alleging that Parnell had approved of the Phoenix Park murders of 1882, was shown in open court to have been based on letters forged by one Richard Pigott. Parnell emerged from this in complete triumph. He had created the most disciplined party ever to sit at Westminster, secured Liberal support and humiliated his Tory detractors. He was unassailable.

Which is why his fall, a little more than a year later, was so traumatic. The relationship with Katharine O'Shea was revealed when Captain O'Shea finally sued for a divorce on grounds of his wife's adultery, naming Parnell as co-respondent. What followed was an epic tragedy, whose emotional resonance is best captured in Joyce's heart-stopping Christmas dinner scene in *A Portrait of the Artist as a Young Man.*

Katharine Parnell (Katharine O'Shea), second wife of Charles Stewart Parnell

There is a furious row between Mr Casey, a dinner guest friend of Dedalus senior, and Mrs Riordan (called Dante; although not an aunt, she was so-called, thus d'auntie – they were, remember, originally from Cork – mispronounced by the young Stephen) which climaxed when Dante, a disappointed old woman who clung grimly to the Church, shouted at Casey of Parnell: 'Devil out of hell! We won! We crushed him to death! Fiend!' She left the dining room slamming the door behind her. Casey was bereft: ' "Poor Parnell!" He cried loudly. "My dead king!" ... Stephen, raising his terrorstricken face, saw that his father's eyes were full of tears.'

Committee Room 15

. . .

THE DRAMA AT THE Dedalus Christmas dinner table proceeded from the fact that the principal opposition to Parnell's continued leadership of the Irish Party came from the higher clergy of the Irish Catholic Church. They were his most formidable opponents, but not his first. Those were the English Nonconformists, the backbone of Gladstone's Liberals, who were scandalised by Parnell's adultery. They made it plain to Gladstone that they could no longer sustain his leadership if he persisted with the Parnell alliance. Gladstone, who was personally untroubled by the whole business, had little choice but to yield.

He wrote to the Irish Party setting out the stark reality. He, Gladstone, was the linchpin of the Liberal alliance. The alliance had been Parnell's crowning achievement to date, on which all hopes of home rule hung. But Gladstone's forced removal as Liberal leader would break the alliance. So his letter to the Irish Party in effect informed them that the continuation of the alliance depended on their dumping Parnell.

They did, by forty-five votes to twenty-eight. After six days of agonised and emotional debate in Committee Room 15 of the House of Commons in December 1890, the parliamentary party voted to oust Parnell and thus save the Liberal alliance. Its crime, in the retrospect of those who stood by Parnell through thick and thin, was to decapitate the Irish leader at the bidding of the English. At this point, the Catholic hierarchy's moral unease could be allowed some oxygen and it swung decisively against Parnell. The Church could hardly afford to be out-moralised by low-church English Protestants and Dissenters.

THE GRAND OLD MAGICIAN'S IRISH POLICY.

THEATRE ROYAL
WESTMINSTER
GREAT LIBERAL
CABINET TRICK

A WONDERFUL REMEDY. No settlement of any question, great or small, can be equitable and permanent which is not approached by all concerned in a perfectly unprejudiced spirit; no person who is in any way affected in health can be for long in a truly unbiassed and judicial frame of mind; there- fore—to secure a lasting and GREAT IRISH PROBLEM it is abso- lutely neces- sary that the satisfactory settlement of the whole English-speaking race should be able to bring the full powers of the mind to bear upon the subject, un- trammelled by any disease or ill-humours of the body.
To gain this end there is no better means than BEECHAM'S PILLS, which are well known to carry off all the gross humours and impurities of the system, and thus, by sweeping and garnishing the temple of the soul, set the mind free to bring all its powers to bear on this, the most momentous question of modern times. Sold everywhere, in Boxes, 1s. 1½d. and 2s. 9d.

William Gladstone (1809–1898), prime minister of Great Britain

Conor Cruise O'Brien, whose grandfather, David Sheehy, was one of the forty-five who voted out Parnell, summarised his grandfather's dilemma in *States of Ireland* (1972):

> *The important thing was to win home rule. The only way of winning home rule was through alliance with an English party. The only party available for such an alliance was the Liberal Party ... Parnell himself had taught them to subordinate everything to that alliance ... If Gladstone refused to co-operate with him, the Liberal alliance would be unworkable, and home rule unattainable in their generation. Therefore they voted against Parnell, not 'at the bidding of an Englishman' but solely in order to win home rule.*

It was a classical political dilemma, but the immediate victors were made to look like shabby assassins. Some terrible things had been said in Committee Room 15, none more bitter than those on the tongue of Tim Healy, and these words, when reported – there were Irish journalists present – were carried back to Ireland, where they enflamed a situation already hot with confused emotion. It was in these circumstances that the overt expression of clerical opprobrium for Parnell the adulterer was so persuasive.

The debates dragged on for days. Attempts to remove Parnell from the chair failed and finally, on Saturday 6 December, the anti-Parnellite majority walked out. Parnell had based his defence on the need for the party to remain independent of English control, even at the cost of losing the Liberal alliance. In Ireland, the anti-Parnellites had a majority of public opinion on their side – outside Dublin. The capital remained loyal to Parnell to the end.

When he returned to Dublin, he went in a torchlit procession to the Rotunda at the top of Sackville Street, where shortly his own memorial would stand, and addressed the crowd:

> *I have not misled you. I have never said that this constitutional movement must succeed. I have never promised you absolute success, but I have promised you this, that if you trust me, I will do all that mortal man can do to perform it. What is the position? ... It is an issue that means the life or death of the constitutional movement ... if Ireland cannot win upon this line within the constitution, if our constitutional movement of today is broken, sundered, separated, discredited and forgotten, England will be*

face to face with that imperishable force which tonight gives me vitality and power, and without which we are broken reeds ...

It was to prove a prescient statement. The constitutional movement was driven into the shadows; the Fenians, to whom Parnell was appealing overtly, would revive and their hour would strike twenty-five years later. Parnell also clarified the immediate issue. It was his leadership, marking the independence of the party, against David Sheehy's political dilemma. The awful necessity of the Liberal alliance was more persuasive in the countryside. Three terrible by-elections were fought over the next year, pitting the two factions against each other. The anti-Parnellites won all three.

At a by-election meeting in Co. Roscommon, Parnell got drenched, contracted a fever and retreated to Brighton, to Katharine O'Shea, and died aged just 46. The Parnell myth turned completely around his operatic personality, never more sedulously nurtured than by Joyce and Yeats, who saw him as the noble stag brought low by scurvy hounds.

After ten years, the party reunited nervously and nearly achieved home rule in 1912, but it was never the same again. Parnell was irreplaceable.

After Parnell

. . .

THE PERIOD BETWEEN THE death of Parnell and the Easter Rising of 1916 is often thought of as the calm after – and then before – the storm. But it was also a time of developments absolutely seminal for the Irish future.

Culture displaced politics, which the fall of Parnell had brought into a bad odour. This bald statement, so often made with little qualification, in fact, requires considerable qualification. But the rise of the Irish language movement, with the ambition to revive the old tongue as a vernacular, was of the first importance. It brought cultural issues back to the centre of nationalist affairs, thus reviving one of the concerns emphasised by the Young Irelanders fifty years earlier. The prime movers were Douglas Hyde and Eoin MacNeill, both scholars. They were largely responsible for the formation of the Gaelic League, which launched itself in 1893.

The Gaelic League was astonishingly successful, and it galvanised a generation. Irish-language classes flourished and the movement spread like wildfire – everywhere except in the remaining native Irish-speaking areas in the impoverished west, where poverty persisted and emigration rates remained distressingly high. The Gaelic League found a popular analogue in the Gaelic Athletic Association (GAA), founded in 1884, and dedicated to the revival of traditional Gaelic sports.

Douglas Hyde's inaugural address to the Irish National Literary Society – the immediate precursor of the Gaelic League – in 1892 set out the aims of both movements and their ancillaries:

> *I would earnestly appeal to everyone, whether Unionist or Nationalist ... to set his face against the constant running to*

> England for our books, literature, music, games, fashions and
> ideas. I appeal to everyone ... to help the Irish race to develop in
> future upon Irish lines ... because upon Irish lines alone can the
> Irish race once more become what it was of yore – one of the most
> original, artistic, literary and charming peoples of Europe.

While the Gaelic League strove mightily, and for the most part
successfully, to remain non-sectarian, the GAA was anything but; it
was dominated by Fenians from the start and was hyper-nationalist.

In the midst of all this, Gladstone returned briefly to power in
1892 and the following year introduced a Second Home Rule Bill in
the Commons, where it passed only to be crushed in the Lords.

Meanwhile, Ireland continued to haemorrhage population
through emigration. Between 1851 and 1921 two and a half million
people left for good. No other country in Europe experienced such
a depopulation. Its rate of outflow was triple that of its nearest
rivals, Norway, Sweden and Scotland – and this at a time of
exceptionally high European emigration generally. Irish emigrants
to Anglophone destinations like North America and Australia had
the advantage of literacy in English – thanks to the nineteenth-
century school system. This partly explains why the Irish took so
readily to public life in their new countries. But for the old country,
emigration was disastrous. As one shopkeeper from Drumcliffe,
Co. Sligo, explained:

> As soon as their children reach the adult age, through the scarcity
> of employment, they join their uncles and aunts and cousins in the
> United States, one son remaining on the farm; and if the parents do
> not get him married before they die, he generally sells out and goes
> too. Thus the country is bleeding to death.

After the second failure of home rule and the split induced by the
issue in the Liberal Party, the Tories were in office for the best part
of twenty years. In the 1890s, they adopted a policy of constructive
unionism, better known as killing home rule with kindness. They
created a Congested Districts Board (although, as we have just seen,
these districts were becoming less congested by the decade) which

sponsored public works schemes in the western counties, building small harbours, extending narrow-gauge railways to remote parts and encouraging cottage industries. Although this was in some respects a counsel of despair, domestic piecework being the very antithesis of modernisation in an industrial age, it wrought a huge and beneficial transformation in Irish life.

Douglas Hyde (1860–1949), Irish academic who served as first president of Ireland

This strategy entailed policies unthinkable in Great Britain, especially government subsidies for public transport. It created holiday resorts like Clifden, Co. Galway; it expanded the national retail economy by expediting the delivery of products from coasts to urban markets. It was, in the opinion of some economists, money ill-spent. But it did have significant achievements in the quality of life for people previously reckoned the poorest of the poor in a poor country. What it did not do was kill home rule with kindness. Nationalism may have been dormant for the moment, but it was a sleeping giant.

Rural revolution

. . .

THE CENTENARY OF THE 1798 rising came around. For most of the previous decade, since the death of Parnell, politics had seemed of little account. Now, however, that changed. The centenary gave advanced nationalists, ever more alienated from the discredited and still disunited Irish Party, an opportunity. Some of this radical nationalism had been stimulated by the ginger of the cultural revival and the sense of greater ownership that it afforded to its enthusiasts. But the centenary also offered an opportunity to the Fenians. They had been low in the water since the New Departure of 1879 had largely neutralised them. But they were still there.

On 2 March 1897, an inaugural committee was formed in Dublin to organise a celebration for the centenary the following year. From the first, the committee was dominated by Fenians and advanced nationalists. Every effort was made to exclude the Irish Party from the plans. The central committee that was formed was composed entirely of advanced nationalists and this was repeated, as far as possible, in the formation of centenary committees around the country, using methods of electing and counting that might not have borne too close a scrutiny.

The big event was a public meeting in Dublin to lay a foundation stone for a statue of Wolfe Tone. It drew an impressive attendance, and while the kudos went mainly to the Fenians, they could not prevent some parliamentary party members from speaking on the platform. For all its misfortunes, the party still commanded the allegiance of most Irish nationalists. But the reopening of this split between advanced and constitutional nationalists – patched up by Parnell in 1879 and warned about by him in 1890 – occurred again. It had consequences.

John Redmond, Irish nationalist
politician, barrister, MP in the House
of Commons and leader of the Irish
Parliamentary Party from 1900 to 1918

The party eventually reunited in 1900 under the leadership of the Parnellite John Redmond, and for the next fifteen years or so it still dominated Irish nationalist politics, with the advanced people confined largely to interesting noises off. But the really transformative action lay, for the moment, in the court of two successive chief secretaries of Ireland who between them effected a rural revolution: Gerald Balfour (1895–1900) and George Wyndham (1900–05).

Balfour passed the Local Government (Ireland) Act 1898, which abolished the old grand jury system and replaced it with local elections to new administrative bodies: county councils, urban district councils and so forth. The grand juries had been largely self-selecting ascendancy vehicles for the conduct of local affairs. Balfour's act was an extension of popular democracy and many an Irish politician got – and still gets – his or her political start in one of these humble forums.

Balfour's successor as chief secretary was George Wyndham. He was a grandson of Lord Edward Fitzgerald and seemed to have inherited some of his forbear's revolutionary zeal. But he was also a British imperialist mandarin at the apogee of empire and he brought that sensibility with him. He wrote of Ireland to a friend:

If only we could turn the river of imperialism into this backwater spawned over by obscene reptiles; if one thing could change these anaemic children into full-blooded men! They are part of the Aryan race ... Ireland a nation. Yes & ah! No.

His great achievement was to oversee the resolution of the Land Question. On 2 September 1902, the landowner John Shawe-Taylor proposed the establishment of a land conference involving all parties to the question to seek a resolution. For once, nationalists and unionists agreed. Lord Dunraven chaired the conference, which prepared proposals for legislation. They represented a dramatic extension of previous Tory land legislation: landlords would sell up their entire estates to their tenants, reserving only their demesne lands as they chose, with the vast purchase prices being advanced by the Treasury, to be repaid by the tenants – now to be proprietors in their own right, with all the traditional protections of English property law – over a period of sixty-eight years in the form of annuities. These charges were set at a level lower than existing rents.

Most landlords sold and were glad to sell for cash in hand. They had wearied of the incessant agrarian agitations and disturbances. Wyndham, thoroughly approving of the entire procedure, got the necessary legislation through parliament, which accounts for its ever after being known – quite correctly – as Wyndham's Act. It needed some supplementary legislation to complete the job, but basically, the most intractable problem in Irish life had been conjured out of existence in a trice.

It was the high-water mark of constructive unionism, which soon fell away. The nationalist demand for self-government could not be appeased. As far back as 1887, Arthur Balfour had realised this way ahead of his contemporaries:

After all, when it comes, I shall not be sorry. Only let us have separation as well as home rule; England cannot afford to go on with the Irishmen in her parliament.

Not everyone saw that far in 1887 – or for another thirty years.

New beginnings: 1905

. . .

THE REUNIFICATION OF THE Irish Party in 1900 demonstrated the enduring nature of Parnell's achievement. Despite all the bitterness of the split, the instinct for unity – drilled into them in the 1880s – still held. It would hold, more or less, although minus the lustre of the Parnell years, for another fifteen years or so. Then a world war, a further great extension of the franchise, a generational change in Irish nationalism and a rebellion in Dublin that would come as if out of a clear blue sky transformed everything. But for the moment, in the early years of the century, the reunited party had made its point. It could not be ignored at the time of the 1798 commemoration, despite the Fenian organisers' earnest desire to do so, and it could not be ignored now.

Nevertheless, there were stirrings on the margins. In 1905, Arthur Griffith, a journalist and printer, founded Sinn Féin, a nationalist ginger group. It was not republican in ambition; rather, Griffith aimed at a solution closer to the Austro-Hungarian *ausgleich* of 1867. But Sinn Féin proved to be protean, undergoing many mutations over the next twenty years and becoming what it was not at the start – the 'brand' for Irish republican separatism after 1916, even though it had had nothing at all to do with the Easter Rising. But the brand name came, ironically, from the British in the first place, as they associated Sinn Féin with all forms of radical nationalism more urgent than that of the party. They were not alone in that.

Griffith was a journalist of real talent. He founded a newspaper, the *United Irishman*, which soon attracted some very distinguished contributors indeed, not least Yeats. It had reach. John Sweetman was a retired Catholic businessman who had financed the paper and some of Griffith's other endeavours. He wrote to George Gavan Duffy, explaining why he had put money into the paper to keep it afloat:

> *I hear the funds of the Sinn Féin daily newspaper are nearly exhausted. I did not subscribe to it at first, as I did not believe that sufficient funds could be obtained and I did not wish to encourage its starting ... Beside the good it directly does through its readers, it is having an effect on the other newspapers and perhaps persons of all political parties might very well subscribe to it for the purpose of keeping it going.*

Sinn Féin was the most prominent but not the only nationalist ginger group established in these years. Also in 1905, there were founded in Belfast the Dungannon Clubs – in commemoration of the Dungannon Convention of the Volunteers (a very different animal then) in 1782. The clubs were outright republican but largely confined to Ulster. Still, they would produce influential people in time.

Of more immediate and urgent interest in Ulster in 1905 was the first meeting of the Ulster Unionist Council 'to form an Ulster Union for bringing into line all local Unionist associations in the province of Ulster'. It marked the increasing solidarity of Ulster unionists and their effective separation from their southern unionist brethren, whom they were abandoning to their own devices. It was the beginning of concerted and concentrated unionist opposition to further nationalist ambition.

Their defensive caution was required, for in 1906 the Liberals returned to power in Westminster in a landslide, thus arousing the ghost of home rule. For the moment, the sheer size of the Liberal majority did not leave them dependent on Irish Party votes, but all concerned – not least the Ulster unionists – knew that this could change, as indeed it did. For the moment, however, the Liberals could ignore home rule, that hot potato that had split their party and delivered them the best part of twenty years in opposition.

So, in the first decade of the twentieth century, there was a quickening in both nationalism and unionism, at the influential margins of the former and the regional heart of the latter. The two political traditions were growing ever further apart, despite some denial on the nationalist side about the seriousness of unionist intent.

One nationalist with no illusions was another journalist of waspish talent, D.P. Moran, whose paper, *The Leader*, had been a success since its foundation in 1900. Now, in 1905, he published a book, *The Philosophy of Irish-Ireland*, in which he stated with brutal clarity his core belief that the Irish nation was Catholic: 'the foundation of Ireland is the Gael, and the Gael must be the element that absorbs'. Protestants could take it or leave it. In the latter case, the only solution was partition, 'leaving the Orangemen and their friends in the north-east corner'. Increasingly, the Ulster Unionist Council came to agree with Moran.

Arthur Griffith, Irish nationalist and economist

Home rule again

. . .

IN TWO ELECTIONS IN 1910, the Liberals lost their overall majority and were once more, as in the mid-1880s, dependent upon the Irish Party to secure a parliamentary majority. The radicalism of the outgoing administration, and especially that of the chancellor, David Lloyd George, had precipitated a constitutional crisis. The House of Lords had refused to pass Lloyd George's 1909 budget, in defiance of every customary precedent which gave the Commons sole authority over money bills. In retaliation, the Lords were neutered, their power reduced from veto to a mere two-year delay on any legislation.

This bore materially on Ireland, for naturally Redmond demanded of Asquith, the prime minister, that which Parnell had demanded of Gladstone thirty years earlier: a home rule bill for Ireland in return for parliamentary support. Thus was the old Liberal alliance restored. The Third Home Rule Bill was introduced and passed in the Commons in 1912; predictably, the Lords rejected it, but now could only delay its implementation until 1914. Redmond had achieved that which had eluded even the great Parnell.

It was as if the lassitude of the years after 1906 had dissipated in this hour of triumph. John Dillon, Redmond's deputy, had written to his leader in 1908: 'An effort must be made to put some life back into the movement. At present it is very much asleep, and Sinn Féiners, Gaelic League etc., etc., are making great play.'

Indeed they had been, with Sinn Féin's policies of Irish members abstaining from Westminster, setting up an assembly in Dublin and passive resistance to British rule appearing vigorous – if not yet wholly persuasive with the nationalist electorate – as against the Irish Party's perceived apathy. No more. The Home Rule Bill was an hour of vindication and triumph for the entire constitutional movement, its apogee. John Redmond was the man of the hour.

Irish unionists were horrified. They had chosen Sir Edward Carson as their leader in 1910. A Dubliner, he was one of the most brilliant lawyers of his day. MP for Trinity College and a former Conservative cabinet minister, he had made his name by his evisceration of Oscar Wilde in a famous legal action in 1895. Now, fifteen years later, Carson found himself at the head of a movement ever more concentrated in Ulster, where he found an efficient lieutenant in James Craig, the chief organiser of much of what followed.

In 1911, Carson addressed 50,000 men from unionist clubs and Orange lodges at Strandtown in east Belfast:

> *With the help of God, you and I joined together ... will yet defeat the most nefarious conspiracy that has ever been hatched against a free people ... We must be prepared ... the morning home rule passes, ourselves to become responsible for the government of the Protestant province of Ulster.*

Carson used his Tory connections well. He was lucky. The Tory leader was Andrew Bonar Law, whose father had been a Presbyterian minister in Coleraine and who was a partisan for the Ulster unionist cause. Bonar Law came to Belfast on Easter Tuesday 1912 and addressed a crowd of 100,000 loyalists:

> *Once more you hold the pass, the pass for the empire. You are a besieged city. The timid have left you; your Lundys have betrayed you; but you have closed your gates. The government have erected by their Parliament Act a boom to shut you off from the help of the British people. You will burst that boom.*

The resistance increased, culminating on 28 September 1912 – 'Ulster Day' – with the mass signing of the Ulster Solemn League and Covenant, a pledge to use any and all means to frustrate the introduction of home rule. The covenant was signed by a total of 471,414 men and women. Some signed in their own blood.

Edward Carson (9 February 1854 – 22 October 1935), Irish unionist politician speaking in Ulster in 1912

In the small hours of 25 April 1914, 216 tons of rifles and ammunition were landed for the Ulster Volunteer Force, a militia, at Larne, under the complaisant gaze of the authorities. The unionists were prepared to resist by force if necessary and now had the means to do so. A similar attempt to land arms near Dublin for the Irish Volunteers, a counter-militia, was not winked at by the authorities, and in the resultant clashes, four men died. One striking incident took place at the Curragh, a British army camp south of Dublin. A number of officers made it plain that they would resign their commissions rather than coerce Ulster. For the first time since 1688, the Crown could not rely utterly on the loyalty of its army.

The Ulster unionists were not bluffing: they meant it, although nationalists persisted in their belief that it was all a sham. After all, was not home rule now the settled law of the land, albeit delayed for two years? In 1914, the Lords' delaying power would expire and the Home Rule Act (Ireland) 1914 would become established law.

But by the second half of 1914, the world had changed beyond recovery.

Lockout and citizen armies

. . .

THE PERIOD BEFORE THE outbreak of World War I was remembered in romantic nostalgia as the late Edwardian afternoon, the last glow of summer before the Fall. In fact, it was, among other things, a time of great social turbulence. This was especially true in Dublin, a city which had stagnated in the course of the nineteenth century. Once-elegant Georgian houses and streets, abandoned by the retreating ascendancy, had decayed into horrifying slums. Many of the middle classes had fled the city for the more salubrious suburban townships, where the writ of the Dublin Corporation did not run and the residents could establish semi-independent townships with lower rates. The excellent public transport system enabled them to commute in and out of the city as they required.

It was this system that was the trigger for the most celebrated labour dispute in Irish history. Dublin had largely missed the Industrial Revolution and was, by the early twentieth century, more a commercial and professional city than an industrial one. The urban poor, crammed into the horrific city-centre tenements that had once been the homes of the privileged, had very few skills: the majority were casual labourers, carters and dockers. Women earned pittances as washerwomen or domestic servants, or were prostitutes in a city notorious for its brothels, which drew the eager custom of the British military. The city's death rate was the highest in the United Kingdom.

In 1909, James Larkin arrived in Dublin. Originally from Liverpool of Irish extraction, he was a radical trade unionist and had come fresh from Belfast, where he had led a dock strike. He founded the

Irish Transport and General Workers' Union, to unionise not just the skilled artisans of the city but the unskilled majority. From the beginning, he was opposed tooth and nail by William Martin Murphy, the leading figure in the Dublin Employers' Federation; Murphy was bent upon smashing Larkin's fledgling union. He was also the owner of the *Irish Independent* newspaper and principal shareholder in the Dublin United Tramway Company, one of Victorian Dublin's more successful enterprises.

Barefoot boys holding up *Daily Herald* sheets reading
'Murphy Must Go' in front of large crowd

The company employed drivers and conductors who were at most semi-skilled and often not even that. Larkin recruited them in large numbers. In 1913, Murphy presented them with a stark choice: leave the union or face dismissal. On 21 August he dismissed 100 men. Other employers followed Murphy's lead. On 26 August, Larkin called all tramway workers out on strike. He held the men spellbound with his fiery oratory. Countess Markievicz recalled:

> Listening to Larkin, I realised that I was in the presence of something that I had never come across before, some great primeval force, rather than a man. A tornado, a storm-driven wave, the rush into life of spring and the blasting breath of autumn, all seemed to emanate from the power that spoke.

The authorities banned a meeting fixed for Sunday 31 August, but Larkin sneaked past the police guard, appeared on the balcony of the Imperial Hotel – proprietor, William Martin Murphy – and harangued the crowd. What followed was a police riot, known ever after as Bloody Sunday. It was merely good fortune that only one person died.

The strike, or lockout, held. The workers and their families endured terrible hardship as their meagre wages were suspended. British trade union help proved inadequate. A plan to send starving children to England was scuppered by the Catholic Church authorities on the grounds that they might end up in Protestant homes! Eventually, the men were starved back to work in January 1914. It had been a Pyrrhic victory for Murphy; as George Russell wrote in an open letter to the employers:

> The men whose manhood you have broken will loathe you ... It is not they – it is you who are blind Samsons pulling down the pillars of the social order.

While the Lockout was at its height in November 1913, there were formed in Dublin two militias: one to protect the strikers, the Irish Citizen Army, and the other a militia entitled the Irish Volunteers, ostensibly to defend home rule – but against whom was not immediately clear. The Irish Volunteers were a mirror image of the UVF. Within the Volunteers, the Fenians were busy and soon established their men in positions of influence. In general, these men were middle or lower middle class, many hostile to Larkin for his socialism while they emphasised nationalism instead. (Tom Clarke was a notable exception, admiring Larkin.) The national interest must take precedence over sectional interests: it was to be a theme in the years to come.

The Volunteers were visible, the Fenians within much less so, being conspiratorial by nature. They were a minority within Fenianism itself, concealing their purposes not only from the head of the Volunteers but even from the Supreme Council of the IRB, which styled itself the Military Council and resolved on a military rising against British rule in Ireland while London was tied up at war in Europe.

Which it was: in August 1914, the Great War began.

The Great War

...

THE WAR WAS FOUGHT between the Allies – France, the UK, Russia, Italy and, from early 1918, the United States – and the Central Powers – Germany, Austria-Hungary and Turkey. Redmond, as the leader of Irish nationalism and with home rule secured, albeit suspended for the duration, fully backed the war effort. He rose to his feet in the House of Commons on the night of 3 August 1914 and declared:

> *I say to the government that they may tomorrow withdraw every one of their troops from Ireland ... The armed Catholics of the South will only be too glad to join arms with the armed Protestant Ulstermen.*

Recruiting posters appeared all over Ireland, with Redmond's face prominent on them. He had secured control of the Irish Volunteers, which he renamed the Irish National Volunteers. Over 200,000 Irishmen volunteered and more than 30,000 of them died. The UVF was welcomed and reconstituted as the 36th (Ulster) Division of the British army with its command structure virtually intact. But Kitchener, the wooden-headed secretary for war, did not extend a similar indulgence to nationalist volunteers, who were dispersed in the newly formed 10th and 16th Divisions.

Redmond then went beyond his pledge of support in the Commons. At an unscheduled speech in Woodenbridge, Co. Wicklow, he said:

> *I say to you – Go on drilling and make yourselves efficient for the work, and then account for yourselves as men, not only for Ireland itself, but wherever the fighting line extends, in defence of right, of freedom and religion in this war (cheers).*

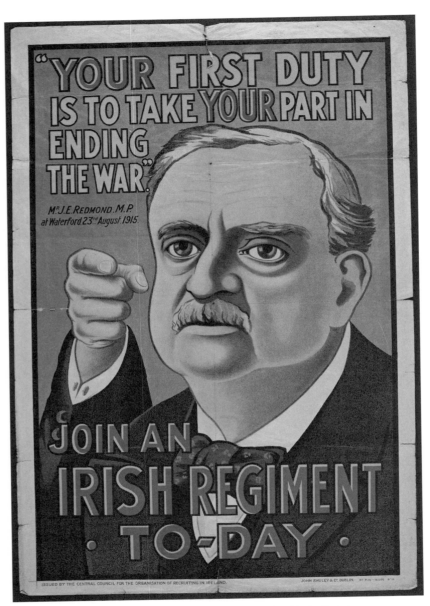

A recruitment poster with Redmond's image produced by the Central Council for the Organisation of Recruiting in Ireland, September 1915

For the more radical members of the Volunteers, this was too much. They might be prepared to defend Ireland but they would not fight abroad for the British Empire. Led by Eoin MacNeill, they withdrew from the Irish National Volunteers and reconstituted themselves as a separate body retaining the simple original title, Irish Volunteers. They were about 11,000 men, leaving Redmond with the remaining 170,000.

Of the British army volunteers, Ulster supplied about half the total, and about 57 per cent of Irish recruits were Catholic. However, doubts grew about whether home rule would ever be applied, all the more so when a new wartime coalition was established in London in 1915; it included many Conservatives, diehard in their previous opposition to the measure. Redmond's attempt, per Woodenbridge, to construct a wider British patriotism based on the inclusion of Irish home rulers drew ever-increasing scepticism from that quarter but also from more radical nationalist elements in Ireland.

In the war itself, the casualties were frightful. Europe had not seen slaughter on this scale since the seventeenth-century wars of religion. The National Volunteers lost, among many others, the promising poet Francis Ledwidge and two MPs, William Redmond (John's brother) and the brilliant young academic Tom Kettle. At the battle of the Somme in July–September 1916, the 36th Ulster suffered horrific casualty rates, pals from little adjacent terraced streets dying side by side. This was only weeks after the sensational Easter Rising in Dublin, which further deepened the conviction of many in Protestant Ulster that the Catholic south was irredeemably treacherous and existentially hostile to Britain, Redmond's emollient words notwithstanding.

As the war dragged on, Prime Minister Asquith was deemed to be not up to the task of war leadership and was replaced by the energetic David Lloyd George, a Liberal but one obliged to preside over a cabinet of ever-increasing Conservative and unionist temper. In 1917–18, this government made one final attempt to settle the Irish Question by means of a convention which sought an accommodation between moderate unionists and nationalists, as if it did not have enough to do to manage a huge war that was going badly. The times were against any convention: moderates on both sides were too few in numbers and influence to bridge the gap. The result was a dangerous vacuum.

By the time the war ended in November 1918 with a victory for the exhausted Allies, the situation in Ireland – and especially in the nationalist south – had been transformed. The post-war world was hardly recognisable. Ex-servicemen, the survivors of the flames, returned home to an often frosty reception. The situation there had been radicalised by the Easter Rising and the executions that followed, and also by a ham-fisted and desperate attempt by Lloyd George in April 1918 to extend military conscription to Ireland, from which it had been previously and wisely excluded. But the sheer loss of life at Passchendaele in the autumn of 1917 and the final, furious German assault on the Western Front in early 1918 prompted the move.

The threat of conscription instantly united all sections of Irish nationalism in opposition to it. Inevitably, it redounded more to the benefit of the radicals, now lumped together under the Sinn Féin rubric (even though Sinn Féin had had nothing to do with the Easter Rising). Even the Catholic Church hierarchy, traditionally cautious in such matters and institutionally suspicious of the radicals, joined the protest. It was a moment of mass withdrawal from the British state. Conscription was never introduced; a few months later, the war was won with the now-prostrate Germany having played its best and last card. But nationalist Ireland was effectively already lost to Britain.

The Easter Rising: an Ireland transformed

. . .

SHORTLY AFTER THE GREAT European War broke out, a faction in the IRB – otherwise the Fenians – resolved on a rebellion against British rule while Britain was distracted by the conflict. They styled themselves the Military Council. Its two prime movers were Tom Clarke, a veteran of the dynamite campaign in the 1880s for which he had spent fifteen years in prison, and Seán MacDermott, a radical cultural and political activist from a young age and a gifted organiser. Its principal spokesman was Patrick Pearse, who gave the graveside oration in 1915 for O'Donovan Rossa, another old radical Fenian, delivering one of the greatest perorations in Irish political oratory:

> *Life springs from death; and from the graves of patriot men and women spring living nations. The Defenders of this realm … think that they have pacified Ireland. They think that they have purchased half of us and intimidated the other half. They think that they have foreseen everything, think they have provided against everything; but the fools, the fools, the fools – they have left us our Fenian dead, and while Ireland holds these graves, Ireland unfree shall never be at peace.*

The chief military planner was the sickly Joseph Mary Plunkett, and the Military Council was joined in early 1916 by James Connolly, who had succeeded Jim Larkin as head of the ITGWU and had formed a small militia, the Irish Citizen Army, to protect workers against further state violence. Its numbers were exiguous but Connolly was a natural commander.

The Rising was planned for Easter Sunday. A shipment of German arms had been arranged by Roger Casement, but was intercepted off the Kerry coast and the ship carrying it later scuttled. Casement came ashore only to be spotted and arrested. With their plans in disarray, the Military Council finally showed its hand to Eoin MacNeill, the leader of the Irish Volunteers, who was horrified at the recklessness of what was planned. He immediately issued a countermanding order, cancelling all Volunteer mobilisation that weekend. The Military Council resolved to go ahead anyway and the Rising started, a day late and with reduced numbers, on Easter Monday.

Some principal buildings in Dublin city centre – notably the General Post Office in Sackville Street, which became the principal rebel garrison – were invested. Pearse stepped out onto the pavement at the front of the GPO and read out the Proclamation of the Republic, hastily composed in Liberty Hall in the previous few days. It became a defining document for the Irish nation:

> *In the name of God and of the dead generations from which she receives her old tradition of nationhood, Ireland, through us, summons her children to her flag and strikes for her freedom.*
>
> *Having organised and trained her manhood through her secret revolutionary organisation, the Irish Republican Brotherhood, and through her open military organisations, the Irish Volunteers and the Irish Citizen Army ... and, supported by her exiled children in America and gallant allies in Europe ... she strikes in full confidence of victory.*

The Rising was doomed from the start, as Connolly admitted. Fewer than 2,000 men and women mobilised. But it was a magnificent theatrical gesture and was soon regarded as the founding moment of the modern republic. The British got troops up to the city on the Tuesday and a gunboat up the Liffey on the Wednesday, which fired artillery shells into Sackville Street. Also on the Wednesday, an outpost of the garrison at Boland's Mills in the south east of the city centre – whose commander was one Éamon de Valera, of whom more would be heard – inflicted severe casualties at Mount Street Bridge on British reinforcements marching in from Kingstown (Dún Laoghaire).

POBLACHT NA H EIREANN.

THE PROVISIONAL GOVERNMENT

OF THE

IRISH REPUBLIC

TO THE PEOPLE OF IRELAND.

IRISHMEN AND IRISHWOMEN: In the name of God and of the dead generations from which she receives her old tradition of nationhood, Ireland, through us, summons her children to her flag and strikes for her freedom.

Having organised and trained her manhood through her secret revolutionary organisation, the Irish Republican Brotherhood, and through her open military organisations, the Irish Volunteers and the Irish Citizen Army, having patiently perfected her discipline, having resolutely waited for the right moment to reveal itself, she now seizes that moment, and, supported by her exiled children in America and by gallant allies in Europe, but relying in the first on her own strength, she strikes in full confidence of victory.

We declare the right of the people of Ireland to the ownership of Ireland, and to the unfettered control of Irish destinies, to be sovereign and indefeasible. The long usurpation of that right by a foreign people and government has not extinguished the right, nor can it ever be extinguished except by the destruction of the Irish people. In every generation the Irish people have asserted their right to national freedom and sovereignty; six times during the past three hundred years they have asserted it in arms. Standing on that fundamental right and again asserting it in arms in the face of the world, we hereby proclaim the Irish Republic as a Sovereign Independent State, and we pledge our lives and the lives of our comrades-in-arms to the cause of its freedom, of its welfare, and of its exaltation among the nations.

The Irish Republic is entitled to, and hereby claims, the allegiance of every Irishman and Irishwoman. The Republic guarantees religious and civil liberty, equal rights and equal opportunities to all its citizens, and declares its resolve to pursue the happiness and prosperity of the whole nation and of all its parts, cherishing all the children of the nation equally, and oblivious of the differences carefully fostered by an alien government, which have divided a minority from the majority in the past.

Until our arms have brought the opportune moment for the establishment of a permanent National Government, representative of the whole people of Ireland and elected by the suffrages of all her men and women, the Provisional Government, hereby constituted, will administer the civil and military affairs of the Republic in trust for the people.

We place the cause of the Irish Republic under the protection of the Most High God, Whose blessing we invoke upon our arms, and we pray that no one who serves that cause will dishonour it by cowardice, inhumanity, or rapine. In this supreme hour the Irish nation must, by its valour and discipline and by the readiness of its children to sacrifice themselves for the common good, prove itself worthy of the august destiny to which it is called.

Signed on Behalf of the Provisional Government,

THOMAS J. CLARKE.

SEAN Mac DIARMADA. THOMAS MacDONAGH.
P. H. PEARSE. EAMONN CEANNT.
JAMES CONNOLLY. JOSEPH PLUNKETT.

The Proclamation of the Provisional Government of the Irish Republic
issued at the GPO in Dublin on Easter Monday, 24 April 1916

By Thursday, the GPO garrison was increasingly untenable because of British artillery fire. Much of Lower Sackville Street was in flames. Other garrisons saw a little action during Easter Week, and Jacob's Biscuit factory, a formidable and near impregnable industrial building near the Grand Canal, saw none. Fighting dragged on until the middle of Saturday; the GPO had been evacuated on Friday evening and the formal surrender took place in mid-afternoon the following day.

The British military was now in control, with politicians sidelined and preoccupied with the world war. The British military commander was Sir John Maxwell, an officer of little distinction and less sense. He had a free hand; he established military courts and court-martialled the leaders of the Rising, having fifteen of them shot. One more, Casement, was later hanged for high treason. Of the garrison commanders, only de Valera – who had been born in New York – escaped the firing squad.

The executions changed the public mood. At first, there was little public sympathy for the rebels, but that changed quite suddenly. The novelist James Stephens spotted this contemporaneously:

> *The truth is that Ireland is not cowed. She is excited a little ... She was not with the revolution, but in a few months she will be, and her heart which was withering will be warmed by the knowledge that men have thought her worth dying for.*

Eventually Asquith, still (but not for much longer) prime minister, came to Dublin and put a stop to the executions. Many of those not executed were interned, principally at Frongoch in north Wales. It was here that young Michael Collins, who had been in the GPO, first came to the notice of others. These internees were released within a year and returned to an Ireland transformed. All elements of radical nationalism were now badged – erroneously – by the British as Sinn Féin. The name stuck and they gradually re-formed that party and began the process of pushing Redmond's Irish Party aside as the voice of Irish national aspiration. The conscription crisis of early 1918 effectively completed the process.

The new Sinn Féin and the conscription crisis

. . .

THE PARTY THAT ARTHUR Griffith had founded in 1915 – Sinn Féin – reconstituted itself in the wake of the Easter Rising. It now embraced all shades of radical nationalist opinion more 'advanced' than the Irish Party. The Irish Party had grown old and complacent. The new Sinn Féin represented a generational change. Men who had been young in Parnell's heady time were middle-aged and old and all too snug sitting in safe, uncontested Westminster seats. In 1917, Griffith stood aside as Sinn Féin leader to allow Éamon de Valera to succeed him.

In the same year, the MP for North Roscommon James O'Kelly died. He had had a colourful life: a member of the French Foreign Legion, he had fought in Algeria and Mexico; in the defence of Paris against the Prussians in 1870; for the American army against Sitting Bull; and had been a military prisoner in Cuba. He had been everywhere except North Roscommon, where he seldom showed his face. Sinn Féin ran a candidate to replace him: George Noble Plunkett, a papal count and connoisseur of fine art, whose son Joseph had been executed after the Rising. The Irish Party vote was split but it didn't matter. Plunkett won a clear majority of the votes cast and was returned.

He was followed later in the year by Joe McGuinness in nearby South Longford and then, sensationally, by de Valera himself in East Clare to fill a vacancy left by the death of Willie Redmond in Flanders. W.T. Cosgrave won in Kilkenny city and Griffith in East Cavan in 1918. The Irish Party had a few consolation victories here and there but the overall trend was clear. This was confirmed in the

Sinn Féiners rioting in the streets of Dublin, demanding the release of Sinn Féin prisoners

general election called in December 1918 after the end of the war. Sinn Féin swept the board in nationalist Ireland, winning seventy-three seats to the Irish Party's six, most of the latter in Ulster, where the party was best organised.

In the South Longford by-election, the brilliant slogan coined was 'Put him In to get him Out' and was attached to the candidate Joe McGuinness, who was still languishing in Lewes jail. De Valera, only recently out of prison himself, caught the new public mood:

> *You have no enemy but England ... Although we fought once and lost, it is only a lesson for the second time ... Every vote you give now is as good as the crack of a rifle in proclaiming your desire for freedom.*

The Easter Rising had been an utterly transformative event, radicalising nationalism generally. In addition, a big widening of the franchise brought a younger generation into the electorate. The conscription crisis in spring 1918 had been decisive, for it prompted an unprecedented display of nationalist unity, right across the spectrum. When the Military Services Act became law, the ailing Irish Party withdrew from Westminster in protest, thus tacitly conceding Sinn Féin's point about abstention. The nationalist public wondered why it shouldn't support the real abstentionist party, Sinn Féin, rather than the reluctant recent convert which had for so long been a noisy booster for the British war effort.

There was a general strike and large demonstrations. Even the Catholic Church hierarchy, from the Archbishop of Armagh down, supported the protest. It had traditionally been suspicious of advanced nationalism. But the advanced position was rapidly becoming mainstream. A pledge to oppose conscription was drafted by de Valera and signed by nearly two million people. In the end, conscription was not applied, but the damage had been done.

This was especially the case in relation to unionist Ulster, where every further iteration of an advanced nationalist position was ever more alienating. The slaughter of the 36th Ulster on the Somme during the summer had entered unionist and Protestant folk memory as surely as the siege of Derry. If unionism had been prepared to go to the brink of civil war against home rule, what were they now to make of Sinn Féin's demand for a separatist republic?

By early 1919, the pre-war standoff between nationalism and unionism stood revealed with even greater clarity than before. The Irish Convention had failed, effectively marginalising the moderates on both sides. The two traditions were more entrenched than ever. What was more, it was a time of lawlessness and violence right across Europe, as previously stable regimes fell apart under the pressures of war. It was not just Ireland, but Ireland was already a tinder box. Winston Churchill summed it up in a memorable passage from his self-serving book, *The World Crisis*:

> *The whole map of Europe has been changed ... But as the deluge subsides and the waters fall short we see the dreary steeples of Fermanagh and Tyrone emerging once again. The integrity of their quarrel is one of the few institutions that has been unaltered in the cataclysm which has swept the world.*

War of Independence
and treaty

. . .

ON 21 JANUARY 1919, the Sinn Féin deputies returned at the December general election met in the Mansion House in central Dublin and constituted their meeting as the First Dáil, or Irish Assembly. They honoured their election pledge and did not go to Westminster. The Dáil instead adopted a Declaration of Independence.

> *Whereas the Irish people is by right a free people:*
>
> *And whereas for seven hundred years the Irish people has ... repeatedly protested in arms against foreign usurpation:*
>
> *And Whereas English rule in this country is ... based upon fraud and maintained by military occupation against the declared will of the people:*
>
> *And Whereas the Irish Republic was proclaimed in Dublin on Easter Monday, 1916, by the Irish Republican Army acting on behalf of the Irish people ...*
>
> *Now, therefore, we, the elected representatives of the ancient Irish people, do, in the name of the Irish nation, ratify the establishment of the Irish Republic ...*

On the same day, there was an ambush at Soloheadbeg in Co. Tipperary. Two RIC men, guarding a cargo of explosives, were shot dead by members of the Irish Volunteers. This was largely a freelance, maverick operation: there was no mandate for further violence, and it remained to be seen if the Dáil would retrospectively endorse this action. In fact, Soloheadbeg – regarded as the first shots fired in the War of Independence – was typical of the conflict that followed for the next two years. The Dáil had uncertain control over its decentralised military, whose actions depended on the vigour and initiative of dynamic local commanders. Some areas remained quiet; some were heavily involved, especially in Munster.

Police wanted poster for Dan Breen, one of those involved in the Soloheadbeg ambush in 1919

A Dáil delegation was dispatched to the post-war Paris peace conference called to settle the affairs of a battered and exhausted Europe following the carnage of the Great War. Despite its best efforts, the delegation gained little traction. It was one thing to reorder the map to accommodate the disparate peoples of the defeated Central Powers, and quite another to break up the metropolitan state of a victorious one. It happened, but not because of anything said or done in Paris. What mattered now was what happened in Ireland.

De Valera was not present at the meeting of the First Dáil, having been imprisoned in England under the terms of an entirely fictitious 'German Plot' dreamed up by the viceroy, Lord French. In February, however, Michael Collins – now emerging as the key figure in Irish nationalist life, both on the political and military sides – helped him to escape and returned him to Ireland. From there, Dev went to the United States to drum up money and support for the republic.

Collins now began his campaign of intimidation and assassination against RIC men in remote areas, against known and suspected British agents, against G Division of the Dublin Metropolitan Police (responsible for internal espionage), and against whatever arm and sinew of the British state in Ireland was within his reach and that of his men. The war in the countryside escalated during 1919 with Collins only partly in control, the rest being the work of those energetic local commanders already noted.

In the first half of 1920, the British were so stretched that they created Crown militia forces called, respectively, the Black and Tans (because of the colour of their uniforms) and the Auxiliaries, officially a police reserve but actually an ill-disciplined group none too squeamish about answering the IRA in kind. Their campaign of terror led to a tightening of organisation in the IRA to create mobile 'flying columns', of which the 3rd West Cork brigade under the command of Tom Barry, a British ex-serviceman, became the best known.

The Auxiliaries and Black and Tans, frustrated by the hit-and-run tactics of men such as Barry, took it out on civilians and towns. They burned the small town of Balbriggan, near Dublin, and the centre of Cork. The lord mayor of Cork, Tomás MacCurtain, was murdered in his bed. His successor, Terence McSwiney, was arrested and died in Brixton Prison after a seventy-four-day hunger strike.

A truce was declared in July 1921, with both sides exhausted by the stalemate. In October, a Dáil delegation went to London. Although returned from America, de Valera, the president of the Dáil and the unquestioned leader of Irish nationalism, did not go. The delegation was headed by Arthur Griffith and Michael Collins. They finally agreed a treaty with Lloyd George in December which granted Ireland dominion status within the British Commonwealth but not a full republic. The agreement split nationalist Ireland, with passions high on both sides. The cabinet narrowly agreed to the terms of the Treaty, as did the Dáil. But a majority of the IRA and a large and influential minority of politicians, led by de Valera himself, disowned it and held out for the full republic.

By now, Ireland was split in more ways than one. The island had been partitioned in the face of the intractable Ulster question.

The partition of Ireland

. . .

THE POST-WAR BRITISH government was led by David Lloyd George, widely praised as 'the man who won the war', but it was a coalition. The Liberal Party had split at the time of Asquith's defenestration in 1916 and it was the minority under the Welsh Wizard who were now in government with a phalanx of Tories. The government reacted to the mayhem in the south by implementing military reprisals while trying for yet another political solution in Ireland.

This led to the Fourth Home Rule Act, better known as the Government of Ireland Act 1920. It proposed the partition of the island – and also of the historic province of Ulster. The three outlying Ulster counties – Cavan, Monaghan and Donegal, with their local Catholic/nationalist majorities – were ceded to the south. In the north, what was left of Ulster, a new statelet was created called Northern Ireland. It contained the largest area, denominated by county preference, with a comfortable unionist/Protestant majority. The rest of the island was to become Southern Ireland, with its own assembly and representation at Westminster.

The act was a dead letter in the south from the moment it was passed because of the War of Independence and the defiance of the Dáil. But it stuck in the north; Northern Ireland was established and a border with the south was now in place. There was much agonising among unionists about the abandonment of their brethren in the south, but not *too* much. Ulster unionists soon became very content with their snug demography and assured local majority.

The local minority – the nationalists/Catholics now trapped in the unionist statelet – were not. Trouble followed fast. In April 1920, nationalists gained possession of the Londonderry Corporation for the first time under a new and fairer electoral system that more accurately reflected political allegiances. Loyalists, fearing abandonment at the western margin of the new Northern Ireland and in a city so embedded in Protestant myth and memory, revived the local UVF. Intense sectarian rioting broke out. The UVF took control of the historic small city within the walls. The *Derry Journal* reported:

> *The Long Tower, an exclusively Catholic district, was kept for hours under a deadly fire from the City Walls ... At least three men were shot dead.*

Troops were deployed, which only made matters worse. They too fired into nationalist areas below the walls, killing six. Soon the trouble spread to Belfast, with its strong Protestant majority, and intensified. Catholics were hunted out of the shipyards. One recalled:

> *The gates were smashed down with sledges, the vests and shirts of those at work were torn open to see if the men were wearing any Catholic emblems, and woe betide any man who was.*

King George V and Queen Mary pass through the streets of Belfast when opening the Ulster parliament

Men were chucked in the harbour. Belfast plunged into outright inter-communal warfare. Catholic expulsions from workplaces continued, numbering over 10,000 men by one estimate. For the next two years, until early 1922, violence convulsed the new Northern Ireland. In March 1922, sixty-one people died in Belfast alone. All shades of nationalism from the IRA in the south – and its northern units – to the new Dáil administration in Dublin tried to subvert the new northern political entity. Meanwhile, internal violence escalated there and showed no signs of stopping.

The new Belfast administration replied with some of the most severe repressive measures anywhere in the world. A Special Powers Act effectively gave the Minister of Home Affairs *carte blanche* to do as he liked. The Royal Ulster Constabulary was formed out of the local remains of the RIC, augmented by a militia, the B Specials, who were little more than the UVF in uniform. There were elections to the new Belfast parliament in May 1921, predictably won by the Unionist Party, as was always intended. King George V, against the advice of his entourage, came to a disturbed Belfast to open the parliament in June and made a conciliatory speech.

Yet there were still more murders and disturbances. The IRA assassinated a Unionist MP. Internment without trial was introduced. But the violence and what was a virtual sectarian civil war raged on; it seemed beyond the control of any administration. And then suddenly, it stopped. The treaty split in the south was coming to a head.

Green against green

...

AT 4.29 A.M. ON the morning of 28 June 1922, the newly formed
National Army of the Irish Free State opened fire on the Four Courts,
recently invested and garrisoned by anti-treaty republican Irregulars,
with one of two eighteen-pound artillery pieces borrowed from
the British. These were the first shots in the Irish civil war, fought
between pro- and anti-treaty forces who had, until less than a year
earlier, been jointly fighting the British.

The basic question at issue was that, under the terms of the treaty,
Irish public representatives in the new dominion had to swear an
oath of allegiance to the British monarch. For the Irregulars, it was
too much – a betrayal of the republic proclaimed in 1916 to which
the IRA had sworn an oath. The pro-treaty position was that Ireland
now had effective independence from Britain. The occupation of the
Four Courts by Irregulars was regarded by Britain as a violation of
the treaty and the new provisional Dublin government was under
intense pressure from London to resolve the issue.

The field guns had been borrowed from the British army in
Marlborough Barracks in Dublin on 27 June. Major-General Emmet
Dalton of the Free State army had gone to the barracks to receive
them from the 17th battery, Royal Field Artillery, still stationed there
pending the final British evacuation. They were standard British
army eighteen-pounder QFs (quick-firing) and they soon made a
breach in the walls of the Four Courts. In little more than forty-eight
hours, the garrison's position became untenable.

Before evacuating the building, the Irregulars set fires, one of
which eventually reached the Public Record Office – housed since
1867 in a corner of the complex – and detonated a cache of gelignite

stored there. It caused a huge explosion, whose plume of smoke was seen rising all over the city. An eyewitness recorded:

> *Black as ink, shot up 400 feet into the sky, a giant column of writhing smoke and dust ... It spread into an enormous mushroom some 200 feet up and glared into the sun with lurid reds and browns, through which could be seen thousands of white snowflakes, dipping, sidling, curtsying, circling ...*

These were the ashen remains of priceless documents going back to the twelfth century.

The garrison surrendered and the fighting moved to Sackville Street, doing severe damage to the side of the street left relatively unscathed by the 1916 rising. Cathal Brugha – *le brave des braves* – emerged from the burning Hammam Hotel and fell mortally wounded in a hail of bullets. Limerick and Waterford cities quickly followed Dublin in yielding to the Free State army. Cork city followed on 11 August.

The explosion at the Four Courts during the Irish civil war, 1922

The next day, Arthur Griffith, president of the Dáil government, died suddenly of a stroke; he was only fifty-one. On 22 August, Michael Collins, the charismatic commander-in-chief of the Free State army and chairman of the provisional government established under the treaty, died in an ambush in west Cork. William T. Cosgrave now became head of the Free State administration and did not scruple to use draconian special powers against the remaining Irregulars. Prisoners were executed without trial in reprisal for Irregular actions; in all, there were seventy-seven such executions in the course of the civil war, something that the British could not even have contemplated, and the predictable source of generational bitterness thereafter.

By early 1923, it was clear that the Free State had won this nasty little war. The Irregulars were reduced to a regional rump in the south – the so-called 'Munster Republic'. But the region was taken from behind in a clever amphibious operation that landed Free State troops in Cork. Although well armed, the remaining Irregulars lacked public support, as one of their leaders explained to Liam Lynch, the Irregular commander:

> *Our principal weakness then is that we have lost by the opposition of the people, our cover, our sources and intelligence, our supplies, transport … The republican forces may have military successes, they cannot hope to beat the people.*

In the end, they did not even have the military successes. Lynch was killed in a fight in the Knockmealdown Mountains in Co. Waterford which was effectively the *coup de grâce*. On 24 May, the Irregular leadership issued a ceasefire order and allowed de Valera to publish this message: 'Military victory must be allowed to rest for the moment with those who have destroyed the Republic.'

The civil war was over, but the passions that had ignited it were not. De Valera now faced his wilderness years, imprisoned for a while by his former comrades and facing political oblivion. But Ireland had not heard the last of this serpentine, brilliant man.

The Irish Free State

...

KEVIN O'HIGGINS, THE Irish Free State's first home affairs minister and widely regarded as the hardest-working and most talented member of the new government, described its beginnings in memorable terms:

> We were simply eight young men ... standing amidst the ruins of one administration, with the foundations of the other not yet laid, and with wild men screaming through the key-hole. No police was functioning through the country, no system of justice was operating, the wheels of administration hung idle, battered out of recognition by the clash of rival jurisdictions.

In May 1923, a year after O'Higgins made this assessment, the Free State had won the civil war and established itself. The price was high: perhaps 4,000 dead; a debt of £17m; a further £30m in material destruction; a legacy of intense bitterness in a nation now divided. Yet Irish democracy survived. The Free Staters formed themselves into a political party, Cumann na nGaedheal (the Club of the Irish), and had the basic support of the small Labour Party, the Farmers' Party and some independents in the Dáil. Sinn Féin, although the second-largest party, refused to enter the Dáil because they would be obliged to take the hated oath of allegiance to the king.

The survival of Irish democracy – if only just – stood in stark contrast to post-imperial states in Europe, almost all of which succumbed to fascism of one sort or another. But de Valera, although now released from prison, chafed at the political impotence imposed upon him by Sinn Féin's policy of abstention from the Dáil. In 1926, he split Sinn Féin and formed a new political party, Fianna Fáil

(Soldiers of Destiny), which accepted the basic legitimacy of the Free State and eschewed violence, although still remaining staunchly republican.

In July 1927, there was a general election in which Fianna Fáil won forty-four seats, leaving the Sinn Féin rump with only five. Cosgrave's party won forty-seven, a paltry advantage which left it reliant on the support of smaller parties. Still, Fianna Fáil refused to take their seats. Then, on 10 July, republican radicals assassinated Kevin O'Higgins and forced everyone's hand. Cosgrave pushed through a bill obliging all future Dáil candidates to swear to take their seats if elected. De Valera agonised, but his desire for power overcame his scruples.

He promptly declared the oath to be 'an empty political formula', although one that had been worth a civil war five years earlier. On 11 August, Fianna Fáil deputies arrived at the Dáil in a body, revolvers bulging in their pockets. But there was no violence. When presented with the oath, de Valera – with Jesuitical cleverness – placed a sheet of blank paper over the text, signed it and told the clerk: 'Remember, I have signed no oath.'

Eamon de Valera and Fianna Fáil members outside Dáil Éireann (1927)

In 1932 the Northern Ireland parliament settled itself at Stormont, in solidly Protestant east Belfast. It is a large neo-Grecian pile set on rising ground in pleasant parkland. Seldom has a more exiguous assembly had a more ostentatious home. At that, the building was a pared-down version of an even more megalomaniacal complex which had to be abandoned because of the worldwide economic contraction that followed the Wall Street crash of 1929.

But these were locust years in Northern Ireland. The troubles of 1920–22 had polarised and embittered social, sectarian and political life. Catholics were approximately one-third of the population but were regarded by unionists as a subversive fifth column. There was little market for unionist moderation or accommodation. The government of Sir James Craig abolished proportional representation, which the British had urged on the new statelet, and returned to the securely majoritarian straight vote.

Nationalists refused to participate in the new regime, allowing unionists to gerrymander constituencies to their advantage. A Boundary Commission – the great hope of all nationalists – made only minimal and unimportant changes to the new border, thus securing the territorial integrity of the northern state. But these inter-war years were economically disastrous: heavy industry, the backbone of Ulster's success, started a decline accelerated by the economic crash and the resultant high levels of unemployment. Even before the crash, unemployment stood at more than 20 per cent.

Grass grew in the shipyards. Workman Clark, the 'wee yard', closed altogether in 1935. There were brief displays of inter-sectarian labour cooperation, but things soon reverted to the established pattern. Northern Ireland was a house divided.

Fianna Fáil in power

. . .

COSGRAVE'S GOVERNMENT WAS ORTHODOX and conservative. Its conservatism was a product of the Wyndham Land Act of 1903, which had effectively ended the landlord system by vesting ownership of the former tenancies in the tenants, turning them into owner-proprietors. This immediately created a conservative rural lower-middle class, who were the backbone of Cosgrave's party.

The one great spending project that the Cosgrave government did embark upon was the hydroelectricity generating scheme at Ardnacrusha, on the Shannon just north of Limerick. Built by the German engineering firm of Siemens-Schuckert, it was completed in 1929. Within ten years, it was supplying 87 per cent of the state's electricity requirements. Otherwise, the government adhered strictly to a tight-money, low-taxation economy with minimal welfare services. This conservatism suited both the new farming class and the ex-unionists, who were glad of the economic stability thus displayed.

Then came the Wall Street crash of 1929, followed by the greatest international depression of modern times. There was a general election in 1932 and despite Cosgrave's rather hysterical smearing of Fianna Fáil as 'reds' – communists, in a country where Marxism of any kind had practically no purchase – de Valera was elected at the head of a minority administration. The transfer of power was peaceful and orderly, extraordinary considering the rivals had fought each other in the civil war only ten years earlier. It was probably Cosgrave's finest achievement.

De Valera wasted no time in unpicking the terms of the 1921 treaty. He removed the oath of allegiance and reduced the office of governor-general to a cipher. A snap election in 1933 delivered him an overall majority, increasing his policy options. Domestically, he improved welfare payments slightly and subsidised public housing schemes. Most of all, he withheld payment of the land annuities, that is the loans repayable to London in respect of the sums advanced to the farmers under the Wyndham Act, funds that ultimately came from the Treasury.

This started the Economic War. The United Kingdom responded to the withholding of the annuities by slapping a 20 per cent tariff on two-thirds of the Free State's exports, 90 per cent of which went to the UK. De Valera retaliated by erecting a tariff wall, behind which he hoped that domestic Irish industry might flourish by import substitution. This conflict was driven by ideology, not by economics, and was not a battle of equals.

The policy caused great anguish among farmers, businessmen and workers, all of whom in one way or another were dependent on the British market. In opposition, an Army Comrades' Association – the Blueshirts, Ireland's tepid attempt at fascism – was formed under the clumsy leadership of Eoin O'Duffy, former head of the police, who had plotted a *coup d'état* to prevent de Valera's accession to power. To make matters worse, de Valera released a lot of IRA prisoners and the two sides faced off angrily. The IRA showed little gratitude for de Valera's gesture and showed open contempt for any public opinion not favourable to them. Nascent Irish democracy was in peril.

De Valera did a U-turn on the IRA following some especially unsavoury murders, re-imprisoning activists under the 1931 Public Safety Act and adopting other draconian powers. On the other side of the scale, he also introduced a new republican constitution which was ratified by referendum in late 1937 and which made a formal claim to the territory of Northern Ireland. He also ended the Economic War, although in this he was pushing an open door. Chamberlain's government in London, alarmed at the deteriorating security situation in Europe since Hitler's arrival in power in Germany in 1933, wished to mend fences in Ireland. For de Valera, the agreement of 1938 was a triumph: the UK dropped its retaliatory tariffs and Ireland – now officially Éire, a republic in all but name – settled the annuities question for a lump sum payment of £10m.

The Royal Navy gave up its three bases at Berehaven, Lough Swilly and Cóbh.

None of these developments were welcomed in Belfast. Inter-communal tensions mounted, not helped by the words of Cardinal MacRory of Armagh:

> The Protestant Church in Ireland – and the same is true of the Protestant Church anywhere else – is not only not the rightful representative of the early Irish Church, but it is not even a part of the Church of Christ.

Amid these rising tensions, there were vicious riots in Belfast in 1935 following the 12 July Orange parades, which flared for more than a month, ending only when the army was deployed. Eight Protestants and five Catholics died; over 2,000 Catholics were driven from their homes. Craigavon called a general election for 1938, which duly confirmed unionist dominance.

Europe stood on the brink of war. Once again, the two parts of Ireland were to go their separate ways.

Irish Blueshirts at the Bluebell cemetery, Dublin, 1934, with Eoin O'Duffy leading the salute

Emergency and Blitz

. . .

ON 3 SEPTEMBER 1939, Britain and France declared war on Germany, following Hitler's invasion of Poland. De Valera, now styled Taoiseach (prime minister), declared Éire neutral. He also secured special wartime powers for the duration of what was euphemistically called 'The Emergency'. Neutrality had massive public support, despite evidence of fatalities in Irish waters caused by the German navy.

Éire was ill-defended, however. The army had only 6,000 regulars, poorly trained and armed. By May 1940, that number had reached 13,500, still nowhere near enough to offer robust defence. However, at first, there seemed little direct threat from Germany, although copious evidence emerged in time of collaboration between elements in the IRA and the Germans, not to mention the presence – soon detected – of German agents in Éire.

The Magazine Fort in the Phoenix Park in Dublin was an army depot, raided successfully by an IRA party in December 1939 which made off with a considerable quantity of small arms and millions of rounds of ammunition.

In a moment that tested de Valera's neutral resolve to the utmost, the British offered a united Ireland in return for Éire joining the war effort. De Valera declined, on the telling ground that he doubted that London could secure 'the assent thereto of the government of Northern Ireland'. Besides, he doubted the sincerity of the British.

Éire practised a policy of neutrality which showed 'a certain consideration for Britain'. Irish army intelligence, under the leadership of the very able Colonel Dan Bryan, regularly sent weather reports to London and intercepted German communiqués. De Valera's government interned any German airmen who crash-landed in its territory while slipping British aviators back across the border.

More than 70,000 men and women from Éire joined the British war effort without any hindrance from the Irish government and won 780 decorations, including seven Victoria Crosses.

There was rigid censorship in support of neutrality. Even at the end of the conflict, news of the death camps was suppressed, and de Valera overplayed his hand by personally offering his condolences to Herr Hempel, the German ambassador, in an excess of diplomatic courtesy. Hempel was no Nazi: he was a diplomat of the old school, formal and correct, and de Valera admired him personally.

The experience of the war in Northern Ireland could hardly have been more different. Craigavon's unionist government, in continuous power for more than twenty years, was ageing and tired. The prime minister himself died in November 1940 and was succeeded by another of the old guard, J.M. Andrews, who proved no more energetic and was ousted in 1943 by a younger generation under Sir Basil Brooke. Their energy was needed, for Northern Ireland faced direct attack.

German reconnaissance had established that Belfast, still an important industrial hub in the British war effort, was poorly defended. So it proved when the Blitz reached it in April 1941. German bombers, predominantly Junkers 88s and Heinkel 111s, dropped 203 metric tons of bombs and 800 firebomb canisters. The city's telephone exchange was wrecked. The main force of the attack fell not directly on the shipyards but on poorly constructed working-class housing just to the north of the docks. Dublin sent fire engines to help the situation, but the water mains had also been damaged and the pressure was inadequate.

At least 900 people died, a rate of death relative to population exceeded in the UK only by London. The attacks continued in May, killing 191, a number that would have been higher had so many not already fled the city for the relative safety of the countryside. Ernst von Kuhren, a war correspondent, reported thus from one of the attacking planes:

> *When we approached the target at half-past two we stared silently into a sea of flames such as none of us had seen before ... In Belfast there was not a large number of conflagrations, but just one*

enormous conflagration which spread over the entire harbour and industrial area ... Here the English had concentrated an important part of their war industries because they felt themselves safe, far up in the North, safe from the blows of the German airforce. This has come to an end.

In time, the United States entered the war and used Northern Ireland as a base for the invasion of Normandy, with a presence of up to 300,000 men in the province. The war turned slowly against Germany after its fatal reverses on the eastern front. The Northern Ireland war economy recovered: Harland & Wolff launched almost

7,000 Admiralty and merchant ships in the final years of the war and repaired or converted over 30,000 vessels while manufacturing over 13 million aircraft parts, over 500 tanks and thousands of guns. The aircraft company Short & Harland completed 1,200 Stirling bombers and 125 Sunderland flying boats.

By VE Day in May 1945, Northern Ireland's mass unemployment of the inter-war years was a distant memory. It had made a belated but notable contribution to the victorious British war effort. Éire had remained studiously, if ambiguously, neutral. The two parts of the island were psychologically as far apart as ever.

Air raid on Dublin, 1 June 1941

Clann na Poblachta
and post-war Ireland

...

IN THE SOUTH, A new party, Clann na Poblachta (Family of the Republic) was formed at the end of the war. It was republican, to the left of Fianna Fáil, and largely composed of ex-anti-treaty IRA men plus a smattering of younger, reform-minded idealists. It spooked de Valera with its early successes in by-elections. Although he had a comfortable Dáil majority secured in 1944, he called another election in 1948 to forestall any further growth in Clann na Poblachta. He lost. To his considerable surprise, the entire anti-Fianna Fáil opposition – ranging from the Clann to ex-Blueshirts and everyone else – were able to cobble together a coalition and formed an inter-party government. The leader of the Clann, Seán MacBride, an ex-IRA chief of staff and son of one of the sixteen martyrs of 1916, became Minister for External Affairs.

John A. Costello of Fine Gael – the party that W.T. Cosgrave's political followers, plus some ex-Blueshirts, had evolved into – became Taoiseach. The leader of Fine Gael, Richard Mulcahy, was not acceptable to the Clann because of his deep involvement on the treaty side in the civil war. He had to be content with becoming Minister for Education.

The most dramatic development in the early days of the inter-party government was the repeal of the External Relations Act, which governed the country's ambiguous constitutional arrangement with the UK. In its place, a republic was formally declared and Éire became the Republic of Ireland in 1949. It declined to join the Commonwealth, suffering no penalty for this refusal. Likewise, it declined to join NATO, despite American pleading, because of the continuing British presence in Northern Ireland.

The inter-party government was largely composed of elderly and middle-aged men who had languished in opposition during the long sixteen years of the de Valera ascendancy, plus the energetic young reformers in the Clann. Of these, the most dynamic and conspicuous was Dr Noël Browne. Elected in the surprise victory of 1948, he was appointed Minister for Health on his first day in the Dáil, aged only thirty-two. He threw himself into a drive to wipe out tuberculosis, which was particularly lethal in the Republic, causing annually 124 deaths per 100,000 compared with 80 in Northern Ireland, 79 in Scotland and 62 in England and Wales.

Dr Noël Browne

Besides, for Browne it was personal. He had lost both parents and three of his sisters to the disease and it had left one of his brothers permanently disabled; he himself had contracted the disease while a medical student in Trinity but had recovered. He expanded sanatorium accommodation by employing the capital of the Irish Hospitals Sweepstakes – an international racket that later was forced to close – and introduced a mass vaccination programme. His enthusiasm was infectious. The county manager for Co. Roscommon recalled him thus:

> *He sprang up from his desk and hurried across the room, shaking my hand warmly, and thanked me for attending so early ... He then set me a deadline [to open a regional sanatorium]; June 30th. It was tough going ... I lost half a stone weight in the process, but it was a labour of love, because (I met him regularly at that time) he was so enthusiastic and appreciative and was obviously working so hard himself.*

The policy was a success and Browne now turned to what became famous as the Mother and Child Scheme. It resurrected an old Fianna Fáil public health policy which had met with the disapproval of the Catholic hierarchy as being an extension of the state into an area that, in its judgement, should be the preserve of the family. The most formidable and influential member of the hierarchy, John Charles McQuaid, the Archbishop of Dublin, led the opposition to the proposal, and de Valera quietly parked it. The Church had previously expressed doubts about the TB scheme, again on the grounds of improper projection of state power, but on this new issue, it left no doubt. The bill proposed to extend free but voluntary antenatal and postnatal state care for mothers and to give free medical care to all children up to the age of sixteen. The secretary to the hierarchy, James Staunton, stated the bishops' belief that the state

> *may help indigent or neglectful parents; it may not deprive 90 per cent of parents of their rights because of 10 per cent necessitous or negligent parents ... Education in regard to motherhood includes instruction in regard to sex relations, chastity and marriage. The state has no competence to give instruction in such matters ...*

The cabinet, mostly composed of observant and submissive Catholics, declined to support Browne in the face of this clerical hostility. Costello himself was conspicuous in this regard, although it was MacBride, Browne's party leader, who delivered the *coup de grâce* in 1951. Browne was forced to resign, sparking a long and agonised debate in the Republic about the proper relationship between church and state. The inter-party government did not long survive this shambles and de Valera returned to power.

The 1950s and the change of generations

. . .

THE TWENTY YEARS AFTER the war were the glory years of unionism. Northern Ireland emerged from the conflict bound ever closer to Britain. But there was a price: the extension of the new British welfare state to Ulster, which the unionist establishment, deeply Tory and reactionary in its social instincts, regarded with suspicion. In particular, the extension of the Butler Education Act of 1944 to Northern Ireland under its 1947 Education Act was hotly contested by both Protestant churches and the Catholic authorities. The former resented the abolition of compulsory Bible instruction in state schools; the latter preferred to retain the independence of its school system and insisted on separate education. All told, however, the act made free education available to the entire population.

The unionist hegemony continued. Lord Brookeborough, as Basil Brooke became in 1952, continued to enjoy comfortable majorities. Nationalists continued to rail against partition but to no avail. No London government, Labour or Conservative, was willing to compel Northern Ireland against the will of its local majority, a position given legislative form in the 1949 Ireland Act passed in response to the declaration of the republic in the south.

In 1956, the IRA revived, if rather feebly, and mounted a six-year, low-level 'border campaign' aimed at subverting the unionist province. It achieved nothing of substance.

If the 1950s were afterwards remembered in unionist Ulster nostalgically as a golden decade, they were a time of despondency in the Republic. Emigration continued at a frightening rate, not least among young, ill-educated men who went to England to work on the building sites in miserable conditions during the post-war rebuilding boom. Young women left as well, to take nursing jobs in the new National Health Service in Britain. They left behind a declining population with dangerously low marriage and reproduction rates: in a pattern constant since the Famine, the population fell continuously until the mid 1960s, when it recovered as the economy recovered.

Until then, the southern establishment seemed impotent in the face of this massive emigration, not to mention the miserable, unfulfilled society the emigrants left behind. Commissions sat and resolved nothing. The haemorrhage was particularly damaging in the poorer western counties, less so in wealthier farming areas such as Co. Kilkenny, where the mixed farming and dairy economy provided local employment. The emigration commissioners made one telling observation in their report of 1954, touching on female emigration:

> For the female emigrant, improvement in personal status is of no less importance than the higher wages and better conditions of employment abroad, and some of the evidence submitted to us would suggest that the prospect of better marriage opportunities is also an influence of some significance.

But it was almost as if the social disaster was willed. The southern economy, whether overseen by Fianna Fáil or a second, brief inter-party government (1954–7), remained doggedly orthodox behind its tariff barriers under successive ultra-orthodox ministers for finance, MacEntee of Fianna Fáil and Sweetman of Fine Gael. Only with the final retirement from active politics of de Valera in 1959 and the arrival in his place of Seán Lemass did real change come. Assisted by T.K. Whitaker, a brilliant civil servant, the new administration – buoyed by Lemass's advance of a new political generation and the gradual ousting of the old, abandoned protectionism – embraced free trade and foreign investment and joined *les trente glorieuses*, the huge international capitalist post-war boom. The results were spectacular and laid the basis for later social and economic advances while marking a distinct generational change.

June 1959 – Seán Lemass receives his seal of office from President de Valera

But until that happened, the shadow of the Mother and Child debacle hung over the Republic. The Catholic Church stood at the apogee of its moral monopoly and social influence. A nasty sectarian campaign in Fethard, Co. Wexford, arose in 1957 when the wife of a failed mixed marriage, a Protestant, took her two children to Northern Ireland and would only bring them back if the children could be brought up in the mother's faith. Local Protestant businesses were boycotted with the support of the local bishop – Staunton, he of the Mother and Child affair – although de Valera, still Taoiseach, to his credit publicly deplored and condemned the whole business.

It was all of a piece with the siege mentality that elevated the ferocious literary censorship of the time to its greatest extent, resulting in the outright banning of some of the leading literary writers of the twentieth century – although, interestingly, not James Joyce, perhaps thought too recherché for the populace. Both parts of Ireland, in their very different ways, looked inwards and were very satisfied with what they saw. But neither arrangement proved remotely durable and in the next ten years, both the Republic and Northern Ireland underwent a transformative change.

All change, all change

...

T.K. WHITAKER WAS thirty-nine when he was appointed secretary of the Department of Finance in Dublin. It was a surprising preferment for such a young man, especially as it meant overlooking candidates more senior in experience, but it proved to be inspired. In 1958, he presented to the government a paper prepared in collaboration with some close colleagues. It was entitled 'Economic Development'. In its opening section, he wrote of a prevailing vicious circle

> *of increasing emigration, resulting in a smaller domestic market depleted of initiative and skill, and reduced incentive, whether for Irishmen or foreigners, to undertake and organise the productive enterprises which alone can provide increased employment opportunities and higher living standards.*

His prescription was in essence simple. Protectionism and import duties would have to yield 'to active participation in a free-trading world'. Lemass, soon to be Taoiseach, welcomed the report, which was later elaborated into the First Programme for Economic Expansion. It proved astonishingly successful. Aiming for an annual target growth rate of 2 per cent, it actually achieved 4.5 per cent between 1959 and 1963. Net emigration began to fall, dropping from 44,427 in 1961 to 12,226 in 1963.

Lemass had been the architect of the siege economy in the 1930s. Now, in his sixties, he was applying the prescriptions of a talented new generation of public servants to unstitch and reverse these policies. An ideology that went back to Arthur Griffith finally yielded to economic reality so that, psychologically, the reforms took some political courage and vision. Inevitability, there were protests from those well satisfied with the old arrangements; they were overborne.

In Northern Ireland, it looked like business as before. In 1960, to enthusiastic crowds, the *Canberra* was launched in the Harland & Wolff yard, a 45,270-ton liner for P&O. Few realised that this was the end of an era, but it was. She was the last liner built in Belfast. Jet planes were transforming long-distance travel. Employment in the shipyard contracted thereafter, as order books went unfilled. Linen also declined, elbowed aside by cheap synthetic fibres from the Far East. Brookeborough's time was up; he had no answers and resigned in 1963, to be replaced by his minister for finance, Captain Terence O'Neill.

3 March 1961 – The new P&O liner *Canberra* is moved to a new berth at the Harland & Wolff Shipyard in Belfast

Like Lemass in the south, O'Neill relied upon talented modernising civil servants to halt the slide. They copied much of what Whitaker and his colleagues did, opening the northern economy to international investment. It worked, and multinational firms flowed in. O'Neill tried, somewhat clumsily, to ease traditional sectarian antagonisms by visiting Catholic institutions and meeting Cardinal Conway of Armagh, with whom he condoled on the death of Pope John XXIII. He also broke a huge taboo by inviting Lemass to come north for a meeting in Belfast.

Lemass jumped at the opportunity and came to Belfast in January 1965. O'Neill managed the visit badly in terms of politics by not telling his cabinet what he was doing until the very last moment, when Lemass was already en route. There was opposition within and without official unionism, and the world began to hear the name of Rev. Ian Paisley more and more. The Lemass visit was reciprocated: O'Neill came to Dublin. But his gestures of friendship were not matched – perhaps they could not be, given the persistence of old attitudes – by practical measures to reduce inter-communal inequalities. Discrimination on overtly sectarian lines continued, especially in the allocation of local authority housing.

Local government elections were not by universal equal suffrage, but by votes weighted quite consciously towards unionist interests; the Corporation in Derry – a Catholic city by population – was flagrantly gerrymandered. The city was also bypassed for the location of Ulster's new university. The Northern Ireland establishment, judiciary, higher civil service, business elite and so on remained overwhelmingly Protestant.

The 1947 Education Act took its time to mature but mature it did, producing the beginnings of a new Catholic middle class, less submissive than their elders and less inclined to put up with the sectarian status quo. A civil rights movement emerged, but it was met by a recrudescence of traditional Protestant opposition. Northern Ireland began its slide to disaster, while the Republic continued to prosper from the Lemass–Whitaker reforms. In that sense, the two parts of the island were once more drawing away from each other. When the northern Troubles broke out properly, they caused a huge tremor of surprise in the Republic, where an unmistakable element of complacency had set in, supposing things to be settling down in a Panglossian manner.

The early 1960s were a false dawn. Northern Ireland was about to descend into the long tragedy of the Troubles. The Republic was to enjoy a few more years of growth until the first oil shock of 1973 brought the international economy to a juddering halt and Ireland's economic renaissance with it.

Troubles

. . .

THE CIVIL RIGHTS MOVEMENT of the late 1960s changed the nature of the nationalist demand in Northern Ireland to seeking equality of rights with the rest of the UK rather than separation and unity, still the goal of republican diehards. A civil rights march in Derry on 5 October 1968 was banned by Belfast. When the ban was ignored, the march was batoned off the streets by an RUC force untrained for such a contingency. Television images went around the world, which woke up to Britain's backyard problem.

There followed some immediate reforms by London but also the gradual rallying of hardline unionism behind Rev. Ian Paisley. O'Neill, the prime minister, represented moderate unionism, but the situation quickly spiralled out of his control. A march by student radicals – People's Democracy – was ambushed and attacked near Derry by the RUC with local Paisleyite assistance; O'Neill was soon ousted, to be replaced by another 'big house' unionist, Chichester-Clark, who was no better.

Derry and Belfast exploded in inter-communal violence in August 1969, necessitating the deployment of the British army to try to restore order. Jack Lynch, now the Taoiseach, made an ambiguous speech to mollify his own Fianna Fáil hardliners in the Republic, but the party effectively split when a plot was discovered on the part of some of his cabinet to import arms for the renascent IRA in the north. The IRA's revival started as simple communal defence of nationalists in areas, especially in Belfast, which were under ferocious siege from superior and vengeful numbers. But soon, the old separatist demand reasserted itself.

The IRA and its political wing split. The Provisionals, who quickly eclipsed the quasi-Marxist Officials, re-established the centrality of the demand for Irish unity. On the unionist side, Paisley still had a long way to go to secure a majority of the Protestant vote but his influence – and his uncompromising sectarian rhetoric – was louder than ever.

The British army, having applied a sticking plaster to stanch the early communal wounds, now made a bad situation worse. It assumed a 'get tough' policy with nationalist demonstrators, and besieged the Belfast Catholic suburb of Ballymurphy for nearly a week in 1971, resulting in the deaths of eleven civilians. Its policy (witting or unwitting) of alienating the entire nationalist community reached a crescendo in January 1972 with the deaths of thirteen unarmed people on a civil rights march in Derry: Bloody Sunday.

In the meantime, Bernadette Devlin rose as the charismatic representative of radical nationalism, earning her stripes by doing time in jail for her activities in Derry in August 1969; the Social Democratic and Labour Party emerged as the voice of moderate nationalism; Chichester-Clark yielded to the bourgeois Brian Faulkner as prime minister of Northern Ireland; there were more institutional reforms, prompted by successive Labour and Tory governments in London; a non-sectarian Alliance party was formed to represent what there was of inter-communal moderation, unsurprisingly without conspicuous success; and the arms importers were tried in Dublin and acquitted, loading pressure on Lynch, which he survived.

Faulkner's government introduced internment without trial in 1971, a botched affair that completed the alienation of the entire nationalist community. The Provisional IRA grew in strength and acquired arms. In March 1972, Heath's Tory government in London had had enough; Stormont was prorogued – in effect, abolished – and direct rule instated. The IRA showed its teeth on 21 July 1972 by setting off twenty-six bombs in Belfast, killing eleven and injuring 130: Bloody Friday. A peace conference at Sunningdale, near London, involved Faulkner's moderate unionists, the Dublin and London governments and the Alliance Party. It created a new power-sharing executive in 1974, which soon collapsed under intransigent pressure from unionist ultras and Paisleyites, including a general strike.

After that, the 1970s were a catalogue of despair and horrors. There were hideous atrocities on both sides as Northern Ireland descended into a vortex of hopeless violence. There were miscarriages of justice in Britain as innocent men and women were fitted up for murders in Birmingham and Guildford committed by the Provisional IRA, the war now carried to 'the mainland'. In the Republic, the IRA murdered Lord Mountbatten, a senior member of the royal family, in 1979. Then, over the next two years, republican prisoners in Northern Ireland jails refused

to conform to prison rules, demanding special category status as political prisoners – culminating in the prison hunger strikes of 1981 which claimed the lives of ten men and inflamed communal passions further.

But the hunger strikes also showed republicans that their campaign needed more than military muscle. Their political wing, Sinn Féin – now reconstituted yet again – began its long march towards electoral capture of the nationalist community. That was visible in hindsight; contemporaneously, all seemed dark as the 1980s began.

Demonstrators run from tear gas during the Bloody Sunday riots, which broke out after British troops shot dead thirteen civilians during a civil rights march in Derry, 30 January 1972

The tide turns, slowly

. . .

ONE OF THE KEY moments in the Sinn Féin change of direction came in October 1981 at the party's ardfheis (conference) when Danny Morrison, one of the emerging leaders – along with Gerry Adams and Martin McGuinness – of the new, northern-orientated leadership, uttered the following words:

> *Who here really believes we can win the war through the ballot box? But will anyone here object if, with a ballot paper in one hand and the Armalite in the other, we take power in Ireland?*

It was a time of very raw emotion, with hunger strikers so recently dead and the final strikes abandoned. Two weeks later, Rev. Robert Bradford, an Ulster Unionist MP and a Methodist minister, was murdered by the IRA. Although the SDLP retained its electoral position as the principal voice of northern nationalism, Sinn Féin began to close the gap. By the middle of 1983, it had risen to 13.4 per cent of the vote, only 4.5 per cent behind the SDLP.

Although this was a low point for the SDLP, from which it soon recovered – at least for the next ten or fifteen years – the seeming surge of Sinn Féin troubled governments both in Dublin and London. The Taoiseach, Garret FitzGerald, began what he called a 'constitutional crusade' to reset the Irish political map. He created a New Ireland Forum, which finally produced three options, all of them rejected by Fianna Fáil under the leadership of the opportunistic Charles Haughey. More importantly, they were rejected out of hand by a peremptory Margaret Thatcher, the British prime minister, in tones of evident exasperation. The British government instead produced a plan for what it called 'rolling devolution'.

Although none of these initiatives led anywhere directly, they put some of the spotlight back on political initiatives, echoing Polonius's remark about 'by indirections find directions out'. In 1985, there followed the Anglo-Irish Agreement between FitzGerald and Thatcher. It copper-fastened direct rule for the moment, although giving Dublin a say in the internal affairs of Northern Ireland for the first time through the permanent presence of some Irish government officials at Maryfield, Co. Down, to give recognition to nationalist aspirations. The deal was bitterly opposed by all shades of unionism – over whose heads it was done – although the protests, while intense for a while, got nowhere.

The violence continued, culminating in the horrific bomb in Enniskillen, Co. Fermanagh, on Armistice Day 1987, killing eleven people watching the commemoration ceremony and injuring a further sixty-three, an atrocity that severely weakened support for the IRA. Sinn Féin reacted by slowly continuing its crawl towards politics. Talks between Gerry Adams and John Hume, the leader of the SDLP, led nowhere at first but once again took the spotlight off the gun. Eventually, in 1993, they produced a joint report which was met sceptically by both governments, not to mention the unionists.

But it led circuitously to the IRA ceasefire of 1994, which, while it only held until early 1996, was a harbinger of the future. New leaders in Dublin and London, Albert Reynolds of Fianna Fáil and the Tory John Major, established a warm personal relationship, which was new and helpful. The president of the United States, Bill Clinton, indicated his sympathetic interest and outraged the British and the unionists by permitting Gerry Adams to enter the US, from which he had previously been banned.

There was a reminder of older and more enduring Ulster realities in the second half of the 1990s in a series of loyalist protests at Drumcree church near Portadown over the contested route of an Orange Order parade. Nonetheless, the momentum was towards some sort of political fudge. This was achieved under yet further new leadership in Dublin and London in the persons of Bertie Ahern and Tony Blair. The American senator George Mitchell, Clinton's appointed umpire, showed the patience of Job in chairing a series of talks which included both governments and most Northern

Ireland parties – including, critically, the Ulster Unionists under the courageous leadership of David Trimble, previously regarded as a hardliner. The loyalist ultras led by Paisley denounced the proceedings as a betrayal.

Nevertheless, an agreement was eventually reached between the negotiating parties in Belfast on Good Friday 1998. There was to be a new Northern Ireland representative assembly, a revised Anglo-Irish agreement with power-sharing and with further north–south institutional structures, and a new British–Irish Council to connect the new structures to those in the rest of the United Kingdom. A referendum in the north endorsed the agreement by a narrow margin; in the south, it was embraced enthusiastically, with the constitutional claim to the territory of Northern Ireland abandoned.

It was not quite the end, but it was the beginning of the end, and 1998 is generally regarded as the moment when the Troubles ceased. There were aftershocks, of course, but by and large, that perception has held. Northern Ireland was one thing before Good Friday 1998, quite another – and better – after it.

The prime minister at the time, Tony Blair, and then-Taoiseach
Bertie Ahern sign the Good Friday Agreement

The Republic to the millennium

. . .

AFTER THE OPTIMISTIC UPWARD blip in the 1960s, in the population, the social economy and what turned out to be false hopes for progress in Northern Ireland, the Republic was badly affected by the two oil crises of the 1970s. They brought the south's recovery to a halt, the price paid for the opening of the economy to world trade.

The 1970s opened with the crisis of the arms trial, in which two cabinet ministers were arraigned and acquitted, along with two associates. It almost split Fianna Fáil, now under the leadership of Jack Lynch, asunder. Charles Haughey, the most powerful of the defendants, went into a kind of internal party exile only to make a spectacular comeback at the end of the decade. Lynch lost power in 1973 to a Fine Gael–Labour coalition but stormed back to victory four years later with a reckless giveaway manifesto which delivered him a record majority. It proved too good for his own good.

After 1977, the outgoing Taoiseach Liam Cosgrave resigned, to be succeeded as Fine Gael leader by the more social democratic Garret FitzGerald. Two years later, to most people's initial surprise, Haughey replaced Lynch as Fianna Fáil leader, preparing the ground for the series of see-saw political contests between the pair that dominated the 1980s. They were a stark clash of opposites: FitzGerald, a brilliant academic, was earnest while conveying an impression of unworldliness. No one ever thought that of Haughey, a gifted, corrupt political animal to his fingertips. He was a tragic figure who betrayed his own talents. Electorally, FitzGerald generally had the better of things in coalition with Labour until 1987, with the Anglo-Irish Agreement the highlight of their government.

Haughey returned in the latter year, in coalition – for the first time ever – with the small Progressive Democrat party, financially orthodox but socially liberal. Eventually, this government, driven on by the tough-minded Minister for Finance Ray McSharry, got a grip on the runaway economy and by a programme of austere orthodoxy prepared the ground for the transformation to come.

The Republic had some distinct advantages. Despite a haemorrhage of talented people in the despairing '80s, there remained a population that was young and Anglophone and well-educated – thanks to the scheme of free secondary education for all introduced back in 1968, probably the most enlightened decision in the history of the state and the great Lemass's finest legacy. Foreign direct investment, especially in pharmaceuticals and later in high tech, began to flow in. In less than a decade, the country was transformed from what had appeared to be a hopeless basket case to a boomtown economy. Social confidence rose giddily – too giddily, as it would transpire, with far too much of the new wealth coming from property speculation financed with borrowed money, a structure that would end in tears in the crash of 2008.

But in the meantime, it was good times on a scale for which the Irish population had no precedent. Inevitably, it went to the head. But there was much that was genuinely positive. Ryanair became a poster boy for the new Ireland. A small, loss-making airline on the edge of Europe grew in barely twenty years into the largest and most profitable such business in Europe, driving a transformation of the entire industry on a continental scale with a ruthlessly cost-cutting, low-fares, no-frills policy that seems normal now but was, like all these things, revolutionary in its day. Its young chief executive, Michael O'Leary, was a business iconoclast, breaking all the rules as when famously dealing thus with a complaining passenger:

> *You're not getting a refund so fuck off. We don't want to hear your sob stories. What part of 'no refund' don't you understand?*

None of this stopped Ryanair's astonishing advance. O'Leary was the most flamboyant and visible member of a new Irish entrepreneurial class. The economy was anchored in the country's enthusiastic membership of the European Union, but socially Ireland was ever more a big branch factory of the booming, post-Cold War American economy of the 1990s, prompting a famous rhetorical enquiry from Mary Harney, a leading politician, as to whether Ireland was closer to Boston than to Berlin. Economically, it aspired to Boston while desiring Berlin-style social benefits – but with a distinctly American aversion to the higher taxes required to fund these benefits.

The changing Dublin skyline

The great achievement of the late 1990s was the Good Friday Agreement in which the Fianna Fáil Taoiseach Bertie Ahern played a crucial role, one not always sufficiently acknowledged in Britain. Although the Celtic Tiger eventually imploded, it changed the Republic forever. It became a freebooting capitalist space, eschewing much in the way of social democracy – planning laws were lax and there was little in the way of coordinated public transport on the European model, for example – while politics remained resolutely local and populist. Viewed overall, even from the other side of the 2008 disaster, the years since the 1960s have been the most transformative in the country's modern history. The despair of the post-Famine generations – the relentless emigration, the sclerotic economy, the sluggishness of social mobility – is long gone from modern memory. There remained enormous problems, such as a church and state entanglement on issues including abortion and same-sex marriage, and economically, the question of affordable housing, but overall the national balance sheet as Ireland entered the new millennium was a positive one.

Epilogue

AN ISLAND ON THE north-western edge of the Eurasian landmass, Ireland had from the eighth millennium BC attracted successive waves of people advancing westwards to make it their home. Newcomers and their descendants brought in new technologies and ideas and in time mixed with the descendants of those who had arrived before them. The related cultures, from the English Pale in the east to the most remote Gaelic lordships, were all a product of importation and blending over the centuries. Until the end of the fifteenth century AD, Europeans were unaware that they could find fresh lands by venturing further west into the Atlantic. Then the age of exploration across the oceans began. The quickening of economic life in western Europe in the sixteenth and seventeenth centuries had much to do with the exploitation of overseas discoveries. The Elizabethan conquest of Ireland made the island a colonial opportunity for the British in the reign of James I, as much as Mexico and Peru were for the Spanish. In Ireland, this opportunity was ruthlessly exploited throughout the seventeenth century and beyond.

The tragedy was that the arrival of the 'New English' administrators and planters from across the Irish Sea coincided with the deadly struggle for supremacy between the supporters of the Reformation and the Counter-Reformation. A much greater blending of these newcomers and indigenous inhabitants occurred than is even realised or admitted today. Nevertheless, particularly in Ulster but in varying degrees across the whole island, conflict arising from religious division blighted the country's development for centuries.

By the late twentieth century, the memory of earlier convulsions and past wrongs was fading fast in the Republic. In Northern Ireland, however, the memory of previous dispossessions and bloodletting remained virulently alive. Here inter-communal suspicion and clashing aspirations, combined with institutional unfairness, plunged the region into chaos. A vibrant civil rights movement, inspired by direct action on the streets overseas, dissolved into sectarian conflict, bloodshed and destruction in 1969. Although troops were sent into Northern Ireland on active service that August, it was not until the spring of 1972 that London stood down Stormont to impose direct rule.

The restoration of devolution in 1974, with an administration in which unionists and nationalists shared power, lasted only a few months. A loyalist general strike brought about its collapse in May. Two more decades of savage bloodshed followed, on occasion spilling over into the Republic, Britain and the European mainland. The 'Troubles' in Northern Ireland became the longest-running conflict in Europe since the end of the Second World War. By the end of the millennium, a total of 3,651 men, women and children had lost their lives in Northern Ireland as a direct result of the violence.

The region turned a corner with the paramilitary ceasefires of the autumn of 1994. Certainly, hatred remained, demonstrated on occasion by further killings and paramilitary violence. Nevertheless, the 'peace process' was under way and a majority in Northern Ireland voted in favour of the Good Friday Agreement in 1998. Attempts to set up a power-sharing devolved administration with a realistic prospect of functioning for more than a few months succeeded best in May 2007 and, after a hiatus of more than a thousand days, again in January 2020.

The restoration of peace in the north was hastened in no small way by the transformation of the south. As long as the 'Free State' appeared to be poverty-stricken and priest-ridden, representatives of the northern majority had rarely felt the need to reconsider their position. At the same time, northern nationalists had to face the fact that, as the south cantered forward towards previously undreamed-of prosperity, Dublin governments quietly consigned to the dustbin the rhetoric of their predecessors on the urgent need to end partition.

By the middle of the twentieth century, it had become plain that a miserably weak economy and a falling population reduced by emigration in the Republic could no longer be blamed on British colonial misrule. Then, under Séan Lemass in the 1960s, a remarkable turnaround began. Multinational firms eagerly took advantage of inducements and the staged reduction in tariffs to set up in the Republic. Employment resulting from the influx of foreign capital not only soaked up large numbers leaving the farming sector but, in addition, virtually wiped out net emigration as a distinctive feature of Irish life. In 1972, 86 per cent of citizens voted in favour of joining the EEC. The Republic's successful application for membership provided an opportunity to widen export markets and benefit from the Community's support funds.

Many of the expected benefits of membership were postponed by the rise in oil prices and alarming fluctuations in the world economy. However, the creation of the Single Market in 1987 coincided with the start of a hectic economic expansion which was widely described as the 'Celtic Tiger'. Irish GDP rose by 36.6 per cent between 1987 and 1993 and by 2000 unemployment, which had reached 17 per cent in the mid-1980s, had fallen to 4.4 per cent. The OECD observed of the Republic in 1999: 'It is astonishing that a nation could have moved all the way from the back of the pack to a leading position within such a short period, not much more than a decade in fact.'

There is no doubt that without a determined drive to upgrade the state's education provision there would have been no Celtic Tiger. The vast majority of those who had exported themselves in the 1940s and 1950s had acquired no more than elementary education at national school and, without formal skills, tended to enter the British labour market on the lowest rung. Sweeping reform was launched by the celebrated announcement, made by Donogh O'Malley, Minister for Education, in September 1966 that the government would make free post-primary education to Intermediate certificate level available for all children in 'academic' secondary, vocational and comprehensive schools.

Meanwhile, Northern Ireland's economy was in a parlous condition. The eruption of violence from 1969 onwards frightened foreign investors away, and, in addition, the leap in oil prices in 1973–4 effectively killed off the briefly flourishing synthetic fibre industry. Yet in 1984 the average material living standard in Northern Ireland was still more than 25 per cent above the level of the Republic. How can this be explained? The answer is that massive financial transfers from the Treasury in London prevented a fall in living standards. As the private sector continued to shrivel, citizens depended to an extraordinary degree on employment in the public service. However, by 1995, living standards north and south were about equal. Then, as the Celtic Tiger began to roar, the Republic left Northern Ireland trailing further and further behind.

Between 1995 and 2005 the Republic's exports quadrupled, output increased by 350 per cent, and personal disposable income doubled. In 2004 the *Economist* concluded that Ireland's quality of life was the best in the world. Even before the world economic downturn of 2008, that assessment has to be treated with caution. Other western European states had an infrastructure – particularly in roads, public transport, health provision and the extension of broadband – which was vastly superior to the one the Republic possessed. In 2001 Ireland had the lowest number of acute hospital beds per capita in the EU, the highest rate of child poverty in the EU, and proportionally more people living in poverty than in any other industrialised country outside the United States.

Certainly, the hectic race towards greater prosperity had its downside. Beautiful riverscapes had been ruined by crude dredging in an economically questionable drive to improve farm drainage. Even loughs in areas of low population were bombarded by urban sewage and agricultural effluent, resulting in acute blooms of deadly blue-green algae – the citizens of Galway had for a time to endure a contaminated water supply from the state's largest lake, Lough Corrib. The abolition of domestic rates following Taoiseach Jack Lynch's electoral triumph in 1977 had left local authorities weak and badly funded for decades to come. The 'brown envelope' culture attached to planning permission proved difficult to eradicate and contributed to a proliferation of unsightly developments and ugly homes erected in the 'Irish hacienda' and 'Toblerone' styles.

In the twenty-six counties, democracy had survived a civil war and the threats posed by Blueshirts and IRA activists between the world wars. In the final decades of the twentieth century, it was imperilled again by financial corruption and the abuse of power. This was at the highest level: it emerged that Taoiseach Charles Haughey had been in receipt of very large payments for favours rendered. However, the corruption infecting political life did not spread to other institutions which played a key role in the development of the state, in particular the civil service and the judiciary. Life in Ireland had become incomparably better than it had been when Taoiseach Seán Lemass had shaken hands with Prime Minister Terence O'Neill in January 1965. The country experienced a remarkable social, cultural and economic transformation over a very short period of time.

Archbishop John Charles McQuaid in his 1971 Lenten pastoral had declared: 'Civil divorce is evil, and contraception is evil ... a curse upon the country'. By then, however, the Catholic Church's moral monopoly was already being eroded by secularisation and modernisation. Three years later, following the highly publicised 'contraception train' from Belfast, the Dáil made a hesitant first step by making birth control available on prescription. Eventually, all attempts to restrict availability were abandoned, and by 1991 the Republic was importing ten million condoms a year. Then followed a stream of revelations about the abuse of children by clergy and religious orders in industrial schools, Magdalene laundries and elsewhere. All this did much to diminish respect for the Church, particularly as members of the hierarchy were so hesitant in making apologies. Vocations dropped by nearly 100 per cent between 1966 and 1996, and between 1970 and 1995 the number of religious in the state declined by over a third. In 1990, 85 per cent of people attended church at least once a week, but just seven years later this was down to 65 per cent.

Civil divorce, rejected by two-thirds in the 1986 referendum, was accepted – admittedly by a tiny majority – ten years later. After the European Court of Human Rights ruled that Ireland's anti-gay laws contravened the 1988 European Convention on Human Rights, Dáil Éireann passed a Bill decriminalising homosexuality on 24 June 1993. Legislation on abortion rights proved more controversial. After concerns that laws prohibiting abortion could be found to be unconstitutional based on a right to privacy, the Eighth Amendment (Article 40.3.3) was added to the Constitution by referendum in 1983. A long campaign ensued to get rid of this amendment. Referendums in 1992 and 2002 failed to win support for change.

Then in 2012, Irish abortion law got worldwide attention on the death in Galway University Hospital of Savita Halappanavar, who had been denied an abortion while suffering a septic miscarriage. At a Citizens' Assembly in 2016–17 the constitutional and legislative provisions were discussed. Substantial reform was recommended and a referendum was called: by 66.4 to 33.6 per cent, the Eighth Amendment was voted down. New legislation in December 2018 brought in abortion services starting on 1 January 2019.

More than 62 per cent voted in a referendum on 22 May 2015 to legalise same-sex marriage and this became law in November. This made the Republic the first country in the world to legalise same-sex marriage through a popular vote. This sea change in opinion in the Republic was not matched in Northern Ireland. 'Northern Ireland you're next' declared a placard held up by a woman in Dublin celebrating the outcome of the May 2018 referendum. The region had not kept step-by-step with Westminster: same-sex marriage was not yet legal and Northern Ireland now had the strictest abortion laws in the UK. Between 2012 and 2015 the Northern Ireland Assembly voted no fewer than five times on same-sex marriage. Only on a fifth vote was it approved (albeit by a slender majority), but the dominant DUP (using a device known as a 'petition of concern') imposed its veto. The initiative passed to Westminster to bring the region into line with the rest of the UK. In July 2019 MPs voted for decriminalisation to take effect if a Northern Ireland Executive had not returned by 21 October. The Assembly did not return by that date and so same-sex marriage became legal on 13 January 2020.

North and south, broadcasters and the print media did much to create a more open, liberal and tolerant society. On RTÉ's *The Late Late Show,* Gay Byrne introduced for discussion topics previously considered taboo. Dermot Morgan and Gerry Stembridge on RTÉ radio satirised Haughey and other politicians with devastating effect in *Scrap Saturday*. Meanwhile, on BBC Radio Ulster David Dunseith vigorously challenged bigotry on *Talk Back*. A group of young lawyers-turned-comedians, calling themselves The Hole in the Wall Gang, lampooned Ulster stereotypes on *Talk Back* and in 1995 made a particularly effective attack on sectarianism in BBC

Northern Ireland's *Two Ceasefires and a Wedding*. Perhaps the most obvious outward and visible signs of an open society in the region were the fearless and penetrating BBC *Spotlight* investigations, and the popularity of often heated discussions on politics and a huge range of controversial topics on both radio and television, presented and chaired by trusted anchors William Crawley and Stephen Nolan.

The position of women in the workplace steadily improved, and growing numbers of women were appointed to public boards and promoted to senior positions in the civil service, the professions and the judiciary. The election of Mary Robinson, and then Mary McAleese, as President of Ireland, and Mary Harney as Tánaiste, would have astonished earlier generations. In Northern Ireland, the Women's Coalition and Sylvia Hermon demonstrated that change was possible, and eventually the DUP, Sinn Féin and Alliance were led respectively by Arlene Foster, Michelle O'Neill and Naomi Long.

Given the breathing space of real peace, Northern Ireland's economy for a time made a remarkable recovery in the wake of the Good Friday Agreement. Early in the new millennium levels of unemployment in the region had dropped to historically low levels. Visible signs of progress down the Lagan valley and into Belfast included the expansion of the Sprucefield complex south of Lisburn; the development of the Titanic Quarter as a financial centre, with Citibank leading the way; the transformation of a run-down part of Belfast City centre to become the 'Cathedral Quarter'; and the opening of the Victoria Centre in March 2008.

The Victoria Centre opened just as the global financial crisis was beginning to reap its terrible harvest. The Irish Republic was hit particularly hard: here light regulation, cronyism, loose ethics, gross corruption, wildly speculative property development and reckless financial incontinence brought with them the threat of imminent collapse. The government felt it had no choice but to guarantee the entire banking system, that is, €440 billion of bank liabilities. The guarantee ran out within a matter of months: locked out of the bond markets, the state was unable to borrow.

On 28 November 2008 agreement was made with 'the Troika' – the European Commission, the European Central Bank and the IMF – to extend to the Republic a bailout of €67.5 billion. In return, the government had to hand over control of its budget, a prescription for swingeing cutbacks for years to come. An *Irish Times* editorial in January 2010 observed: 'We have gone from the Celtic Tiger to an era of financial fear with the suddenness of a Titanic-style shipwreck, thrown from comfort, even luxury, into a cold sea of uncertainty'.

Ireland had been extraordinary because its entire economy after 2000 came to be driven by a property bubble. By 2006 construction accounted for 20 per cent of GDP, banks had dangerous exposures to construction and property concerns, and domestic wages had been driven up to uncompetitive levels. Property prices, after stabilising in 2007, fell dramatically to the year 2010. By the second quarter of 2010, house prices in Ireland had fallen by 35 per cent compared with the second quarter of 2007. David McWilliams, one of the few Irish economists who had warned of the crash to come, wrote on 13 November 2010: 'The case is clear: an economically challenged government, perniciously influenced by the interests of the housing lobby, blew it. The entire Irish episode will be studied internationally in years to come as an example of how not to do things.'

In the Republic, by 2014 the national debt had increased to 117 per cent of GDP due to the bailout of Irish banks, a deep recession which saw a 20 per cent drop in nominal tax revenues and continued weakness in economic growth. The effect of the economic and financial crisis lasted until 2014. The following year, with a growth rate of 6.7 per cent, did mark the beginning of a new period of strong growth. Nevertheless, the state's national debt that year totalled €203.2 billion, 76.7 per cent of GDP, and even though economic growth was sustained, the national debt burden remained heavy – on 17 May 2019 reckoned to be €47,638 per citizen. Though 'ghost estates' were still to be seen, especially in rural towns, alarmingly high property prices in Dublin and its environs signalled a thriving economy. The Republic of Ireland, with a population of nearly 4.8 million, had become a prosperous state, a net contributor to the EU's finances. Of course, dark clouds remained on the horizon. How much damage would result from the UK's exodus from the EU? Was the state over-reliant on the presence of American corporations such as Google? Would the EU force the government to alter its favourable corporation tax rate, thus discouraging overseas concerns from basing themselves in Ireland? Would Dublin governments have the courage to confront vested interests and tackle a grave housing crisis in the greater Dublin area?

In proportion, the impact of the global financial crisis was just as painful in Northern Ireland as in the Republic. And their recovery from 2014 onwards was barely detectable. Ballymena, which for some time gave every appearance of being a boomtown, suffered the closing down in succession of the JTI Gallaher tobacco factory, the Michelin tyre factory and Wrightbus (known for its London Boris buses and once employing 1,400 people). In Belfast the Harland & Wolff yard, which had not built a ship since 2003, went into administration in 2019; it was bought over at the eleventh hour but with employment available only to a tiny workforce. Bombardier, the region's largest manufacturing business, employing 4,000, regularly made significant numbers of its employees redundant, and its future remained uncertain, particularly when it announced plans to sell its aerostructures business. And many asked: would Brexit end its production of components for Airbus?

However, in 2019 manufacturing employment in Northern Ireland, with a population of 1.7 million, stood at around 88,000, the highest it had been since 2003. This accounted for about 11 per cent of employment in the region, at a time when it was just over 8 per cent for the United Kingdom as a whole. Here there was a move away from the domination of a handful of big employers towards smaller niche concerns. As Manufacturing NI chief executive Stephen Kelly explained: 'We no longer have behemoths, we don't have the huge companies. But we do have a raft of successful medium-sized ones and a huge amount of successful smaller companies'. The centre of gravity was moving out of greater Belfast. JW Kane, a machining company in Craigavon, created hundreds of high-value jobs when it was bought over by Singapore Airspace Manufacturing, a supplier of aerospace components. Between them, BE Aerospace in Kilkeel and Thompson Aero Seating in Portadown held around half of the global market for aircraft seats. Also in 2019, more than 40 per cent of global screening and crushing equipment for the mining industry was being made in mid-Ulster, principally by Terex, CDE and Maximus Screening. In the north-west, electronics company Seagate produced about a quarter of the world's read-write heads for computer disks. In 2019 Creative Composites in Lisburn had recently provided 132 jobs and the Dowds group in Ballymoney planned to hire up to seventy. Elsewhere, the creative and film industries were thriving; software and fintech demonstrated growth for companies such as First Derivatives, Allstate, PwC, Citibank and Deloitte. Assisted by the success of the Titanic Experience in Belfast, walking tours of Derry's walls and the encouragement given to HBO to use many Northern Ireland locations for *Game of Thrones*, tourism was thriving in the region more than ever before.

Though its political landscape remained depressingly tribalised, Northern Ireland was largely at peace during the first two decades of the new millennium. Stable devolved power-sharing arrangements proved difficult to bed in, however. A suspension of the Assembly from October 2002 lasted until May 2007, following alterations approved the previous year known as the St Andrews Agreement. Meanwhile, the DUP had displaced the UUP as the largest unionist party. As leader of the DUP, Ian Paisley, became First Minister and the leader of Sinn Féin, Martin McGuinness, Deputy First Minister, the two men bonded so well, smiling constantly, that they were dubbed 'The Chuckle Brothers'. Though Paisley stepped down in May 2008, being replaced by Peter Robinson, the Assembly functioned without interruption until the beginning of 2017.

Then came the 'ash for cash' scandal, dramatically exposed on a BBC *Spotlight* programme on 6 December 2016. This demonstrated that the Renewable Heat Incentive (RHI) as implemented in Northern Ireland effectively subsidised commercial heating boilers burning wood pellets or chips over and above the cost of the fuel. Despite a whistleblower having warned Arlene Foster (then the minister in charge) of RHI's grave shortcomings, the scheme was allowed to go ahead with a bungled subsidy which would cost the taxpayer around £500 million. Thirty-four days later McGuinness resigned in protest and the devolved government fell. Since the general election of December 2019 saw both Sinn Féin and the DUP lose their share of votes, the two parties were eager to restore the power-sharing executive to avoid the threat of an immediate Assembly election. The Assembly returned to work in January 2020. Members of the Assembly ensured that devolution had provided free prescriptions, low university fees and free travel for the retired: it remained to be seen whether or not they could agree to hard decisions about water charges, school amalgamations, rationalised health care provision and the like. Could they work towards easing community tensions to ensure that Northern Ireland would become a stable shared home place?

Even before the start of the new millennium the stereotypical view of a quaint island, as portrayed in such films as *The Quiet Man* and *Darby O'Gill and the Little People*, had been swept aside by (among others) Ryanair, which pioneered low-cost air travel; Riverdance, a troupe which captivated international audiences when Ireland hosted the Eurovision Song Contest; Bono and U2, and Van Morrison, who had good claim to be in the top tier of rock and rhythm-and-blues musicians; Paddy Moloney and The Chieftains, who brought Irish traditional music to a world stage; actors with international reputations, including Colin Farrell, Liam Neeson and Pierce Brosnan; and Séamus Heaney, who not only won the Nobel Prize for Literature but also became the world's best-selling living poet writing in English.

I conclude by recalling an incident which reminds me that for long we Irish have been more concerned about what divides us than what we have in common.

Nearly forty years ago, keen to catch fish in Lough Melvin, I launched a ten-foot flat-bottomed boat at Kinlough, Co. Leitrim. Soon a vicious westerly storm blew up and, unable to row back, I was in imminent danger of being swamped. My only hope was a small island ahead of me. I made it.

Then I realised that this was a place where cultures had met, clashed and blended. The island is an artificial one, a crannóg, constructed during the Iron Age. On it is the ruined castle of the McClancys where in 1588, in a snowstorm, the Armada castaway Francisco de Cuéllar and his men successfully resisted the English

Lord Deputy, Sir William Fitzwilliam. Looking behind me I could see a line of buoys across the lough marking the unlikely frontier between the Irish Republic and Northern Ireland.

Later I reflected that, in addition to arctic char and salmon, this lough is home to four distinct species of trout – sonaghan, gillaroo, ferox and brown trout. Though they spawn in the same rivers, they do not interbreed. In short, there is more genetic diversity in the trout of this medium-sized lake in the north west of Ireland than there is among all humans living on this earth.

Acknowledgements

ONLY AFTER THE LAST episode of the BBC series had been broadcast did I discover that the whole idea of relating the history of the island in numerous short episodes was that of Alison Finch, who subsequently produced all of the programmes. I am particularly grateful to Alison, who by a constant stream of queries worked unceasingly to ensure that listeners – and subsequently readers – who had no previous knowledge of Irish history would not encounter obscurities and unexplained terminology. The radio series is published as a download by BBC Audiobooks and is available at www.audible.co.uk.

My wife, Carol Tweedale, valiantly undertook the task of reading draft episodes to comment on how they might be received by the non-specialist, and her advice urging further clarification was not only deeply appreciated but, I have no doubt, proved vital. Sincere thanks are due to the following for many kindnesses, including drawing my attention to useful sources, reading some of the scripts, and giving me helpful comments as the episodes were broadcast: Colm Croker; Liam Kennedy; Fearghal McGarry; David Hayton; Brian M. Walker; Sean J. Connolly; Trevor Parkhill; the late Bill (W.H.) Crawford; Margaret O'Callaghan; Liviu Cotrau and Adrian Radu; Anne Devlin and Chris Parr; Medbh McGuckian; Victor and Maurice Blease; Douglas Carson; Patrick Speight and Bronagh Hinds; Isabella Evangelisti and Chris Hudson; Errol and Janice Steele; Carol and Richard Hawkins; Barbara and Kieran Fagan; Norbert and Margaret Bannon; Máire Neary; Rosemary McCreery; Jane Conroy and John Waddell; Nonie and Frank Murray; Paula and Oliver Boylan; Ann and Gerry Begley; V. Henry Bell; Babs McDade; John Waugh and Paul Weir; Sharon Rivers and Trevor Moore; Barbara and Peter Tame; Hilary, Pat and Lucy Donnelly; and Brian Lambkin and Kay Muhr. I am also grateful for the assistance of the staffs of the Public Record Office of Northern Ireland, the State Paper Office, the McClay Library in Queen's University, Belfast Central Library, the National Library and the Linen Hall Library.

Jonathan Bardon

Publisher's note

Jonathan Bardon died in 2020 having completed about 60 per cent of the work on this book. His former editor at Gill Books, Fergal Tobin, agreed to complete the adaptation of *A History of Ireland in 250 Episodes*, with the blessing of Jonathan's family. Sadly, Fergal died in February 2023. Fergal had finished working on the text, but the bibliography remains incomplete. We have reproduced the bibliography from *A History of Ireland in 250 Episodes* to provide a guide to some of the references and sources used in this book, however some sources are missing and others may be out of date. We ask for your understanding with this.

Selected bibliography

Adamson, Ian, *Bangor: Light of the World*, Bangor, 1979

Allingham, Hugh, *Translation of Captain Cuellar's Narrative of the Spanish Armada and his Adventures in Ireland, by Robert Crawford*, London, 1897

Bagwell, Richard, *Ireland Under the Tudors*, 3 vols, London, 1885–90

Bardon, Jonathan, *A History of Ulster*, Belfast, 1992

—— *Belfast: 1000 Years*, Belfast, 1985

—— *Dublin: One Thousand Years of Wood Quay*, Belfast, 1984

—— *Belfast: An Illustrated History*, Belfast, 1982

Byrne, F. J., *Irish Kings and High-Kings*, London, 1973

Cabot, David, *The New Naturalist: Ireland*, London, 1999

Calendar of State Papers, Henry VIII: Correspondence

Chambers, Anne, *Granuaile: The Life and Times of Grace O'Malley, c. 1530–1603*, Dublin & Colorado, 1998

Cosgrove, Art (ed.), *A New History of Ireland, II: Medieval Ireland, 1169–1534*, Oxford, 1987

Curtis, E., 'Unpublished Letters from Richard II in Ireland, 1394–5', *Proceedings of the Royal Irish Academy*, xxxviii (1927)

Dasent, G. W., *The Story of Burnt Njal* from the Icelandic of Njal's Saga, London, 1911

Docwra, Henry, 'A Narration of the Services done by the Army ymployed to Lough-Foyle', *Miscellany of the Celtic Society*, ed. John O'Donovan, Dublin, 1849

Dunlevy, Mairéad, *Dress in Ireland*, London, 1989

Ellis, Peter Berresford, *Hell or Connaught! The Cromwellian Colonisation of Ireland, 1652–1660*, Belfast, 2000

—— *The Boyne Water: The Battle of the Boyne, 1690*, Belfast, 1989

Ellis, S. G., *Tudor Ireland: Crown, Community and the Conflict of Cultures, 1470–1603*, London & New York, 1985

Fallon, Niall, *The Armada in Ireland*, London, 1978

Falls, Cyril, *Elizabeth's Irish Wars*, London, 1950

Freeman, A. Martin (ed.), *Annala Connacht: The Annals of Connacht* (AD 1224–1554), Dublin, 1983

Gantz, Jeffrey, *Early Irish Myths and Sagas*, Harmondsworth, 1981

Gillespie, Raymond, *Colonial Ulster: The Settlement of East Ulster 1600–1641*, Cork, 1985

Haddick-Flynn, Kevin, *Sarsfield and the Jacobites*, Cork, 2003

Harbison, Peter, *Pre-Christian Ireland*, London, 1988

Hayes-McCoy, G. A., *Irish Battles: A Military History of Ireland*, London, 1969

—— (ed.), *The Irish at War*, Cork, 1964

—— *Scots Mercenary Forces in Ireland, 1565–1603*, Dublin, 1937

Hill, George (ed.), *The Montgomery Manuscripts*, Belfast, 1869

Kelly, Maria, *A History of the Black Death in Ireland*, Dublin, 2001

Lennon, Colm, *Sixteenth-Century Ireland: The Incomplete Conquest*, Dublin, 1994

Lydon, James, (ed.), *England and Ireland in the Later Middle Ages*, Dublin, 1981

——'Richard II's Expeditions to Ireland', *Journal of the Royal Society of Antiquaries of Ireland*, xciii (1963)

Mac Niocaill, Gearóid, *Ireland before the Vikings*, Dublin, 1972

Macrory, Patrick, *The Siege of Derry*, London, 1980

Mallory, J. P., and T. E. McNeill, *The Archaeology of Ulster: From Colonization to Plantation*, Belfast, 1991

Marsh, Arnold, *Saint Patrick and his Writings*, Dublin, 1966

Maxwell, Constantia, *Irish History from Contemporary Sources (1509–1610)*, London, 1923

McCavitt, John, *The Flight of the Earls*, Dublin, 2005

McCorristine, Laurence, *The Revolt of Silken Thomas: A Challenge to Henry VIII*, Dublin, 1987

McNally, Robert (ed.), *Old Ireland*, Dublin, 1965

Moody, T. W., F. X. Martin and F. J. Byrne (eds), *A New History of Ireland, III: Early Modern Ireland, 1534–1691*, 2nd ed., Oxford, 1986

Moody, T. W., *The Londonderry Plantation, 1609–41*, Belfast, 1939

Moryson, Fynes, *An History of Ireland, from the year 1599 to 1603*, London, 1617; repr. Dublin, 1735

Murray, Robert H. (ed.), *The Journal of John Stevens ... 1689–1691*, Oxford, 1912

O'Connor, Frank, *A Book of Ireland*, London & Glasgow, 1959

Ó Corráin, Donncha, *Ireland before the Normans*, Dublin, 1972

Ó Cróinín, Dáibhí (ed.), *A New History of Ireland, I: Prehistoric and Early Ireland*, Oxford, 2005

O'Donovan, John (ed.), *Annála Ríoghachta Éireann: Annals of the Kingdom of Ireland by the Four Masters, from the Earliest Period to the year 1616*, 2nd ed., Dublin, 1856

O'Kelly, M. J., 'Excavations and Experiments in Ancient Irish Cooking-Places', *Journal of the Royal Society of Antiquaries of Ireland*, lxxxiv (1954)

O'Meara, John J. (trans.), *The History and Topography of Ireland: Gerald of Wales*, Harmondsworth, 1982

Orpen, Goddard H. (ed.), *The Song of Dermot and the Earl: an old French poem about the coming of the Normans to Ireland*, edited with a literal translation, Felinfach, 1994

Perceval-Maxwell, Michael, *The Scottish Migration to Ulster in the Reign of James I*, London & New York, 1973

Ranelagh, John, *Ireland: An Illustrated History*, London, 1981

Reid, J. S., *History of the Presbyterian Church in Ireland*, ed. W. D. Killen, 3 vols, Belfast, 1867

Robinson, Philip S., *The Plantation of Ulster: British Settlement in an Irish Landscape, 1600–1670*, Dublin & New York, 1984

Sayles, G. O., 'The Siege of Carrickfergus Castle, 1315–16', *Irish Historical Studies*, x, no. 37 (Mar. 1956)

Scott, A. B. and F. X. Martin (eds.), *Expugnatio Hibernica: The Conquest of Ireland by Giraldus Cambrensis*, edited with translation and historical notes, Dublin, 1978

Silke, John J., *Kinsale: The Spanish Intervention in Ireland at the End of the Elizabethan Wars*, Liverpool, 1970

Sténuit, Robert, *Treasures of the Armada*, Newton Abbot, 1972

Stevenson, David, *Scottish Covenanters & Irish Confederates: Scottish–Irish Relations in the Mid-Seventeenth Century*, Belfast, 1981

Story, George, *A True and Impartial History of the Most Material Occurrences in the Kingdom of Ireland during the Two Last Years*, London, 1691

Sweetman, H. S., and G. F. Handcock (eds), *Calendar of Documents relating to Ireland, 1171 –1307*, 5 vols, London, 1886

Todd, James H. (ed.), *Cogadh Gaedhel re Gallaibh: The War of the Gaedhil with the Gaill*, London, 1867

Viney, Michael, *Ireland: A Smithsonian Natural History*, Belfast, 2003

Waddell, John, *The Prehistoric Archaeology of Ireland*, Bray, 2000

Woodman, P. C., 'A Mesolithic Camp in Ireland', *Scientific American*, ccxlv (Aug. 1981)

Index

3rd West Cork brigade (IRA), 310
10th Division, British Army, 295
16th Division, British Army, 295
36th (Ulster) Division, British Army, 295, 297, 306

Abercorn, Earl of, 129, 131, 192
Abercrombie, Sir Ralph, 217
abortion, 347, 352–3
Achmutie, Alexander, 130–1
Achmutie, John, 130–1
Act of Settlement, 154, 212
Act of Union, 224–6, 239*ill*, 255
Act to Prevent the Further Growth of Popery (1704), 181, 187
Adair, Reverend Patrick, 157
Adams, Gerry, 342, 343
Address of Protestant Dissenting Ministers to the King, 191–2
Adrian IV, Pope, 50
áes dána, 26
Aethelfrith, 33
Affreca (daughter of Godred, King of Man), 51
Aghalane Castle, 132
Agricola, Gnaeus Julius, 19
Agricultural Revolution, 197
agriculture *see* farming
Ahern, Bertie, 343, 344*ill*, 347
Aidan, 33
Airbus, 356
Albert, Archduke, 120
alcohol, 16, 92, 202, 204
Alexander, Lord Mount, 159
Alexander, Sir William, 133
Alliance party, 339, 354
Allies, 295
Allstate, 357
Amboina, 178
American colonies, 190–2, 198, 199, 200, 206–8
American War of Independence, 209
Anabaptists, 157
Andrews, J.M., 325
Angles, 20, 32, 33
Anglo-Irish Agreement, 343, 345

Annals of Connacht, 62–3
Annals of Inishfallen, 54–5
Annals of the Four Masters, 73–4, 106–7, 111, 121
Annals of Ulster, 65
Anne, Queen, 180*ill*, 181, 183, 187, 189
Annegray, 34
Antrim, 8, 32, 51, 53, 55, 69, 122, 125, 134, 223
Antrim, Lord, 160
Aoife, 15
apprentice boys of Derry, 160, 163, 164*ill*
Ardagh Chalice, 30
Ardee, 60
Ardnacrusha, 321
Ards peninsula, 123
Argideen, x
Argyll, 32, 33
Argyll, Duke of, 189
Armada, 86–9, 93, 358–9
Armagh, 37, 125, 129, 145, 219, 223
Armagh, Archbishop of, 162, 191, 306
Armed Guard, 115
Armourers, 135
arms trial, 345
Armstrongs, 115
Army Comrades' Association, 322
Articlis to be contracted amongst the Societie of the Lewis, 132
Ash, Thomas, 163, 166
ash for cash scandal, 357–8
Asquith, Herbert Henry, 288, 297, 302, 312
Assembly Rooms, 202
Áth Cliath, 41
Athlone, 173–4, 175*ill*
Aughrim, Battle of, 175-6, 194
Austria, 213, 224
Auxiliaries, 310–11

B Specials, 314
badgers, 3
Bagenal, Beauchamp, 204
Bagenal, Sir Henry (Marshall), 100, 101, 102, 103
Baghdad Times, x

Baginbun, 44
baile, 28
bailey, 51
bainne clabair (bonnyclabber), 90
Baker, Major Henry, 163
Balbriggan, 310
Balfour, Arthur, 284
Balfour, Gerald, 283
Ballinasloe, 175
Ballinrees, 20
Ballitore, 220
ballybetaghs, 125
Ballycastle, 80
Ballymena, 269, 356
Ballymurphy, 339
Ballynahinch, 223
Ballyneety Castle, 171
Banagh, 131
Bangor, 34, 123
Bann, 4
Bannockburn, 60
Bantry Bay, 215, 224
Bardon, Captain James, x
Barrington, Sir Jonah, 202
Barry, Tom, 310
Battle of Aughrim, 175–6, 194
Battle of Benburb, 149–50
Battle of Bosworth, 73
Battle of Kinsale, 129
Battle of Naseby, 148*ill*
Battle of the Biscuits, 101
Battle of the Boyne, 168–70
Battle of the Somme, x
Battle of the Yellow Ford, 103, 124
Battys, 115
BBC
Northern Ireland, 353–4
    Radio Ulster, ix, 353
    Spotlight, 354, 357
BE Aerospace, 356–7
Beachy Head, 170
Bealtaine, 17
Beattie, Herbert, ix
Becket, Thomas, 49
Bedford Tower, 201
Belfast, 155, 188, 213, 238, 256, 257, 258, 259, 260*ill*, 261, 268–9, 270–1*ill*, 313–14, 323, 325–6, 335, 336, 338, 339, 354, 356

Belfast Castle, 82
Belfast Chamber of Commerce, 261
Belfast News-Letter, 257–8, 263
Belturbet, 188
Benburb, Battle of, 149–50
Bentinck, Hans Willem, 168
Beresford, Lord Thomas, 230
Beresford, Marcus, 201
Beresford family, 230
Bingham, Sir Richard, 98–9
Birmingham Six, 340
Biscuits, Battle of the, 101
Black and Tans, 310–11
Black Death, 63–7, 179
    see also bubonic plague
Blacksod Bay, 88
Blackwater Fort, 102, 103
Blasket Sound, 87
Blennerhasset, Anne, 145
Bliadhain an Áir (Year of the Slaughter), 195–6
Bliadhain an Áir (Year of the Slaughter), 195–6
Bliain an Áir, 249
Bligh, Captain William, 201
Bloody Friday, 339
Bloody Sunday, 293, 339, 340–1*ill*
Blount, Charles (Lord Mountjoy), 90, 104, 105, 106, 110, 111, 113
Blue Guards, 169
Blueshirts, 322, 323*ill*, 328, 351
Bobbio, 35
Bodley, Sir Josias, 91, 132
Boer War, x
Boland's Mills, 300
Boleyn, Anne, 75
Bombardier, 356
Bonamargy friary, 75
Bonaparte, Napoleon, 224
Bonar Law, Andrew, 289
bonnyclabber (*bainne clabair*), 90
Bono, 358
Book of Common Prayer, 77, 140, 141
Book of Durrow, 30, 33
Book of Kells, 30, 31*ill*, 33
Book of Kildare, 30
Book of Leinster, 37
The Book of the Taking of Ireland (Lebor Gabála Érenn), 15

Border Commission, 115
Borderers, 114–17
Boston News Letter, 190
Bosworth, Battle of, 73
Bothwell Brig, 158
Boulter, Hugh (Archbishop of Armagh), 191
Boundary Commission, 320
Boycott, Captain Charles, 265
Boylagh, 131
Boyle, John, 204
Boyne, Battle of the, 168–70
Bradford, Rev. Robert, 342
Breakspear, Nicholas (Pope Adrian IV), 50
Breen, Daniel, 309*ill*
Bregenz, 35
Brexit, 356
Brian Boru, 38–42
British Army, 295, 297, 306, 338, 339
British Empire, 200–1
British–Irish Council, 344
Britons, 32
Brixton Prison, 311
Brodar, King, 41
Broken Treaty, 177, 181
Bronze Age, 3, 6*ill*, 7*ill*, 11, 12
bronze-working, 12–13, 14
Brooke, Sir Basil (Lord Brookeborough), 129, 325, 331, 335
Brookeborough, Lord (Basil Brooke), 129, 325, 331, 335
Brosnan, Pierce, 358
Browne, Archbishop of Dublin, 76
Browne, Dr Noël, 329–30
Brownlow brothers, 129
Brú na Bóinne, 11*ill*
Bruce, Edward, 60–3, 68
Bruce, Robert (Earl of Carrick), 59, 60, 61
Brugha, Cathal, 316
Bryan, Dan, 324
bubonic plague, 154
    see also Black Death
Burgh, Lord Deputy Thomas, 102
Burke, Richard (Devil's Hook), 98
Burke, Risdeárd-an-Iarainn (Richard-the-Iron), 96, 98
Burke, Ulick MacWilliam, 77

Burley, Lord, 131
Burritt, Elihu, 251
Bush, John, 202
Butler, Edmund, 61
Butler, Piers, 74
Butler, R.A., 331
Butler Education Act (1944), 331
Butlers of Ormond, 73
Butt, Isaac, 263
by-elections
    Clare (1828), 232
    East Cavan (1918), 303
    East Clare (1917), 303
    Kilkenny city, (1918), 303
    Meath (1875), 263
    North Roscommon (1917), 303
    South Longford (1917), 303, 306
Byrne, Gay, 353

caiseal, 28
Caldwell, William, 208
Campion, Edmund, 89, 94
Canberra, 335
Cantrell & Cochrane, 261
Caravats, 228
Carew, Sir George, 107, 132
Carnfree, 25
Carnot, Lazare, 214–15
Carrick, Earl of *see* Bruce, Robert (Earl of Carrick)
Carrickfergus, 57, 82, 105, 124, 155, 167, 169*ill*
Carrickfergus Castle, 52, 55, 61, 71, 82, 105, 122, 123*ill*
Carrick-on-Shannon, 195
Carrowmore complex, 9
Carson, Sir Edward, 289, 290*ill*
Carton, 203
Casement, Roger, 300, 302
Cassels, Richard, 203
Castle Balfour, 132
Castle Coole, 203–4
Castlecaulfield, 142
Castleknock, 154
Castlereagh, 123, 226
Castletown, 203
Cathach, 29
cathair, 28
Cathedral Quarter, 354

Catherine of Aragon, 75
Catholic Association, 229–30, 231*ill*
Catholic Church, 22–4, 32, 75–6, 77, 137, 147, 154, 181, 183, 184, 227, 228, 231, 254, 255, 275, 293, 298, 306, 330, 331, 333, 352
Catholic Emancipation, 214, 224, 226, 227, 229, 230, 232, 235, 236
Catholic Rent, 230
cattle, 3, 8, 17, 90, 91, 131, 194, 197, 210
Caulfield, James, 201
Cavan, 125, 144, 312
CDE, 357
Celestine, Pope, 20
celibacy, 75
Celtic Tiger, 347, 350, 351, 355
Celts, 12, 13–18, 30, 33
Central Powers, 295
cereals, 5, 8, 9, 90
Cessair, 15
Chalmont, Charles (Marquis de Saint-Ruth), 173–6
Chamberlain, Joseph, 322
Charlemagne, 36
Charlemont, 142
Charlemont House, 201
Charles I, King, 139, 140, 147, 151
Charles II, King, 155, 156*ill*, 157, 158–9
Charles V, Emperor, 73, 74
Chesterfield, Lord, 202
Chichester, Sir Arthur, 104–5, 112, 113, 115–16, 119, 121, 122, 129, 131
Chichester-Clark, James, 338, 339
child abuse, 352
Christ Church, 42
Christianity
    break with Roman Church, 75–6
    early Irish church, 22–4, 32
    high crosses, 30
    manuscripts, 29–30
    Saint Patrick, 20–3
Church of England, 186, 255
Church of Ireland, 128, 140, 157, 158, 183, 185, 186, 188, 226, 228, 236, 255
Church of Scotland, 186
Churchill, Lord Randolph, 267
Churchill, Winston, 267, 307
Ciarán, 23
Citibank, 354, 357

Citizens' Assembly, 353
City Swordbearer, 135
civil rights, 336, 338, 340–1*ill*, 348–9
civil war, 148, 150, 255, 260, 307, 314, 315–17, 318, 328, 351
Clann na Poblachta, 328, 329
Clare by-election (1828), 232
Clare Island, 87, 153
Clarke, Margaret, 145
Clarke, Tom, 294, 299
Clarke, William, 144
clerical abuse, 352
Clew Bay, 2, 56, 98, 99
Clifden, 281
Clinton, Bill, 343
Clonmacnoise, 24
Clonmacnoise Cathedral, 22*ill*, 23
Clonmel, 152
Clontarf, 238–9, 242
Clontarf, Battle of, 41–2
Clontibret, 101
clothing, 93–5
clotted milk, 90
Clotworthy, Captain Hugh, 124
Clotworthy, Lady, 157
Clotworthys, 198
Clyn, Friar, 64–5, 67
Cogadh Gaedhel re Gallaibh (Wars of Irish with Foreigners), 35
Cole, Sir William, 145
Colemanstown, 67
Coleraine, 125, 134
Collins, Michael, 302, 310, 311, 317
Colmcille (Columba), 29, 32, 33
Columba (Colmcille), 29, 32, 33
Comber Letter, 159–60
Commission for Defective Titles, 140
Commonwealth, 328
Composition of Connacht, 98
Conall mac Comgaill, 33
Confederation of Kilkenny, 148, 149–50
Confessio, 20
Congested Districts Board, 280–1
Congress of Vienna, 242
Connacht, 56, 57, 96–9, 154, 237
Connaught Telegraph, 264, 265
Connolly, James, 299, 300
Connor, 61
Conolly, William, 203, 205

conscription, 298, 302, 306
Conservative Party, 154, 268, 272, 280,
    289, 297, 312, 339, 343
constitution, 277–8, 322, 352, 353
contraception, 352
Conway, Cardinal of Armagh, 336
Conway, Sir Fulke, 124
Cooke, Dr Henry, 238, 256–7, 258
Cooke, Edward, 225, 226
copper mining, 11
Cordwainers, 134–5
Cork, 57, 71, 250*ill*, 251, 316
Cork Examiner, 249
Corn Laws, 245
Cornwallis, Viceroy,, 226
Corporation (Derry), 336
Cosgrave, Liam, 345
Cosgrave, W.T., 303, 317, 319, 321, 328
Costello, John A., 328, 330
Counter-Reformation, 137, 348
counties, 56
court cairns, 9
Cox, Sir Richard, 195
Craig, James (1st Viscount Craigavon),
    289, 320, 323, 325
Craig, Sir James, 131
Craigavon, Viscount (James Craig),
    289, 320, 323, 325
crannógs, 27, 28, 358
Cranston, Sir William, 115
Crawley, William, 354
Creative Composites, 357
Crom Castle, 132
Cromwell, Oliver, 150–2, 154–5, 157, 159
Cross of Cong, 30
Cruachain (Rathcroghan), 17
Cullen, Paul (Archbishop of Dublin),
    254
Culmore, 166
Cumann na nGaedheal, 318
Cummins, Nicholas, 249–50
Cunningham family, 129
Custom House, 200*ill*

Dagda, 15
Dáil Éireann, 201
Dál Cais, 38
Dál Fiatach, 51
Dál Riata, 32, 33

Dalton, Major-General Emmet, 315
Dalway, Ensign John, 124
Daly, James, 264
Dalyell, Colonel Tam, 155
Darby O'Gill, 358
Davis, Thomas, 242
Davitt, Michael, 264
de Beaumont, Gustave, 240
de Bermingham, John, 62
de Braose, Matilda, 55
de Braose, William (Lord of Limerick),
    53–4, 55
de Burgo, Elizabeth, 59, 60, 70
de Burgo, Richard (Red Earl), 56, 57–8,
    59, 60, 61
de Burgo, William (Brown Earl), 70
de Cobos, Don Alonso, 102
de Cogan, Milo, 46, 47–8, 51
de Cogan, Richard, 48
de Córdoba, Don Luis, 87
de Courcy, John, 51, 53, 57
de Cuéllar, Captain Francisco, 88, 89,
    93, 358–9
de Ginkel, Baron (Godard van Reede),
    168, 172–7, 181
de Lacy, Hugh (Earl of Ulster), 50–2, 53,
    54, 55, 57, 61
de Latocnaye, Chevalier, 203–4
de Leiva de Rioja, Don Alonso
    Martínez, 88
de Luzon, Don Alonso, 87–8
de Mendoza, Don Pedro, 87
de Montmorency, Hervey, 44
de Pointis, Marquis, 165
de Prendergast, Maurice, 44
de Riddlesford, Walter, 48
de Saint-Valéry, Matilda, 54
de Saukville, Jordan, 55
de Valera, Éamon, 300, 302, 303, 306,
    310, 311, 317, 318–19, 321–2, 324, 325,
    328, 329, 330, 332, 333
de Verdons, 57
de Zubiaur, Don Pedro, 107
Declaration of Independence, 308
deer, 3
Defenders, 214, 216, 217, 218, 219, 228
Defoe, Daniel, 187–8
del Águila, Don Juan, 105–6, 107
Deloitte, 357

Democratic Unionist Party (DUP) *see* DUP
Denny, Lady, 87
Derry, 121, 134, 142, 160, 162–7, 169, 258, 269, 306, 312–13, 336, 338, 339, 340–1*ill*, 357
see also Londonderry
Derry Corporation, 336
Derry Journal, 313
Derrynaflan, 30
Devereux, Walter, 82, 84
Devlin, Bernadette, 339
Dillon, John, 273, 288
direct rule, 235, 339, 343, 349
Disraeli, Benjamin, 263, 272
Dissenters, 275
divorce, 75, 274, 352
Dobbs, Arthur, 208
Docwra, Sir Henry, 104, 112
Doe Castle, 148
dóer, 27
dolmens, 9–10
Donaghadee, 124
Donegal, 2, 116, 121, 134, 312
Donegal friary, 75
donjon, 52
Dowds, 357
Down, 122, 123, 124, 125, 223
Downhill, 204
Dowris, 12–13
Dowth, 10
Drake, Francis, 84
Drapers, 135
Drennan, William, 217
Drogheda, 57, 64, 65, 147, 152, 153*ill*, 159, 168
Drumcree crisis, ix, 343
drumlins, 2
Drummond, Thomas, 235–6
Dubh Linn (black pool), 37
Dubhgall's Bridge, 41, 48
Dublin, 37–8, 39–40, 46, 47–8, 49, 57, 61, 64, 201–2, 239, 291–4, 316, 325, 326–7*ill*, 347*ill*
Dublin, Archbishop of, 186, 190–1, 330, 352
Dublin, Archibishop of, 73, 76, 254
Dublin Castle, 37, 55–6, 59*ill*, 74, 81, 87, 98, 100, 142, 201, 214, 255

Dublin Corporation, 214, 291
Dublin Employers' Federation, 292
Dublin Lockout, x
Dublin Metropolitan Police, x, 310
Dublin Militia, 221
Dublin United Tramway Company, 292
Duffy, George Gavan, 286
Dulace Castle, 130*ill*
dún, 28
Dun, Thomas, 62
Dún Ailinne, 17
Dún an Óir (fort of gold), 85
Dunbar, Gavin, 114–15
Dundalk, 57, 60, 61, 62, 63, 64, 71, 147, 167, 168
Dundas, James, 137
Dundrum Castle, 55
Dungannon, 142
Dungannon Clubs, 286
Dungannon Convention of the Volunteers, 286
Dunluce, 80
Dunraven, Lord, 284
Dunseith, David, 353
Dunseverick, 80
DUP, 353, 354, 357, 358

Eagle Wing, 141
East Cavan by-election (1918), 303
East Clare by-election (1917), 303
Easter Rising, 272, 279, 285, 297, 298, 299–303, 306
Economic Development, 334
Economic War, 322
Economist, 351
education, 331, 346, 350
Education Act (1944), 331
Education Act (1947), 331, 336
Edward I, King, 57–8, 60
Edward II, King, 59, 60, 62
Edward VI, King, x, 77
Eighth Amendment (Article 40.3.3), Constitution, 352–3
Elizabeth I, Queen, 77, 78, 79, 80, 81, 82, 83*ill*, 84, 92, 97*ill*, 99, 103, 104, 112, 113, 114, 120, 125
Elliots, 115
Emain Macha (Navan Fort), 14, 17
Emancipation Bill, 233

The Emergency, 324
emigration, 198, 240, 251, 279, 280, 331–2, 334, 346, 347, 349, 350
Emmet, Robert, 227
English Civil War, 148, 150
English Nonconformists, 275
Enniscorthy, 221, 223
Enniskillen, 142, 167, 343
Enniskillen Castle, 100
Erne, Lord, 265
eskers, 2
Essex, Earl of, 104
Established Church *see* Church of Ireland
European Central Bank, 354–5
European Commission, 354–5
European Convention on Human Rights (1988), 352
European Court of Human Rights, 352
European Union, 346, 350
Eurovision Song Contest, 358
External Relations Act, 328
Eyre, John, 204

Falls of Belfast, 208
famines, 61, 62–3, 112–13, 178–9, 195–6, 235
 see also Irish Potato Famine
Fanad, 104
Farmers' Party, 318
farming, 5, 8, 9, 10, 28, 86, 90, 197, 241, 263, 321, 332, 350
Farrell, Colin, 358
Faughart, 62
Faulkner, Brian, 339
Fenians, 253–4, 255, 264, 266, 272, 278, 280, 282, 285, 294, 299
Ferguson, Mr, 157
Fermanagh, 100, 116, 117, 125, 132, 145, 307
Fethard, 333
Fews, 219
Fianna Fáil, 318–19, 321–2, 328, 330, 332, 338, 342, 343, 345, 347
financial crisis (2008), 346, 347, 351, 354–5, 356
Fine Gael, 328, 332, 345
Fine Gall, 38
Finnian, 23, 33

Fionn, 16*ill*
Fir Bolg, 15
First Dáil, 308, 309, 310, 311, 312
First Derivatives, 357
First Home Rule Bill (1886), 272, 273
First Programme for Economic Expansion, 334
First World War *see* World War I
fish, 3
Fishmongers, 134, 135
Fishmongers' Company, 164
Fitton, Sir Edward, 98
fitz Gerald, Raymond 'le Gros,' 44, 48
fitz Godebert, Richard (of Rhos), 44
fitz Stephen, Robert, 44
FitzGerald, Garret, 342, 343, 345
FitzGerald, Garret Mór (Earl of Kildare), 73
FitzGerald, Garret Óg (Earl of Kildare), 73
FitzGerald, Gerald, 84, 85
Fitzgerald, James, 201
FitzGerald, James FitzMaurice, 84–5
Fitzgerald, Lord Edward, 220, 283
FitzGerald, Maurice, 57
Fitzgerald, Robert, 203
FitzGerald, Silken Thomas (Earl of Kildare), 72*ill*, 73–4, 76
Fitzgibbon, John (Black Jack), 211–12, 225, 226
Fitzharding, Robert, 43
Fitzwilliam, Earl, 214
Fitzwilliam, Lord (of Meryon), 202
Fitzwilliam, Sir William, 78, 87, 100, 360
Fitzwilliam Street, 202
flaxseed, 197–9, 206–7, 256
Fletcher, Andrew, 179
flints, 4–5, 6*ill*, 8
Fomorians, 15
Foster, Arlene, 354, 357
Four Courts, x, 315–16
Fourth Home Rule Act, 312
'the Fox,' 52
Franciscans, 75, 137
Free State, 315, 316, 317, 318–19, 322, 349
free trade, 210, 245, 248, 332, 334, 335–6
Freeman's Journal, 263, 273
French, Lord, 310

French Revolution, 211, 213, 216, 219, 223
friaries, 75
Froissart, 70
Frongoch, 302

G Division, Dublin Metropolitan Police, 310
Gaelic Athletic Association (GAA), 279–80
Gaelic language, 32, 33, 70, 115, 209, 249, 279–80
Gaelic League, 279–80, 288
Gaels, 15
Gall, 35
gallóglaigh (gallowglasses), 68–9, 79–80
Galway, 57, 71, 351
Galway University Hospital, 353
Game of Thrones, 357
Gardiner, Luke, 202, 221
Gardiner Street, 202
gay, 352
general elections
   (1880), 265
   (1885), 267, 268
   (1918), 306
   (1944), 328
   (2019), 358
General Post Office (GPO), x, 300, 302
Geoffrey (son of Henry II), 53
Georg, Prince (of Darmstadt), 168
George, Captain, 165
George, Elector of Hanover *see* George I, King
George I, King, 189
George III, King, 211, 212, 214, 225, 227, 229
George IV, King, 211, 233
George V, King, 313*ill*, 314
Gerald of Wales, 30, 44, 47, 48, 53
German Plot, 310
Gilbert, Sir Humphrey, 84
Gilli, Earl, 42
Girona, 88
Gladstone, William, 255, 262–3, 266, 267, 275, 276*ill*, 277, 280, 288
Glenconkeyne, 134
Glenshesk, 81
glib, 94

global financial crisis (2008), 346, 347, 351, 354–5, 356
Godred, King of Man, 51
Goldsmiths, 134–5
gold-working, 12, 14*ill*
Good Friday Agreement, 344, 347, 349, 354
Google, 356
Gormflaith, 39
Gorteenreagh, 12
Government of Ireland Act (1920), 312
GPO, x, 300, 302
Grahams, 115
Grattan, Henry, 211, 212
Grattan's Parliament, 211, 212, 225
Great Clare Find, 12
Great Famine *see* Potato Famine
Great Frost, 194–6
Great War *see* World War I
Greg, John, 208
Gregory XIII, Pope, 84, 85
Greville, 227
Grey, Leonard (Lord Deputy), 74, 85
Grey Friars, 74
Griffith, Arthur, 285, 286, 287*ill*, 303, 311, 317, 334
Grocers, 135
Guildford Four, 340
Gustav Adolph, King, 137

Haberdashers, 135
Hag's Castle, 98
Halappanavar, Savita, 353
Halloween, 17
Hamilton, Richard, 165
Hamilton, Sir James, 123, 124
Hammam Hotel, 316
Hanna, Rev. Hugh, 269
hares, 1*ill*, 3
Harland, Edward, 259–60
Harland & Wolff, 259–61, 326–7, 335, 356
Harney, Mary, 347, 354
Harold, King, 43
Hasculf, Earl, 46, 47, 48
Haughey, Charles, 342, 345–6, 351–2, 353
HBO, 357
Healy, Timothy, 273, 277
Heaney, Séamus, 358
Heath, Ted, 339

Hebrides, 32, 39, 68, 124, 132
Hekla, 178
Hempel, Herr, 325
Henry II, King, 43–4, 49–50, 53
Henry III, King, 55, 57
Henry VI, King, 71
Henry VII, King (Henry Tudor), 73
Henry VIII, King, 73, 74, 75, 77
Hen's Castle, 96
Herder, Johann Gottfried, 242
Hermon, Sylvia, 354
Hervey, Frederick, 204
Hickson, Robert, 259
high crosses, 30
High Tories, 187
    see also Conservative Party
Highland Light Infantry, 269
Hill, Sir Moses, 124
Hitler, Adolf, 322
Hoche, 215
Hogan, Michael (Galloping), 171
The Hole in the Wall Gang, 353–4
Holmes, George, 166
Holywood, 123
Home, Alexander, 116
Home, Sir John, 116
home rule, 263, 264, 265, 266, 267, 268,
    270, 272, 277, 278, 280, 286, 288–90,
    293–4, 295, 297, 307
Home Rule Act (Ireland) (1914), 290
Home Rule Bills, 267, 268, 272, 280,
    288–9
homosexuality, 352
horses, 14
Howth, 37, 64
Huguenots, 167, 168, 175, 186, 197
Hume, John, 343
Hume, Sir Gustavus, 203
hunger strikes, 340–1, 342
hunter-gatherers, 5
Hyde, Douglas, 279–80, 281ill

ice age, 1–3
Iceland, 34
Ill Week, 114
Imbolg, 17
IMF (International Monetary Fund),
    355
Imperial Hotel, 293

Industrial Revolution, 238, 240–1, 256–
    61, 291
Ingram, John Kells, 243
Inishbofin, 153
Inishturk, 153
Inniskillingers, 167
Insurrection Act, 216
internment, 314, 339
Invincibles, 266
Iona, 30, 33, 34
IRA, 310, 311, 314, 315, 322, 324, 328, 331,
    338–9, 340, 342, 343, 351
    see also Provisional IRA
Iraq, x
Ireland Act (1949), 331
Ireton, Henry, 152
Irish Citizen Army, 293–4, 299
Irish Constabulary, 235
Irish Convention, 307
Irish Council, 103, 136
Irish Great Council, 70
Irish Hospitals Sweepstakes, 329
Irish House of Commons, 203, 214
Irish Independent, 292
Irish Land League, 266ill
Irish language see Gaelic language
Irish National Literary Society, 279,
    280
Irish National Volunteers, 295, 297
Irish Party, 275, 282–3, 285, 286, 288,
    302, 303, 306
Irish Potato Famine, 196, 244–53, 258,
    272
Irish Republican Brotherhood, 253, 254,
    294, 299, 300
Irish Revolution, 272
Irish Times, 355
Irish Transport and General Workers'
    Union, 292, 299
Irish Volunteers, 209–11, 290, 293–4,
    295, 297, 300
Irishtown, 264
Ironsides, 152
Irregulars, 315–16, 317
Isabel, Infanta, 120
Isabella (daughter of Richard fitz
    Gilbert de Clare), 57
Islamic Turkish Empire, 186
Ivar the Boneless, 37

Jackson, John, 11
Jacobites, 163, 165, 167, 168–9, 170–5, 176, 181, 184, 189
Jacob's Biscuit factory, 302
Jaffe Centre, ix
James I, King, 113, 115, 119, 120, 121, 122, 124–5, 128–9, 131, 132, 133, 136, 140, 147, 183, 348
James II, King, 159, 160–3, 164, 165, 167, 169–70, 181, 183
James III, King, 189
John, King, 53–5, 57
John of Athy, 62
John of Desmond, Sir, 84
John of Salisbury, 50
John the Wode, 47, 48
John XXIII, Pope, 336
Johnston, Major-General Henry, 221
Johnstons, 115
Joyce, James, 274, 278, 333
Joyces, 96
JTI Gallaher, 356
Jugendstil, 259
Jutes, 20
JW Kane, 356

Kelly, Stephen, 356
Kettle, Tom, 297
Kilkenny, 57, 64, 65, 150, 236
Kilkenny city by-election (1918), 303
Killybegs, 88, 102
Kilroot, 185
Kilwarden, Lord, 227
Kilwarlin Wood, 146
King, William (Archbishop of Dublin), 186, 190–1
kings, 25–8, 36, 38, 50, 53
Kinsale, 105–6, 107–10, 111, 124, 129
Kirk of Scotland, 140
Kirke, Major-General Percy, 166
Kitchener, Lord, 295
Knocklayd, 80
Knowth, 10
Knox, Andrew, 137
Knox, John, 140
Knox family, 201

La Bague, 44

La Bonne, 44
La Tène, 14
La Trinidad Valencera, 87–8
Labour Party, 318, 345
Lagan valley, 256, 257, 259, 354
Laggan district, 190
Lake, General Gerard, 216, 217, 218*ill*, 223
Lancaster, Duke of, 71
land annuities, 284, 322
Land League, 264
land reform, 262, 263–5, 266, 266*ill*, 284, 321
Langford, Captain Roger, 124
Lanyon, H.O., 261
Larkin, James, 291–2, 293, 294, 299
Larkin, Jim, x
The Late Late Show, 353
Laud Annals, 61–2
Lavia, 88
Lawrence, Colonel Richard, 154
Leadbetter, Mary, 220
The Leader, 287
Lebor Gabála Érenn (*The Book of the Taking of Ireland*), 15
Ledwidge, Francis, 297
Leinster, 17, 39, 41, 43, 44, 47, 48, 50, 57, 70, 73, 217, 237
Leinster House, 201
Leitrim, 88
Leix, 77
Lemass, Seán, 332–3, 334, 336, 346, 349, 352
Leslie, Henry, 140, 141
Lewis, 132
Lia Fáil (Stone of Destiny), 17
Liberal Party, 263, 266, 268, 273, 274, 275, 277, 278, 280, 286, 288, 297, 312
Liberty Hall, 300
Liffey, 201
Limerick, 38, 57, 171, 173*ill*, 176–7, 194, 316
   see also Treaty of Limerick
Limerick, Treaty of, 177, 181, 183
Lindisfarne, 33
Linen Hall, 198
linen industry, 197–9, 201, 207, 256–7, 259, 261, 335
lios, 28

Lir, 15
Lisburn, 142
literacy, 206, 280
The Little Book on English Policy, 71
The Little People, 358
Livingston, John, 141
Lloyd George, David, 288, 297, 298, 311, 312
Local Government (Ireland) Act (1898), 283
London Companies, 192
Londonderry, 134, 135, 190, 198, 204
    see also Derry
Londonderry Corporation, 312–13
Long, Naomi, 354
Lough Corrib, 351
Lough Foyle, 104
Lough Key, 56–7
Lough Melvin, 358
Lough Neagh, 5, 37, 55, 105, 194, 205
Loughbrickland, 146
Loughinsholin, 134
Loughrea castle, 57
Loughros More Bay, 88
Louis XIV, King, 160, 162, 169, 170, 173, 181, 186
Loveday, John, 204
Lowry-Corry, Armar, 203
loyalism, 221, 265, 269, 289, 313, 343, 344, 349
    see also unionism
Lug the Long-Handed, 15, 17
Lughnasa, 17
Lundy, Lieutenant-Colonel Robert, 163
Lurgan, 142
Lynch, Jack, 338, 339, 345, 351
Lynch, Liam, 317

Mac Aodhagáin, Conor, 67
Mac Aodhagáin, Hugh, 67
mac Dubhghaill, Alexander, 69
MacBride, Seán, 328, 330
MacCabes, 69
MacCarthy, Dermot (King of Desmond), 51, 77
MacCarthy, Lieutenant-General Justin, 167
MacCarthys, 107
MacClancys, 88

MacCurtain, Tomás, 310–11
MacDermott, Seán, 299
MacDonleavy, Rory, 51
MacDonnell, Alexander, 183
MacDonnell, James, 80
MacDonnell, Randal, 157
MacDonnell, Sir Randal Arannach MacSorley, 124
MacDonnell, Sorley Boy, 80, 81
MacDonnells, 69, 80, 84, 88
MacDowells, 69
MacEntee, Seán, 332
Mackie's, 261
MacMahon, Hugh (Bishop of Clogher), 184
MacMahon, Hugh Roe, 100
MacMurrough, Aoife, 44, 46
MacMurrough, Dermot, 43–7, 49*ill*
MacMurrough, Murtagh, 47, 48
MacMurrough-Kavanagh, Art, 69, 70
MacNeill, Eoin, 279, 297, 300
MacQuillan, Rory, 75
MacRory, Cardinal, 323
MacRorys, 69
MacSheehys, 69
MacSweeneys, 69, 81, 104, 119, 121
Máel Mórda, 38, 39, 41
Magazine Fort, 324
Magdalene nurseries, 352
Magennis, Sir Conn, 142
Magennises, 138, 157
Maguire, Conor, 142
Maguire, Cúchonnacht, 120, 121
Maguire, Hugh, 100, 101
Maguires, 145
Major, John, 343
Mallory, J.P., 3
mammals, 3
Manannán mac Lir, 15
Manchester Martyrs, 255
mantles, 93–4, 95*ill*
Manufacturing NI, 356
manuscripts, 29–30
Mar, Earl of, 189
Markievicz, Countess, 293
Marlborough Barracks, 315
Marsh, Dr Jeremiah, 188
Marshal, William (William the Marshall), 57

Mary, Queen (wife of King George V), 313*ill*

Mary, Queen (wife of William of Orange), 160, 161*ill*

Mary I, Queen of England and Ireland, 76*ill*, 77

Matchett, Ellen, 145

Mathew, Fr Theobald, 245

Maximus Screening, 357

Maxwell, Sir John, 302

Maynooth Castle, 74

Mazzini, 242

McAleese, Mary, 354

McBride, John, 188

McClancys, 358

McClelland, Sir Robert, 131, 135

McGuinness, Joe, 303, 306

McGuinness, Martin, 342, 357

McManus, Terence Bellew, 254

McQuaid, John Charles (Archbishop of Dublin), 330, 352

McSharry, Ray, 346

McSwiney, Terence, 311

McWilliams, David, 355

Meagher, Thomas Francis, 254

Meath by-election (1875), 263

Meath Militia, 221

Medbh, 15

megalithic monuments, 9–11

Mellifont Abbey, 113

Merrion Square, 202

Mesolithic humans, 5

metalworking, 11, 14, 17, 26, 28, 30

Metropolitan Police, 235

Michelin, 356

Míl, 15

Military Council (IRB), 294, 299, 300

Military Services Act, 306

Mitchell, George, 343–4

Moate, 195

Monaghan, 100, 125, 312

Monasterboice, 24

monasteries, 23–4, 29, 30, 33, 34, 35, 75

Monea Castle, 132

Monro, Major-General Robert, 146, 149–50

Monroe, James, 214–15

Montgomery, George, 137

Montgomery, Lord, 155

Montgomery, Sir Hugh, 122, 123, 124

Mooghaun hill fort, 12

Moore, Frank Frankfort, 269

Moore, Sir Garret, 113

Moran, D.P., 287

Morgan, Dermot, 353

Mormaer of Mar, 41

Morrison, Danny, 342

Mortimer, Roger, 70

Moryson, Fynes, 90, 91, 92, 112–13

Mosse, Dr Bartholomew, 202

Mother and Child Scheme, 330, 333

motte castles, 51

Mount Gabriel, 11

Mount Sandel, 4–5

Mount Street Bridge, 300

Mountbatten, Lord, 340

Mountjoy, 142

Mountjoy (ship), 166, 167

Mountjoy, Lord Deputy *see* Blount, Charles (Lord Mountjoy)

Mountjoy Square, 202

Moylurg, 65

Mulcahy, Richard, 328

Mulholland, 256

Municipal Gallery of Modern Art, 201

Munster, 84–5, 86, 228, 236, 237

Munster Plantation, 103

Munster Republic, 317

Munsterian Ice Age, 2

Murchad, 39, 41

Murphy, Fr John, 221

Murphy, Johnny, x

Murphy, William Martin, 292–3

Murrisk and Achill Island, 56

Mussenden, Bateson and Company of Belfast, 208

Naseby, Battle of, 148*ill*

Nassau, Count Henry, 168

The Nation, 242, 243

National Covenant, 141, 146, 158

national schools, 235

NATO, 328

Neeson, Liam, 358

nemed, 27

Neolithic humans, 8, 9, 10

neutrality, World War II, 324–5, 327

New Departure, 264, 282

New English, 348
New Ireland Forum, 342
New Ross, 57, 221, 223
Newgrange, 10
Newry, 142, 146
Newtownards, 123
Newtownbutler, 167
Nine Years War, 100–2, 121
Njal's Saga, 42
Nolan, Stephen, 354
Normandy, 43, 49, 53, 57, 326
Normans, 25, 42–51, 53, 57, 63, 70, 72, 96, 123*ill*, 147, 239
North, Lord, 210
North Cork Militia, 221
North Roscommon by-election (1917), 303
Northern Ireland, 255, 312–14, 320, 322, 324, 325, 326–7, 328, 329, 331, 333, 335–45, 348–9, 350–1, 353, 354, 356–8
Northern Ireland Assembly, 353, 357, 358
Northland House, 201
Norwich, Bishop of, 55
Nuestre Señora de la Rosa, 87

oath of allegiance, 315, 318, 319, 321–2
Oath of Supremacy, 128
oats, 90
O'Boyles, 119
O'Brien, Conor, 74
O'Brien, Conor Cruise, 276–7
O'Brien, Donal (King of Thomond), 51
O'Brien, Murrough, 77
O'Cahan, Lord, 95
O'Cahan, Manus Roe, 144
O'Cahans, 121
O'Carroll, from Ulster, 48
Ochiltree, Earl of, 129
Ó Cianáin, Tadhg, 120, 121
O'Connell, Daniel, 226–30, 232, 233, 235, 236, 237–9, 242, 243, 251, 253, 256, 263, 272
O'Connell, Seán, 154
O'Connell Street, x
O'Connor, Cathal Crobhderg, 54, 55, 56, 57
O'Connor, Finola, 75
O'Connor, Murchad, 51

O'Connor, Rory, 43, 44, 46, 47, 48, 50, 51, 54
O'Connors, 77
O'Dempseys, 77
O'Doherty, Sir Cahir, 121
O'Dohertys, 88
O'Donnell (Lordship of Tír Conaill), 69
O'Donnell, Calvagh, 78, 79
O'Donnell, Catherine, 78
O'Donnell, Red Hugh, 100, 101, 102, 104, 105, 106–10, 111–12, 119
O'Donnell, Rory, 113, 119
O'Donnells, 29, 81, 90
O'Donnells (Tír Conaill), 78
O'Driscolls, 107
O'Duffy, Eoin, 322, 323*ill*
OECD, 350
Offaly, 77
O'Flaherty, Donal, 96
O'Flahertys, 56, 71
Ó Gráda, Cormac, 252
O'Hanlons, 121
O'Higgins, Kevin, 318, 319
oil crises, 337, 343, 344*ill*, 345, 350
O'Kelly, James, 303
O'Kelly, Professor Michael, 10
Old English, 147, 148
Old Pretender, 189
O'Leary, Michael, 346
O'Mahony, John, 253, 254
O'Malley, Donogh, 350
O'Malley, Gráinne (Granuaile), 96–9
O'Malleys, 56, 87
O'More, Rory, 201
O'Mores, 73, 77
O'Neill, Conn Bacach, 74, 77, 78, 120
O'Neill, Conn (Lord of Castlereagh), 138
O'Neill, Conn MacNeill, 122–3
O'Neill, Gordon, 175
O'Neill, Hugh, 100–2, 103, 104, 105, 106–10, 111–12, 113, 119–21, 137
O'Neill, Lady, 123, 205
O'Neill, Matthew, 78
O'Neill, Michelle, 354
O'Neill, Owen Roe, 148, 149–50
O'Neill, Shane, 78–82, 90
O'Neill, Sir Brian McPhelim, 82

O'Neill, Sir Phelim, 138, 142, 144, 154, 157
O'Neill, Terence, 335–6, 338, 352
O'Neills, 112
O'Neills (Clandeboye), 78
Orange Order, 214, 217, 219, 226, 228, 343
Orchard County, 129
O'Reilly, Philip, 144
O'Reillys, 144
Ormonde, Earl of, 102
O'Rourke, Cathal, 65
O'Rourke, Matthew, 65
O'Rourke, Tiernan (King of Bréifne), 43, 44, 48, 50–1
O'Rourkes, 88
Orr, William, 216–17
O'Shea, Captain William, 272, 274
O'Shea, Katherine, 273, 274, 278
Ostia, 121
Ó Súilleabháin, Eoghan Rua, 209
O'Sullivans, 107
Oswald, 33
O'Toole, Laurence, 46
Oulart Hill, 221

Paddy Moloney and The Chieftains, 358
Page, Kathleen, ix
Paintstainers, 135
Paisley, Rev. Ian, 336, 338, 339, 344, 357
Palaeolithic humans, 5
Pale, 71, 78, 100, 147, 348
Palladius Patricius, 20
The Parallel; or Persecution the Shortest Way to prevent the Growth of Popery in Ireland, 187–8
Parnell, Charles Stewart, 262*ill*, 263, 264–5, 266, 267, 268, 272–9, 282–3, 285, 288, 303
Parnell Square, 202
partition, 287, 311, 312, 331, 349
passage tombs, 9, 10, 11*ill*
Passchendaele, 298
Patrick, Saint, 20–3
Paulet, Sir George, 121
Peace Preservation Force, 235
Pearce, Edward Lovett, 201
Pearse, Patrick, 299, 300
Peel, Robert, 232–3, 235, 237, 244, 245

Peep o' Day Boys, 218
Penal Laws, 181–3, 189, 224
People's Democracy, 338
Petty, Dr William, 153–4
Philadelphia, 206, 207, 208
Philip II, King of Spain, 86, 88, 102
Philip III, King of Spain, 105, 112, 120
Philip of Spain, King, 77
Phillips, Sir Thomas, 134
The Philosophy of Irish-Ireland, 287
Phoenix Park, 266, 273–4, 324
Phoenix Society of Skibbereen, 255
Phytophthora Infestans, 244, 252
Picts, 20, 32, 33
pitchcapping, 220, 222*ill*
Pitt, William (the Younger), 214, 224, 225, 227
Pius V, Pope, 120
Plantation of Munster, 86
Plantation of Ulster, 115–16, 122–36, 137–8, 139, 144, 155, 169, 184–5, 190, 256
Plunkett, George Noble, 303
Plunkett, Joseph Mary, 299, 303
Poag, John, 208
poets (*filí*), 25–6
Poor Law, 196
Poor Law Act (1838), 237
Pope Adrian IV, 50
Pope Celestine, 20
Pope Gregory XIII, 84, 85
Pope John XXIII, 336
Pope Pius V, 120
porcellanite, 8
Portadown, 144, 269
portal tombs, 9–10
A Portrait of the Artist as a Young Man, 274–5
potato blight, 244–52, 263
Potato Famine, 196, 244–52, 258, 272
potatoes, 194, 240, 241, 244–52
Powel, Samuel, 206–7
Powerscourt House, 201
Presbyterianism, 140–1, 157–8, 184–6, 187–9, 190, 191–2, 206, 211, 213, 237, 258
Price, Elizabeth, 145
Prince of the Asturias, 102
Prince of Wales, 208

Prince of Wales (later George IV), 211
Printed Book, 125
Proclamation of the Republic, 300, 301*ill*
Progressive Democrats, 346
property speculation, 346, 354, 355
Protestant Ascendancy, 193
Protestantism, 137, 138, 140, 151, 186, 188, 201–2, 214, 242, 261, 268, 271, 323, 331, 333, 336
Provisional IRA, 338–9, 340
    see also IRA
Prussia, 213, 224
Prussia, King of, 227
Public Record Office, 315–16
Public Safety Act (1931), 322
Pue's Occurrences, 194
Purcell, Richard, 194
PwC, 357
Pynnar, Captain Nicholas, 132–3

Quakers (Society of Friends), 250–1
quarters, 125
Queen Mab, 15
Queen Maeve's tomb, 9
Queen's Colleges, 242
Queen's Island, 259
The Quiet Man, 358

Radio Ulster, ix, 353
Ragnall, 37
Raleigh, Walter, 86
rapparees, 172–3
ráth, 28
Rathcroghan (Cruachain), 17
Rathfarnham, 151
Rathlin Island, 35, 60, 84
Rathmore, 60
Raymond 'le Gros' fitz Gerald, 44, 48
redemptioners, 208
Redmond, John, 283, 288, 289, 295–6, 297, 302
Redmond, William, 297, 303
Redshanks, 160
Reformation, 76, 77, 84, 140, 348
Reginald's Tower, 46
regium donum, 158
Renewable Heat Incentive, 357
Republic of Ireland, 328

Reynolds, Albert, 343
Ribbonmen, 228
Richard fitz Gilbert de Clare (Strongbow), 44–5, 46–7, 48, 49, 50, 57
Richard fitz Godebert of Rhos, 44
Richard II, King, 70–1
Richard the Lionheart, 53
Richmond Penitentiary, 239
ring forts, 28
riots, 248, 258, 268–9, 270–1*ill*, 323, 341*ill*
River Boyne, 195
River Shannon, 38, 154, 170, 172, 173–4, 194
River Swilly, 81
Riverdance, 358
Robert, King of Scots, 59
Robert fitz Stephen, 44
Robert the Bruce (Earl of Carrick), 59, 60
Robespierre, 213
Robinson, Mary, 354
Robinson, Peter, 357
Robinson & Cleaver, 259
Rock of Doon, 121
Rockfleet Castle, 98
Rodney's Glory, 209
Roman Empire, 18, 19, 21
Rossa, Jeremiah O'Donovan, 254, 299
Rotunda Lying-in Hospital, 202
Roundheads, 150
Routh, Sir Randolph, 245
Royal Avenue, Belfast, 257*ill*
Royal Field Artillery, 315
Royal Irish Academy, 201
Royal Irish Constabulary, 235, 269, 308, 310
Royal Irish Linen Warehouse, 259
Royal Navy, 323
Royal Ulster Constabulary, 314, 338
RTÉ, 353
Russell, George, 293
Russell, Lord John, 245, 251
Rutland Square, 202
Ryanair, 346, 358

Sackville Street, 300, 316
Saint Columbanus, 34–5
Saint Patrick, 20–3, 37

Saint-Ruth, Marquis de, 173–6
same-sex marriage, 353
Samhain, 17
A Sample of Jet-black Prelatic Calumny, 188
A Sample of True-Blew Presbyterian Loyalty in all Changes and Turns of Government, 188
Sancta Maria Rata Encoronada, 88
Sarsfield, Patrick, 170, 171, 176, 177
Saxons, 20
Schomberg, Duke of, 167, 169
Schwabe, Gustav, 259–60
scowbankers, 206
Scrap Saturday, 353
Scullabogue, 221
Seagate, 357
Seán an Díomais (Shane the Proud) *see* O'Neill, Shane
Second Home Rule Bill (1893), 280
Second World War *see* World War II
Secret Ballot Act (1872), 263
Serua, 178
servitors, 128
settlements, 28
Shakespeare, William, 15
shamrock, 92
Shanavests, 229
Shane's Castle, 205
Shankill Road, 269
Shawe-Taylor, John, 284
Sheehy, David, 276, 278
Sheil, Richard Lalor, 229
ship building, 259–61, 320, 335
A Short History of Ireland, ix
Shovell, Sir Cloudsley, 168
Shute, Samuel, 190
Siddons, Sarah, 205
Sidley, Sir Ralph, 115
Sidney, Sir Henry, 80, 81, 98
Siemens-Schuckert, 321
Sigurd, Earl (the Fat), 41, 42
Silken Thomas FitzGerald (Earl of Kildare), 72*ill*, 73–4, 76
Singapore Airspace Manufacturing, 356
Single Market, 350
Sinn Féin, 285–6, 288, 298, 302–7, 308, 318–19, 341–2, 343, 354, 357, 358
Sir John of Desmond, 85

Sirr, Major, 220
Sitric Silkenbeard, 38, 39, 41, 42
Sitric the Squinty, 37
Skeffington, Sir William, 74
Skellig Michael, 23
Skellig Rock, 23–4, 37
Skelton, Rev. Philip, 195
Skibbereen, 249–50, 251
Skinners, 135
Sligo, 57
Sligo Bay, 88
Sligo Castle, 101
Sloan, James, 219
Smailholm, George, 131
Smerwick, 84–5, 86
Smith, Ann, 145
Smith, Sir Thomas, 82
Smith, Sir Thomas (son), 82
smokesilver, 71
Social Democratic and Labour Party (SDLP), 339, 342, 343
Society of United Irishmen, 213–14, 216–17, 220–3, 242–3
sóer, 27
Solemn League, 158
Soloheadbeg, 308–9
Somerled, 69
Somme, x, 297, 306
The Song of Dermot and the Earl, 43
South Carolina, 208
South Longford by-election (1917), 303, 306
Southern Ireland, 312
Special Powers Act, 314
Spenser, Edmund, 85, 94
Spotlight (BBC), 354, 357
Spottiswood, James, 137
Sprucefield complex, 354
SS Oceanic, 260*ill*
St Andrews Agreement, 357
St Enoch's Presbyterian Church, 269
St Gall, 30
St Gallen, 35
St Leger, Sir Anthony, 68, 77
St Mary's Abbey, 61, 73
St Moling, 65
St Patrick's Cathedral, 170
St Peter's (Drogheda), 152
St Saviour's Priory, 61

Stanley, Edward, 235
Staunton, James, 330, 333
Stembridge, Gerry, 353
Stephens, James, 253–5, 302
Stevens, John, 171, 174
Stewart, Ezekiel, 192
Stewart, Reverend Andrew, 136
Stone Age, 3, 4–8, 9–10
Stormont, 320, 339, 349
Story, George Rev., 167–8, 176
Strangford, 82
Strangford Lough, 194
Streedagh, 88
Strongbow (Richard fitz Gilbert de Clare), 44–5, 46–7, 48, 49, 50, 57
Success, 208
Sunningdale peace conference, 339
surrender and regrant scheme, 77
Sussex, Earl of, 79, 80
Sven, King of Denmark, 39
Sweetman, John, 285–6, 332
Swift, Jonathan, 185, 188, 189*ill*
Synge, Edward (Archbishop of Tuam), 184
Synod of Ulster, 185

Talbot, Richard (Earl of Tyrconnell), 159, 160, 176
Talk Back, 353–4
Tara, 17, 25, 238
Teach Moling, 65
Terex, 357
Test Act (1673), 158
Thatcher, Margaret, 342, 343
Theoderic, King of Burgundy, 34
Thingmote, 49
Third Home Rule Bill (1912), 288–9
Third Reform Act (1884), 266
Thompson Aero Seating, 356–7
Three Bullet Gate, 221
The Times, 238, 273–4
tin, 11, 12
Tipperary, 155, 157
Tír Conaill, 69, 75, 91, 100, 104
Tír Eóghain, 74, 77, 102, 103, 104
Tisdall, Dr William, 188
Titanic, 260
Titanic Experience, 357
Titanic Quarter, 354

Tithe Rent Charge (Ireland) Act, 236
Tithe War, 234*ill*, 236
Todd, John, 137
Tone, Theobald Wolfe, 213, 214–15, 224, 282
Tories *see* Conservative Party
Torrans, John, 208
townlands, 125, 128
Tralee Bay, 87
tramway workers strike, 292–3
Treaty of Limerick, 177, 181, 183
trees, 2–3
Trench family, 175
Trevelyan, Charles, 244, 245
Trevelyan's corn, 244
Tribes of Galway, 57
Trim Castle, 51–2
Trimble, David, 344
Trinity College Dublin, 128
Troika, 354–5
The Troubles, 338, 344, 349
Tuatha Dé Danann, 15, 16*ill*
tuberculosis, 329–30
Tully Castle, 132, 145
Turgeis, 37, 38*ill*
Turoe Stone, 17
Two Ceasefires and a Wedding, 354
Tyrconnell, 125, 134
Tyrone, 125, 129
Tyrone House, 201

U2, 358
uí néill, 32–3
uisce beathadh (whiskey), 91
Ulster, 4, 14, 17, 51, 60, 69, 77–82, 91, 99, 100–4, 113, 115–17, 121, 183–6, 187, 188, 190, 191, 197–8, 206, 207, 216, 217, 223, 232, 237–8, 256–61, 267, 268–71*ill*, 286, 306–7, 312, 320, 331, 336, 343, 348
Ulster Custom, 262
Ulster Day, 289
Ulster Plantation *see* Plantation of Ulster
Ulster Solemn League and Covenant, 289
Ulster unionism, 286, 287, 289, 290, 312, 342, 344, 357
Ulster Unionist Council, 286, 287

Ulster Volunteer Force, x, 290, 295, 313, 314
undertakers, 86, 116, 128, 129, 130–2, 136, 137
unemployment, 320, 327, 350, 354
unionism, 258, 267, 268–9, 270, 271, 280, 284, 286–7, 289–90, 297, 306–7, 312, 331, 336, 338, 339, 343
see also loyalism
Unionist Party, 314
United Irishman, 285–6
United States, 326
Usher, John, 195

Valmy, 213
Van Morrison, 358
van Reede, Godard (Baron de Ginkel), 168, 172–3, 174
Venables, Colonel Robert, 155, 157
Vesey, Major, 221
Vesey-Fitzgerald, William, 232
veto crisis, 227, 229
Victoria Centre, 354
Victoria Channel, 257–8, 259
Vikings, 35–42, 43, 47–8, 49, 57, 68, 69, 239
Villiers-Stuart, Henry, 230
Vindicator, 238, 248
Vinegar Hill, 223
von Kuhren, Ernst, 325–6
Vormärz (pre-March), 242
Vox Hiberniae, 20

Walker, Patrick, 179
Walker, Rev. George, 163–4, 165, 168
Walkington, Dr Edward, 185
Wallace, William, 58–9
War of Independence, 309, 312
War of the Roses, 72–3
Wars of Irish with Foreigners (*Cogadh Gaedhel re Gallaibh*), 35
Waterford, 38, 44–6, 47, 57, 64, 70, 71, 230, 316
Waterloo, 213
Wellington, Duke of, 232, 233
Wentworth, Thomas, 139–40, 141
Wexford, 152, 154, 217, 220–1, 223
Whigs, 227, 233, 235, 236, 237, 245
Whitaker, T.K., 332, 334, 335–6

White Linen Hall, 257, 259
White Star Line, 260
Whiteboys, 228, 236
Whiteside, Donald, x
wild boar, 3
Wild Geese, 181
Wilde, Oscar, 289
William, Duke (the Conqueror), 43
William III, King (William of Orange), 159, 160, 161*ill*, 167, 168–9, 170–1, 176, 181, 202, 204
William of Orange *see* William III, King (William of Orange)
Winchester, 20
wine, 91, 92
Wingfield, Richard (Viscount Powerscourt), 201
Wodrow, Robert, 188
Wolfe, Rev. Richard, 227
Wolff, Gustav, 260
women, 354
Women's Coalition, 354
Woodenbridge, 295, 297
woodkerne, 134, 137
Woodman, Peter, 4
Woollen Act (1699), 198
Workman Clark, 261, 320
The World Crisis, 307
World War I, 294–8, 310
World War II, 324–7
Wrightbus, 356
Würtemberg-Neustadt, Duke of, 168
Wyndham, George, 283–4
Wyndham Land Act (1903), 321, 322
Wyndham's Act, 284

Year of the Slaughter (*Bliadhain an Áir*), 195–6
Yeats, W.B., 278, 285
Yellow Ford, Battle of the, 103, 124
York, Sir Edward, 101
York Street, 256, 269
York Street Flax and Weaving Company, 261
Young Ireland movement, 242–3, 251, 253, 254, 279
Young Italy, 242

z Donína, Jaroslav, 95